STAFF DEVELOPMENT IN OPEN
AND FLEXIBLE LEARNING

'This book will find an important niche as a reference source among all those engaged in the transformation of our educational practices from the selective to universal accessibility.'

Dató Dr Gajaraj Dhanarajan
President and Chief Executive Officer,
Commonwealth of Learning

As institutions and organisations around the world move to more open and flexible delivery of educational and training programmes, there is increasing need for effective forms of staff development to encourage and support change. Staff development is critical not only in helping teachers and trainers acquire and improve their knowledge and skills in alternative modes of delivery, but also in helping to shape the policies, procedures and attitudes that are needed for more learner-centred approaches.

This book draws together the experiences, insights and findings of some of the world's leading staff developers in open and flexible education. It is designed to provide an overview of the trends, influences and events which are shaping the work of these professionals, and the policy changes, processes and outcomes they are helping to bring about in this expanding field.

The contributors offer frameworks, strategies and practical advice for the organisation and implementation of staff development in various educational settings, open applications and cultural contexts around the globe.

Colin Latchem is Head of the Teaching and Learning Group at Curtin University of Technology, Australia. **Fred Lockwood** is Senior Lecturer in Educational Technology and Head of the Professional Development in Educational Technology Programme at The Open University, UK.

ROUTLEDGE STUDIES IN DISTANCE EDUCATION
General editors: Desmond Keegan and Alan Tait

STAFF DEVELOPMENT IN OPEN AND FLEXIBLE LEARNING

*Edited by Colin Latchem
and Fred Lockwood*

London and New York

First published 1998
by Routledge
11 New Fetter Lane, London EC4P 4EE

Simultaneously published in the USA and Canada
by Routledge
29 West 35th Street, New York, NY 10001

Typeset in Goudy by Keystroke, Jacaranda Lodge, Wolverhampton
Printed and bound in Great Britain by TJ International Ltd, Padstow, Cornwall

British Library Cataloguing in Publication Data
A catalogue record for this book is available from the British Library

Library of Congress Cataloging in Publication Data
Staff development in open and flexible learning / edited by Colin
Latchem and Fred Lockwood.
(Routledge studies in distance education)
Includes bibliographical references and index.
1. Distance education.   2. Open learning.   3. College teachers—In-service training.
I. Latchem, C. R. (Colin R.)   II. Lockwood, Fred.   III. Series.
LC5800.S83   1998
378′.03—dc21   97–30930
CIP

ISBN 0–415–17376–0 (HB)
ISBN 0–415–17390–6 (PB)

CONTENTS

CONTENTS

CONTENTS

ILLUSTRATIONS

Figures

Tables

CONTRIBUTORS

Szarina Abdullah is Professor in Library and Information Science and Associate Rector of Distance Education at Institut Teknologi Mara, Malaysia. She has researched and published in the fields of library and information science, scientometrics and distance education. She was the chief investigator for the 1996 Malaysian government-commissioned *National Survey on Reading Habits and Reading Interests among Students in Malaysian Institutions of Higher Learning* and was responsible for a Ministry of Education Malaysia and IDP Education Australia report, *Professional Development for In-service Teachers through Distance Education*. E-mail:drszarina@psmb.ibm.edu.my

Eli Bitzer is the Director of Academic Staff Development and Professor at the University of Free State, Bloemfontein, South Africa. He was President of the South African Association for Research and Development in Higher Education in 1992–93, and in 1997, he received the SAARDHE Johann Pauw Award for his contribution to academic life in South Africa. He has published and presented papers internationally in the field of academic staff development. E-mail:baovdw@rs.uovs.ac.za

Liz Burge is Professor of Adult Education at the University of New Brunswick in Fredericton, New Brunswick. She was the 1996–97 President of the Canadian Association for Distance Education/Association Canadienne de l'Education à Distance. Drawing upon her extensive experience in distance education, she writes, researches, runs practitioner workshops, teaches graduate courses in distance and adult education, and generally tries to 'walk the talk' in her practice. She is co-author of *Classrooms with a Difference: Facilitating Learning on the Information Highway* (Chenlierye-McGraw-Hill, 1997). E-mail: burge@unb.ca

Jocelyn Calvert has been Professor of Distance Education at Deakin University since 1989. During the 1980s she was a Director in the British Columbia Open University. A keen student of contemporary developments in higher education, she is currently involved in academic planning and quality management. Her academic interests in open and distance education have included the foundations of research, patterns of academic dialogue, electronic networks, collaboration and quality and standards. E-mail:jocelyn@deakin.edu.au

Gajaraj Dhanarajan is President and Chief Executive Officer of the Commonwealth of Learning in Vancouver, Canada. A Malaysian citizen, Professor Dhanarajan was formerly the Director of the Opening Learning Institute of Hong Kong. He is Secretary General of the Asian Association of Open Universities. During the past fifteen years, Professor Dhanarajan has helped to establish several distance education systems in South and Southeast Asia. He has a distinguished international career as a distance learning research strategist and has a world-wide reputation for his global understanding of the directions that open and distance learning are taking.

Terry Evans is Director of Research in the Faculty of Education at Deakin University, where he also teaches and supervises postgraduate students. Professor Evans is the author of *Understanding Learners in Open and Distance Education* (Kogan Page, 1994) and the co-editor of nine books, including *Opening Education: Policies and Practices from Open and Distance Education* (Routledge, 1996) and *Shifting Borders: Globalisation and Open and Distance Education* (Deakin University Press, 1997). E-mail:tevans@deakin.edu.au

Anne Forster is a specialist in the design of instructional systems for distributed learning. She has held a number of academic and managerial educational technology positions in the UK, Canada, the USA and Australasia. Her research and development interests include alternative delivery systems for education and training and strategic development and instructional design for networked interactive learning and teaching. She has recently been the primary investigator in international comparative analyses of telematic initiatives and a study of information technology in the management and delivery of Australian higher education. E-mail:forster@agsm.unsw.edu.au

Richard Freeman is a freelance consultant in the production of learning materials and in staff development in writing, editing and assessment. His publications include *Quality Assurance in Training and Education* (Kogan Page, 1993) and, with Roger Lewis, *Writing Open Learning Materials* (Framework Press, 1995). Recent publications include *Managing Open Systems* (Kogan Page, 1997) and, with Roger Lewis, *Planning and Implementing Assessment* (Kogan Page, in press). He was formerly Course Director of the Open College in the UK. E-mail:r.d.freeman@dial.pipex.com

Charlotte N. Gunawardena is Associate Professor of Distance Education and Instructional Technology in the Organisational Learning and Instructional Technologies programme at the University of New Mexico, USA. She teaches graduate courses in distance education, instructional design, adult learning and cross-cultural training. She is the Project Director for a Star

Schools distance learning evaluation project funded by the US Department of Education. Her current research examines learning styles, learner-centred learning, social presence, and collaborative learning in interactive distance learning systems. E-mail:lani@unm.edu

Cathy Gunn is Educational Technologies Adviser at the University of Auckland in New Zealand. Prior to this, she worked on educational software development and evaluation at the Institute for Computer-based Learning at Heriot-Watt University, Edinburgh. Her research interests lie in learning psychology, computer-assisted education, and the development of a holistic framework for formative and summative evaluation of the educational impact of innovative products. E-mail:ca.gunn@aukland.ac.nz

Neil Haigh is Director of the Teaching and Learning Development Unit at the University of Waikato, Hamilton, New Zealand. He also works with staff in other organisations to help them learn to use thinking methods and tools that can assist them to solve workplace problems more effectively. He has a long-standing interest in the 'mental life' of teachers and how the character of their thoughts and thinking change and develop during their teaching careers. E-mail:nhaigh@waikato.ac.nz

David Hawkridge is Professor of Applied Educational Sciences at the Institute of Educational Technology at the UK Open University. He is also the Director of the Institute's MA in Open and Distance Education Programme. He was Director of the Institute between 1970 and 1988. He has advised on distance education in Canada, China, Egypt, El Salvador, Finland, Germany, Hong Kong, Israel, Italy, Jamaica, Mauritius, the Netherlands, Norway and the USA. E-mail:d.g.hawkridge@open.ac.uk

Lindsay Hewson is a Senior Lecturer in the Professional Development Centre at the University of New South Wales, Sydney, Australia. His research interests are in the appropriate application of technology to teaching and learning and the staff development issues arising from this. His professional background includes over twenty years as a teacher and lecturer in education and design, and twelve years in commercial television and film production. He is currently teaching about uses of information technology in teaching and research on a postgraduate programme in higher education and co-developing interactive software for effective online teaching on the Internet. E-mail:l.hewson @unsw.edu.au

David Kember is the Coordinator of the Action Learning Project in the Educational Development Unit, Hong Kong Polytechnic University. The Action Learning Project is an inter-institutional initiative which supports action research projects by academics in the seven Hong Kong universities. The projects take as their focus particular aspects of the academics' teaching. He has previously held educational development positions in Britain, Fiji,

Papua New Guinea and Australia. He has written five books, the most recent being *Open Learning Courses for Adults: A Model of Student Progress* (Educational Technology Publications, 1995). He has also written numerous journal articles in the fields of student learning, action research, distance education and instructional design. E-mail:etkember@hkpucc.polyu.edu.hk

Badri N. Koul is the Head of the Distance and Open Learning Division in the Tertiary Education Commission of Mauritius. He was formerly a Pro Vice-Chancellor at the Indira Gandhi National Open University (IGNOU) in India and the founder of IGNOU's Staff Training and Research Institute of Distance Education (STRIDE). He conceived, developed and implemented the STRIDE staff development programmes leading to postgraduate programmes in distance education which were introduced in India in 1987 and offered internationally in 1995. He also established the *Indian Journal of Open Learning*.

Colin Latchem is Associate Professor and Head of the Teaching Learning Group at Curtin University of Technology, Perth, Western Australia. He was the National President of the Open and Distance Learning Association of Australia between 1995 and 1997 and formerly a member of the Academic Programmes Board of Open Learning Australia of which Curtin is a shareholder. His research interests include strategic planning and management for educational change, academic staff development, educational technology and open and distance education, and internationalising the curriculum. E-mail:c.latchem@info.curtin.edu.au

Daryl Le Grew is the Deputy Vice-Chancellor and Vice-President (Academic) at Deakin University in Victoria, Australia. Professor Le Grew has been instrumental in integrating new university structures, rationalising the academic profile of the university and establishing the entrepreneurial Deakin Australia and Deakin International. He has also been responsible for facilitating course development and the re-engineering of Deakin for electronic learning, and the development and delivery of courses, programmes and electronic learning in response to the needs and demands of multi-campus and flexible learning environments. E-mail:jocelyn@deakin.edu.au

Roger Lewis is BP Professor of Learning Development at the University of Lincolnshire and Humberside in Hull, England. He previously worked for the UK Open University, the National Extension College and the Open College. He has published many open learning resources for students and tutors, including the UK National Council for Educational Technology Open Learning Guides series. He gained most of his own qualifications through open and distance learning. His current position involves the strategic and systematic implementation of open learning in a multi-campus institution. E-mail:ROGER@milner_a.humber.ac.uk

Fred Lockwood is a Senior Lecturer in the UK Open University Institute of Educational Technology, where he is involved in course planning, production, presentation and evaluation. He was formerly Deputy Director of the Institute and he is heavily involved as a consultant to many other open and distance teaching centres around the world. Over the past three years, he has conducted over 500 staff development activities in more than a dozen countries. He is Series Editor of the Kogan Page Open and Distance Learning Series, and the editor of *Open and Distance Learning Today* (Routledge Studies in Distance Education, 1995). E-mail:f.g.lockwood@open.ac.uk

Diana Mak's background is in social work education and social welfare administration. She is the Professor and Head of the Department of Applied Social Studies at the Hong Kong Polytechnic University, where she is responsible for a full range of educational programmes for social workers and early childhood educators.

Hilary Mar has extensive experience in educational publishing, distance/open learning materials development and educational consulting. Between 1982 and 1994 she led a team of instructional designers, editors and production staff at the Hong Kong Polytechnic University. Since 1995 she has been engaged in consulting activities and is currently participating in a telecommuting and telecommunications research project at the University of Toronto.

Claire Matthewson is the Director of International Projects at the Centre for Distance Education, Simon Fraser University, Canada, and the former Director of University Extension at the University of the South Pacific. She was Founding President of the Pacific Islands Regional Association for Distance Education (PIRADE) and has undertaken major consultancies in the Pacific region. She has recently completed a short history of distance education in the South Pacific for the Sasakawa Foundation. In 1994, she received the Elizabeth Powell Award from the American National University Continuing Education Association for exceptional contribution to the field of cross-cultural research and publication. E-mail:ccmatt@es.co.nz

Patricia McWilliams has been responsible for Commonwealth of Learning (COL) training programmes since 1992 and is now the COL Senior Training Officer. This work entails managing and operating training programmes in the theory and practice of distance education in various Commonwealth countries and working on major projects funded by organisations such as the Commonwealth Youth Programme, the Asian Development Bank and the Canadian International Development Agency.

Louise Moran is a consultant in open and flexible learning. She was formerly Director of the Flexible Learning Centre at the University of South Australia and, prior to that, held the positions of Director of Course Policy and Director of Educational Services at Deakin University, Victoria. She co-edited

Collaboration in Distance Education: International Case Studies (Routledge, 1993) with Ian Mugridge and was responsible for the 1995 Department of Employment, Education and Training/Deakin University Centre for Academic Support report: *National Policy Frameworks to Support the Integration of Information Technologies into University Teaching/Learning.*

Ian Mugridge was formerly Principal of the British Columbia Open University and Senior Consultant, Higher Education, at the Commonwealth of Learning (COL). He is now COL's Director of Programmes, responsible for Commonwealth-wide initiatives in areas such as research, quality assurance and training. He holds an honorary doctorate from the Open Learning Institute, Hong Kong, and is a frequent contributor to the literature of open and distance learning.

David Murphy is Senior Course Designer at the Open University of Hong Kong (formerly the Open Learning Institute of Hong Kong), a position he has held since 1994. Prior to that, he spent over two years at Deakin University, Australia, and was at Hong Kong Polytechnic from 1985 until 1991. His experience includes planning and administration, course designing and writing, tutoring, staff development, research and evaluation, and he is the author of over fifty journal articles, book chapters, books and conference papers. E-mail:dmurphy@oliv1.oli.hk

Daryl Nation is Associate Professor and Deputy Head of the School of Humanities and Social Sciences at Monash University in Australia. He divides his time between policy development, research and teaching. He has over twenty years' experience in teaching at a distance and extensive experience of integrating a variety of media into teaching. He has co-edited *Critical Reflections on Distance Education* (Falmer Press, 1989), *Reforming Open and Distance Education* (Kogan Page, 1993) and *Opening Education* (Routledge, 1996). E-mail:daryl@mugc.cc.monash.edu.au

Jennifer O'Rourke is a consultant and researcher in adult education and open and distance learning. Her experience includes programme planning and management, evaluation, research, organisational development and instructional design for universities and colleges, organisations and ministries of education in Canada, the Caribbean, Africa and Southeast Asia. She lives on Gabriola Island, British Columbia. E-mail:jorourke@islandnet.ca

Jo Osborne has worked as an instructional designer in several different environments. Starting as an industrial trainer in the UK pharmaceutical industry, she moved into tertiary education, working at the (then) Hong Kong Polytechnic. She is currently Coordinator of the Instructional Development Unit at the University of Tasmania. Previously principally concerned with the development of study materials for off-campus students, she has developed a research interest in the sharing of study resources between on- and off-campus teaching modes. E-mail:josborne@cult.utas.edu.au

Mary Panko is the Training Leader at UNITEC Institute of Technology in Auckland, New Zealand. She directs the staff development programme and the Graduate Diploma in Higher Education, in addition to developing management training courses for the institution. One of her major directives is encouraging the appropriate use of new technology by teaching staff. Previously, she lectured at Robert Gordon's University in Scotland, as well as establishing and coordinating their Interactive Teaching Centre. E-mail:mpanko@unitec.ac.nz

Ross Paul is President of Laurentian University in Sudbury, Ontario, Canada. He has written extensively on management issues in open and distance learning and has a particular interest in student support and the management of technology. He was the founding president of Consorcio Red de Educacion a Distancia (CREAD), the international distance education consortium for all of the Americas, and is presently North American Vice-President of the International Council on Open and Distance Learning (ICDE). E-mail:rpaul@nickel.laurentian.ca

Christine Randell is the Professional Development Coordinator at the South African Institute for Distance Education (SAIDE). She has been a driving force behind the formation of a professional development consortium of six major institutions/organisations in South Africa. Launched in May 1997, the consortium aims to improve the professionalism and quality of distance education practitioners. She is also currently involved in joint initiatives for the development of management staff in open and flexible learning programmes. E-mail:saide@icon.ca.za

Bernadette Robinson of the School of Education, UK Open University, has worked as a practitioner and researcher in open and distance education for over twenty years. She has wide experience of training and staff development in a number of countries, most recently in South Africa, Colombia, Mongolia, Indonesia and the UK. She has produced many training materials and courses, organised workshops and acted as consultant to distance education projects and institutions on behalf of international agencies. E-mail:b.robinson @open.ac.uk

Derek Rowntree is Professor of Educational Development at the UK Open University. His contributions to staff development include working as a pedagogical consultant on course teams, his workshops on setting up and running learning systems and, not least, his many books, e.g. *Developing Courses for Students* (Paul Chapman, 1982); *Educational Technology in Curriculum Development* (Paul Chapman, 1982); *Assessing Students: How Shall We Know Them?* (Kogan Page, 1987); and *Preparing Materials for Open,*

Distance and Flexible Learning: An Action Guide for Teachers and Trainers (Kogan Page, 1994). E-mail:d.g.f.rowntree@open.ac.uk

David Sewart is Director of Regional Academic Services at the UK Open University, responsible for the tuition and counselling of the university's 150,000 students and for the 7,500 part-time Associate Lecturers who provide this service. He has written extensively on student support services and staff development for those engaged in supporting students in distance education. He is Professor of Distance Education, was Vice-President and President of the International Council for Distance Education for some thirteen years, and compiled and edited the conference proceedings for ICDE's 1988 Oslo Conference and 1995 Birmingham Conference. E-mail:d.sewart@open.ac.uk

Barbara Spronk is Executive Director of the International Extension College in Cambridge, England. She was previously Associate Professor of Anthropology at Athabasca University, Canada. She has managed projects in northeast Thailand and western Canada, and has served as a consultant and course developer in participatory approaches to education for development at the University of Calgary. She is also a past-president of the Canadian Association for Distance Education/Association Canadienne de l'Education à Distance. E-mail:iec@dial.pipex.com

Konai Helu Thaman is a Tongan academic and the former Pro Vice-Chancellor of the University of South Pacific (USP), a regional university owned by twelve Pacific island nations. She is currently Professor of Pacific Education and Culture and Head of the School of Humanities at USP. Konai is also a well-known Pacific poet, with five collections of poetry published. E-mail:thaman_k@usp.ac.fj

Ross Vermeer is a Course Designer in the Educational Technology and Publishing Unit of the Open University of Hong Kong (formerly the Open Learning Institute of Hong Kong). He has lived and worked in Hong Kong for six years, two at the Chinese University of Hong Kong, and four at the OUHK. His interests lie in multimedia and online course materials development. E-mail:rvermeer@di1.di.hk

Rebecca H. Zittle has an MA in distance education and instructional technology from the University of New Mexico, USA. She is currently working as an evaluator on a three-year programme funded by the US Department of Education. As well as evaluation, her interests include faculty development and distance education in developing countries. E-mail:rzittle@unm.edu

FOREWORD

Ours is a remarkable century not only for the spectacular achievements in science, agriculture, health, exploration, communication and technology, but also for the expressions of concern and the attempts to ameliorate the inequalities for many in terms of justice, fair play, individual rights and freedoms and, perhaps, most importantly, *equal opportunities for all* with regard to educational access. The last needs emphasis because educational access, as we know, from time immemorial has been a most important agent of change. Notwithstanding the progress that has been achieved during the last fifty years, there are still more people in the world today who remain either totally or functionally illiterate than those who can read, write and use their education for a useful purpose. This is a concern that not only bothers political leaders and educational providers of those countries where illiteracy is endemic, but also the many in other parts of the world where extremely high levels of literacy have been achieved. In an increasingly interdependent world, one person's educational deprivation is another's security threat.

In Jomtien in 1990, at the start of the last decade of this century, global leaders pledged to make *education for all* universal by the year 2000. Sadly, the gap between our *desire* to provide education for all and our *ability* to do so is huge. Resources, social and personal impediments, pedagogic challenges and the sheer magnitude of the task, all contribute to make this aspiration difficult to achieve in the remaining years of the present century. On the positive side, however, the political will of nations coupled with the rapidly evolving technologies of computing, information and electronics offer widespread hope that solutions are available to minimise the gap between aspiration and achievement. One such solution especially builds on the experience of distance education techniques and open learning principles to take learning beyond and often outside school and campus walls, to learners wherever they may be. Recent studies and reviews strongly recommend that nations need to pursue the use of distance education if the twenty-first century agenda of universalising educational access is to be achieved.

To explore and exploit the opportunities presented by the new political, social and technological environments, we need people with the knowledge and skills to become the 'new teachers'. It is in this context that this book, edited by Latchem and Lockwood, will find an important niche as a reference source among all those engaged in the transformation of our educational practices from the selective to universal accessibility. In three parts, the book conveys the views, knowledge, skills and insights of some thirty-eight experienced practitioners of distance and open learning on matters relating to staff development.

At a time when the fundamental relationship between societies, institutions, teachers and learners are changing, those of us who are right in the middle of these changes will find this book a very helpful source of support.

G. Dhanarajan
President and CEO
Commonwealth of Learning

PREFACE

It may not always be easy to explain to someone from outside academia what staff developers do or why indeed such persons are needed. The lay person might be surprised to learn that 'traditionally there has been a disregard of training for teaching in higher education' (Brew 1995: 4). Furthermore, many teachers, and indeed many students, have traditional perceptions and expectations of teaching and learning while so much of what is new and challenging has no precedent – the changes necessitated by mass systems of higher and further education, the changing demography of students, the pressures for more open and flexible learning, information and communications technology, internationalisation and global market competition between institutions. Such changes not only require staff development in order to develop new knowledge, skills and attitudes in teaching and learning but also to foster leadership and management which is responsive to the educational, economic and technological demands of the marketplace.

For those unfamiliar with the particular learning context of this book, it may be useful to elaborate on the terms 'open' and 'flexible' learning. Open learning has been defined as

> an approach rather than a system or technique; it is based on the needs of individual learners, not the interests of the teacher or the institution; it gives students as much control as possible over what and when and where and how they learn; it commonly uses the delivery methods of distance education and the facilities of educational technology; it changes the role of the teacher from a source of knowledge to a manager of learning and a facilitator.
>
> (Johnson 1990: 4)

Taylor *et al.* (1996: xi) suggest that the term 'flexible' refers to

> practices which utilise the capacities for learner–learner and teacher–learner interaction made possible through recent developments in communication and information technology (CIT) to provide

increased 'openness' in both on- and off-campus delivery of educational programs ... we use the expression 'flexible modes of delivery' to capture this combination of philosophy and technology and quite explicitly recognise that this combination frees the provision of educational programs from both geographical and time constraints.

Such distinctions are useful, but the important points to be made here are that such practices and uses of technology are educationally and socially defensible and that staff development is needed to support reform in the delivery of higher education.

Beaty (1995) suggests that staff development is about the learning of individuals and the learning of organisations. Institutions may invest enormous resources in training staff to use new methods and technology, but unless the institutional strategic focus is clear and staff have been enabled to recon-ceptualise their roles as teachers and those of the learners, the desired reforms and improvements will not occur. In her book *Rethinking University Teaching: A Framework for Effective Use of Educational Technology*, Laurillard (1993) suggests that change and quality come through effective organisational infrastructure, collaboration, cyclical review, addressing the context of the entire teaching and learning process and reflecting upon experience and knowledge, not least in the realm of technology.

Educational development requires informed reflective practice and institutions to become 'learning communities', capable of developing the vision, policies and procedures that will ensure that the best of the cultural traditions of higher and further education and the new modes of delivery and technology can be harnessed to serve in specific contexts. Staff developers have a critical role in helping institutions to identify and anticipate external opportunities and threats and internal capabilities and weaknesses, plan and prepare for change, and cope with change as it occurs. In providing such support, staff developers often have to combat problems of scarce resources, scepticism and low morale among staff, and ensure that change is driven by the educators rather than the imperatives of economic rationalism or the 'silicon veneer' of technological determinism. They also need to promote leadership and management skills at all levels of the enterprise. The stance and energies demonstrated by senior and middle managers are crucial in educational change, not least in maintaining open communication and a critical sharing of views in regard to strategic options, implementing change and academic practice.

Helping an educational institution to realign itself for competitive advantage and success can at times be a difficult and frustrating experience. In one case that came to the notice of the editors, an institution invited an internationally renowned staff developer/change agent to develop a vision and strategy for its future. He involved about fifty senior, influential staff in the envisioning process and together, they examined the external factors, targeted new opportunities, established the critical success factors and developed a vision and proposals for more open, flexible and global delivery. Despite being arrived at through an apparently exemplary process, these proposals were considered too radical by senior management, who quietly set them to one side, claiming that they had more pressing matters to address. However, other institutions around the world are not putting such proposals 'to one side' but are actively promoting changes in delivery. At the time of completing this book, the most recent data from the International Centre for Distance Learning indicated that there were about 1,000 institutions around the globe offering open, distance and flexible learning courses. The number of recorded programmes and courses has grown from approximately 3,000 in 1991 to over 33,000 in 1997; and teacher and trainer involvement in alternative modes of delivery is growing at an amazing rate.

However, the vast majority of tertiary staff, while skilled in the more conventional forms of course and programme delivery, have limited experience of approaches which place student needs, choice and learning at the centre of the enterprise and use self-instructional materials in technologies ranging from print to the Internet. Given this situation, it is surprising that a search of the ERIC database revealed relatively little literature in staff development for open, distance and flexible education. Two recent and extremely useful books – Brew (1995) and Webb (1996) – examine the nature and directions of staff development but neither specifically addresses staff development for open and flexible learning. We therefore felt that there would be need for such a publication and we set out to identify staff developers working in various contexts around the world, who could describe the trends, influences and events which shaped their work, the policy changes, processes and practices they were helping to bring about, and the lessons they had learned in the process. We sought contributions from the Indian Ocean, Asian and Pacific regions as well as from Europe and North America to ensure that we included the experiences and insights of staff developers working in developing countries, with indigenous peoples and in cross-cultural and economically constrained contexts, as well as those who could depend upon Western knowledge and sophisticated educational and technological infrastructure for their work.

Part I of the book, Staff Development in Context, looks at the changing environment within which various levels and forms of staff development are needed. Daryl Le Grew and Jocelyn Calvert examine the developments in Australia and other countries which are profoundly changing the nature, organisation and work of universities. They argue for leaders, planners and decision-makers to be closely and continuously involved in staff development and the processes of change. Ross Paul, viewing the world from a Canadian base, warns about the dangers of political leaders expecting quick fixes, rapid responses and simplistic solutions from open and flexible learning. He argues that distance educators must participate more fully in debates about the reform of traditional education. Roger Lewis, writing from a UK perspective, looks at issues of staff development in conventional institutions moving towards open learning and suggests that institutional managers have to empower staff to bring about change in an environment currently characterised by low trust and low energy. Bernadette Robinson, drawing upon her extensive international experience as a staff developer, expresses concern that staff development for open and distance education may be all too often viewed as a cost rather than an investment and recommends a more strategic perspective on staff development. Terry Evans and Daryl Nation draw upon their experiences as researchers and teachers in open and distance education at two of Australia's major distance education institutions and discuss the power of research to inform reflection and educational development. Patricia McWilliams and Ian Mugridge of the Commonwealth of Learning (COL) explore the magnitude and complexity of the staff development needs of developing countries moving to adopt distance and open learning systems and how COL has sought to meet these needs.

Part II, Staff Development in the Organisation, looks at ways in which staff development has been introduced into, and organised within, various distance and dual-mode institutions around the globe. Colin Latchem and Louise Moran write of the progressive blurring of distinction between on- and off-campus delivery evident in Australian universities and argue for new synergy between staff development and instructional design and face-to-face and technology-based delivery. Badri Koul, drawing on his experiences at India's Indira Gandhi National Open University, describes the ideological differences and institutional inertia which had to be overcome in helping this institution move into distance education and argues for staff development to be embedded within a human resource strategy. Szarina Abdullah, describing how one Malaysian university sought to achieve the paradigm shift into dual-mode delivery, explains the strategies and processes that helped the staff move through the 'Resistance' and 'Exploration' stages of transition once the government and the Rector had set the vision. Hilary Mar and Diana Mak describe a similar process at the Hong Kong Polytechnic University, arguing that the change agents for open and flexible learning have to come from within. American contributors, Charlotte Nirmalani Gunawardena and Rebecca Zittle, show that teaching in an interactive distance education environment may require skills not commonly found in staff teaching on-campus programmes and describe how some American universities are helping their staff adopt more learner-centred approaches. Claire Matthewson and Konai Helu Thaman write of staff development in the multicultural environment of the University of the South Pacific and discuss the important issues of cross-cultural transfer and the submergence of, or 'commodified adding to', other cultures by the dominant educational model of a globalised curriculum. Writing to a similar agenda, Barbara Spronk draws on her Canadian experiences of developing and delivering distance and open programmes for First Nations peoples and suggests that staff developers need to help managers, administrators and lecturers see the world through 'two pairs of eyes'. Christine Randell and Eli Bitzer describe the urgent problems confronting educational reformers and distance educators in South Africa, how staff involved in some innovative programmes are developing models of learning support well suited to the South

African context and the associated staff development needs and priorities. David Sewart of the UK Open University, like Badri Koul, sees the need to integrate staff development into the institutional human resource strategy and argues that ultimately, it is only the staff who deliver open and distance education who can provide the unbeatable competitive advantage. Jo Osborne, writing from her experiences at the University of Tasmania, discusses the need to be wary about making assumptions about students' understandings of flexible learning and discusses the variety of ways in which lecturers and students can use distance education material in on-campus settings.

Part III, Staff Development in Action, draws upon the experience of practitioners in regard to specific open, flexible and technology-based projects. The opening chapters by David Kember and by Neil Haigh complement each other and present compelling arguments for a reconsideration of the forms that staff development activities may take. David Kember challenges the positivistic approach to course design and the technical-rational approach typical of some instructional designers. He advocates action research as a basis for staff development and describes an inter-universities project wherein staff are empowered to reflect upon, monitor and assume responsibility for their own investigations and practices. Neil Haigh offers his personal account of a sensitive approach to staff development which combines 'public general knowledge' with 'personal practical knowledge' as his institution moves towards more flexible forms of teaching. He describes his work with colleagues as they examine their assumptions about teaching and learning, extend their repertoire of teaching methods and skills, become more sensitive to learner needs and investigate the quality of their teaching. Liz Burge and Jennifer O'Rourke describe how their colleagues, moving from conventional forms of teaching to teaching at a distance with new technologies and with little or no staff development support, acquired the skills they believed were needed. This small qualitative study illustrates the broad range of staff perceptions and needs that staff developers must be sensitive to. The chapters by David Murphy and Ross Vermeer and by Cathy Gunn and Mary Panko describe how the creation of teaching material, in a CD-ROM format and within a Flexible and Open Learning Course respectively, provided vehicles for staff development. David Murphy and Ross Vermeer assess the staff development benefits in terms of 'linkage', 'openness', 'leadership', 'ownership' and 'rewards'. Cathy Gunn and Mary Panko discuss their attempts to empower participants on a flexible and open learning course through an understanding of organisations, educational principles and new technologies, and argue that if students are to take more charge of their learning, so too must the managers and teachers of their programmes. Anne Forster and Lindsay Hewson outline the technical and pedagogical skills that staff need to master as they progress from being merely 'aware' to being 'competent' in their use of the Internet. In their chapters, Derek Rowntree and Fred Lockwood share their experiences of providing staff development and offer practical advice that is consistent with the foregoing chapters. Derek Rowntree provides a guide to offering staff development programmes in which the staff developer is the 'guide on the side', rather than the 'sage on the stage'. Fred Lockwood takes the task of assembling a course proposal as a vehicle for staff development and describes a game designed to stimulate discussion and decision-making. David Hawkridge describes the UK Open University Master's degree which uses electronic tutoring and the World Wide Web to help distance educators place themselves, their colleagues and their institutions at the forefront of developments without disrupting their careers, leaving home or losing income. The final chapter, by Richard Freeman, serves to remind us that open and flexible learning projects need to be completed within budget and to a deadline. His explanation of project management and quality assurance procedures provides a useful practical note on which to conclude.

Inevitably there are some contradictions and differing views within this book, but this is to be expected given the varieties of organisations and cultures within which the contributors are operating. However, the contributors broadly concur on the compelling reasons for changing the what, where, when and how of teaching and learning and that there are major resistances to changing management and teaching practices and using technology which need to be addressed if there is to be the much-heralded paradigm shift within universities and colleges. To summarise the findings in this book broadly, a systemic organisational shift to more open and flexible learning requires:

- environmental scanning, a clear vision, strategic planning and priority setting;
- total and public commitment to, and understanding of the ramifications of, the vision and strategic plan by everyone from the vice-chancellor or president down;
- a reshaping of policies, structures, practices and conditions supportive of the desired changes;
- the institution to be a 'learning community' based upon informed 'reflective practice';
- senior and middle managers to be continuously involved in the change processes and sharing the 'pain and the gain';
- staff development to be closely aligned to the institutional strategic plan and embedded within the institutional human resource strategy;
- staff development to have status and adequate resourcing;
- a combination of centralised and devolved staff development;
- the teaching school or support centre to be the focus of change, rather than the individual;
- an accommodation between the new ways of doing things and the teachers' beliefs and skills leading to a negotiated redefinition of staff roles and functions;
- reward and recognition systems which reflect these new roles and functions and honour risk and innovation;

- new synergies and partnerships within and between institutions, sectors and nations.

This book enables the reader to do what would be physically quite impossible: that is, to spend some hours in the company of experienced distance and open educators from around the globe as they discuss the issues of staff development for organisational and educational change. We hope that their practices, researches, speculations and suggestions will provide useful insights and guidance in supporting moves to more learner-centred, resource-based open and flexible learning.

Colin Latchem and Fred Lockwood

References

Beaty, E. (1995) 'Working across the hierarchy', in A. Brew (ed.), *Directions in Staff Development*, Bristol, PA, and Buckingham, UK: Society for Research into Higher Education and Open University Press.

Brew, A. (ed.) (1995) *Directions in Staff Development*, Bristol, PA, and Buckingham, UK: Society for Research into Higher Education and Open University Press.

Johnson, R. (1990) *Open Learning: Policy and Practice*, National Board of Employment Education and Training Commissioned Report No. 4, Canberra, Australian Government Publishing Service.

Laurillard, D. (1993) *Rethinking University Teaching: A Framework for the Effective Use of Educational Technology*, London: Routledge.

Reid, I. (1984) *The Making of Literature: Texts, Contexts, and Classroom Practices*, Adelaide: Australian Association for the Teaching of English.

Taylor, P.G., Lopez, L. and Quadrelli, C. (1996) *Flexibility, Technology and Academics' Practices: Tantalising Tales and Muddy Maps*, Higher Education Division, Department of Employment, Education, Training and Youth Affairs, Evaluations and Investigations Program, Canberra, Australian Government Publishing Service.

Webb, G. (1996) *Understanding Staff Development*, Bristol, PA, and Buckingham, UK: Society for Research into Higher Education and Open University Press.

ACKNOWLEDGEMENTS

The editors are grateful for the valuable assistance given by Sheila Alley, Michelle Robert-Libia and Anna Boyd of the Teaching Learning Group at Curtin University, for their assistance in the publication of this book.

Figure 9.1 on p. 88 is taken from *Managing Organisational Change: A Guide for Managers* by C.D. Scott and D.T. Jaffe (London: Kogan Page, 1990).

Part I

STAFF DEVELOPMENT IN CONTEXT

1

LEADERSHIP FOR OPEN AND FLEXIBLE LEARNING IN HIGHER EDUCATION

Daryl Le Grew and Jocelyn Calvert

Among the features of the new face of higher education are the 'flexible and open curriculum'; 'student (or) client focus'; 'lifelong learning'; 'multimedia integration'; 'pro-active planning and positioning'; 'strategic partnering'; and 'global networking and referencing' (Le Grew 1995: 1). These and other contemporary developments in higher education are increasingly interpreted as reflecting profound change in character and function rather than simply an expansion and diversification of the higher education system (Scott 1995). Furthermore, the transformation needed to serve the 'Information Age' is said to demand 'new delivery systems for learning, new paradigms for financing, and new models for higher education' (Dolence and Norris 1995: 7). The consequent rethinking of teaching and learning is leading to fundamental changes in the organisation and work of universities and the distribution of their resources.

This chapter starts from the premise that the challenges and changes facing higher education are part of the economic, political and social transformation reflected in the global economy and the age of information. Furthermore, these changes are real and enduring, and what leaders, planners and decision-makers need to know about open and flexible learning is intricately bound up with how they conceive the contemporary university and its place in the world. It is our contention that higher education leaders need to be familiar with, and actively engaging in, a number of contemporary debates.

We also see this presenting a major challenge for open and flexible learning professionals. It is often lamented by such practitioners that leaders, planners and decision-makers do not pay attention to these important developments and indeed, do not always acknowledge that anything important is happening. Or alternatively, that they enthusiastically proclaim new initiatives without making necessary organisational changes or allocating the resources needed. Thus, in the last part of our chapter, we consider how leaders learn and the implications of this for the work of open and flexible learning professionals.

The global economy and the information society

Sophisticated communications and information technologies are converging and networks are forming a global system for human interchange that transcends national and cultural boundaries. Electronic trade and commerce create global markets for even the most local of products and new products designed directly for global markets are promoted and traded on international electronic networks. Resource development and management, production and manufacturing systems, and marketing programmes are coordinated globally, increasingly by international consortia and corporations that seem well able to transcend differences in regional and national socio-political systems. In addition, convergent and increasingly intelligent technologies are transforming conventional processes of resource and product development. Production processes that formerly were localised and labour-intensive are increasingly automated and flexible. Services have the major share of the market in the economies of post-industrial societies.

New information services and the free-ranging 'super highway' environment allow for complex interactions wherein business, art, education and entertainment converge. Thus the old media taxonomies are shifting rapidly as innovative software enables the construction and creative use of global information systems. *Inter alia*, these new realities have established a dynamic, global 'community without propinquity' (Webber 1963) that pays scant attention to old boundaries. This global community lays its complex and constantly shifting web over those other communities that are defined and bound by geographic, ethnic and cultural factors.

These developments have impact that reverberates from nation to community to individual, and there are good outcomes and bad, winners and losers. Cultural diversity may be blurred by standardised and homogenised services and products, both economic and cultural. Alternatively, any person, group, organisation, community or nation can differentiate itself by presenting distinctive qualities in the form of cultural and intellectual services and products that are attractive to, and assessable by, others. As Bottomley (1995: 224) suggests, 'regions that (previously) flourished . . . now often languish as the new international division of labour sees manufacturing move to developing nations with lower labour costs' and global economic restructuring is changing the map to reflect a 'new geography of inequality'.

For individuals, the changes mean contending with continual change and less security of employment. At the same time, there is potentially more opportunity in this more flexible business environment. With new communication services, individuals have vastly increased, almost anarchic access to information. The positive prospect is for more freedom of exchange, greater sharing and human interchange and, leaving aside the potential for exploitation or distortion, the creation of a wider community that is only partly propinquitous and almost totally dependent upon increasing levels of technological integration and innovation.

Higher education for the information age

In this last decade of the twentieth century, universities are also undergoing great change. While there are differences among countries in the maturity of their higher education systems and in the extent to which they can meet the demand for traditional places, the factors stimulating change are similar and the key factor is a dramatic rise in participation.

One reason for this is a change in aspiration. Global communications, information exchange and mobility have lifted the expectations of communities in regard to personal achievement, community development and quality of life. International focus on social justice has raised the consciousness and expectations for equity and access for communities that are disadvantaged and oppressed – no more so than in education where, quite rightly, more people, regardless of their personal and community histories, are coming to regard access to higher education as desirable and as a right. In most developed economies, public policy over recent decades has slowly become attuned to this social revolution.

Even more potent is the recognition, in public policy, of a connection between education and the successful development of integrated and sophisticated regional and national economies that can compete internationally in the emergent global economy. Thus, in combination with more pragmatic economic and labour market policies, many governments have encouraged and invested in education as a route to jobs. Add to this increasing pressure on professional associations, corporations, agencies and employers to sponsor continual retraining so that they can remain competitive and competent, and it is not difficult to understand the high participation and retention rates in all levels of education and training. Dolence and Norris (1995: 7–8) claim that, for a nation to remain competitive, every member of the workforce should spend the equivalent of one year in full-time study in every seven years of work. If this learning was to be carried out in a conventional classroom context, a country such as Australia would need to build, by the year 2000, forty-two new university campuses, each accommodating approximately 30,000 students, at a total cost of A$14.8 billion. This estimate assumes 1.3 million full-time equivalent learners in an Australian workforce of 8.9 million, and does not allow for the enrolment of any international students.

There is broad agreement internationally on the changes these world developments would mean for universities. Steeples (1990: 101–2), writing on the American situation, cited fewer school leavers, an ageing population, less public funding, greater participation of minority groups, the global economy, the technology and knowledge explosions and the adoption of marketplace parlance by academia as features of 'an era of instability and competition'. Scott (1991), from a British perspective, explored the consequences for universities of the development of mass higher education. He foresaw universities as part of a broadly constituted knowledge industry, more reliant on targeted and special purpose funding, operating under a managerial regime. They would offer non-traditional programmes for a heterogeneous student body, with emphasis on liberal, technical, caring and enterprise professions, and increasing reliance on technology for teaching. The 'Hoare Report' (Higher Education Management Review Committee 1995: 23–4) listed, among the pressures facing Australian universities, 'demands . . . for more accountability and better performance'; 'more direct competition' with other universities as well as the vocational education and training and the private sectors; 'the end of assured government funded growth in undergraduate places'; 'a working, teaching and learning environment . . . reshaped by . . . new information technology and communications'; 'mass participation . . . and increasing diversity of the student population, and the requirement for economy of operations and acquittal of social justice objectives'; and the 'internationalisation of higher education'.

Open and flexible higher education

Just as a principal characteristic of the new global economy and the information age is flexibility, so, at the same time, are the changes in universities and the environment in which they operate defined by flexibility (Bottomley 1995). Australia's Deakin University provides one example of a university that has built on its dual-mode origins and embraced the changes described above. It caters for more than 60,000 students, of whom half are studying through the university's commercial arm, Deakin Australia. Only 12,408 are full-time, on-campus students; 43,000 or 72 per cent are off-campus. Of the students in regular programmes, 37 per cent are aged 30 and over and the great majority are in clearly applied areas of study. Deakin was named Australian University of the Year in 1995 for its integration of technology into undergraduate teaching and learning, and it has invested heavily, in part with special grants, in software development and computer communication and can evidence good results in terms of adoption.

We argue, however, that open and flexible higher education is not just a matter for open universities and those that feature distance education; all universities are faced with the issues of how they will relate to a wider clientele and incorporate new methods. And indeed, there is evidence that they are addressing these issues. For example, when the Australian National Council on Open and Distance Education, reconstituted from eight government-designated distance education centres, invited all Australian universities to become fee-paying members, thirty-one of thirty-eight universities accepted the offer. And in the UK, where the Open University was once the only major distance education option, the plethora of advertisements for courses 'by distance learning' suggests that almost everyone is doing it. In fact, the vulnerability of the UK OU in the face of competition has prompted some public breast-beating (Rumble 1992).

Recognition of the need for universities to transform themselves to cater for new students with new methods is not new. Ten years ago, Bok wrote about 'non-traditional students . . . flocking to Harvard', particularly for 'education for professional development' (1986: 116). 'The great challenge of continuing education will be to make it central to the activities of every professional school without stifling the innovative, flexible qualities that have enabled it to grow so successfully in the past' (p. 128). Duke (1992: 5), writing more recently, takes a more extreme view, contending that 'mainstream [continuing education] . . . heralds a new paradigm of the university'. Although there will undoubtedly be variations in the degree to which universities broaden their horizons, we do not envisage the situation predicted by Slee (1990: 90) that higher education in the UK 'will be sharply defined into four sectors': 'Ivy Leaguers' catering for the 'traditional student market', 'giant civics offering a range of services tailored flexibly to the needs of a range of regionally based clientele', 'a national network of distance- and open-learning centres covering professional updating, training and development' and 'a handful of specialist research institutions'.

The broad changes outlined above have an impact on the curricula, teaching and learning methods, and organisation and work of universities. For example, a competitive environment commends strategic alliances and universities are aligning themselves with corporations, professional associations, schools, vocational institutions and other universities in the development and delivery of courses. Even broader alliances will be necessary as institutions realise that they cannot create the resources needed to compete in globalised information environments and combine in national and international consortia to achieve critical mass in infrastructure and intellectual fire power. Such consortia will carry other non-academic partners – publishers, media companies, information technology providers, administrative service providers, public relations and marketing agencies. International partnerships of this kind will provide opportunities to package together the best of content and academic and administrative services and deliver flexibly to wherever the students and other organisations may be. Being outside the realm of these various international consortia will be difficult for individual institutions, yet negotiating the way in through the maze of local and national legislation, international protocols and agreements needed for such collaboration will require special skills as yet underdeveloped in the realm of higher education.

In another example, alliances for teaching and learning, along with a more diverse range of students with varied backgrounds and motivations, entering and leaving education at different points and times, require articulated programmes of study. Credit transfer, recognition of prior non-formal learning and foundation and bridging courses are blurring traditional educational boundaries. Many secondary schools and vocational institutions are now teaching university introductory programmes under licence. Credit transfer agreements mean that vocational and higher education courses are more neatly articulated, and laddering undergraduate and postgraduate awards is now practised widely. Institutions are becoming skilled at designing bridging and interpretation programmes that facilitate cross-sectoral movement, both ways. Awards are being linked more flexibly into particular training outcomes, employment levels and professional accreditation goals. These localised arrangements are rapidly moving into national and international dimensions.

In addition, movement towards internationalisation across ethnic and cultural boundaries demands that curricula and teaching styles recognise cultural and epistemological differences. These concern not just content but context, learning styles and even contradictory attitudes and interpretations of curricular issues. Much more of the academic and educative content and styles of the institution will be influenced by the range of its international programmes and partnerships. More programmes will be jointly produced and adapted for twinning and co-educational arrangements with students and staff learning to tolerate difference and often ambiguity. The challenge will be to devise more creative learning frameworks that can hold the differences yet still produce a source of coherence to the various students.

Add to these a variety of modes and media for learning and major issues loom for staff development, technical support and administrative systems. These are exacerbated by the shrinkage of traditional funding. Leaders, planners and decision-makers do not have an easy task.

Executive development in higher education

A review in the UK found that leadership and management development in higher education was not conceived in terms of career development and tended to focus on categories of staff in short courses for specific purposes. The principal types of programme were 'national short courses and seminars', 'locally organised in-house programmes on management themes' and 'European programmes and conferences' (Middlehurst 1995: 110). Davies (1995), reviewing a number of reports of management development programmes, commented that national programmes raise awareness of issues and developments and demonstrate the commitment of the programmes' sponsors, but are not perceived as leading to effective transfer of learning back into the workplace. On institutionally organised programmes, he commented that one-off events tend not to be valued while programmes that involve a series of related activities are better regarded. He also saw value in programmes designed for individual needs involving self-managed learning and counselling.

Middlehurst (1995: 110) also observed, however, that lists of formal provision do not really capture where much learning takes place. Among her examples of activities with developmental properties are 'running workshops . . . making presentations at conferences . . . participating in external committees . . . acting as governor or director for outside organisations, [and] preparing for external review at departmental or institutional level'. It is broadly reported that non-formal learning plays a major role.

A third approach involves using real problems as a focus for group development. One long-term programme coupled a review of leadership in

8

Swedish universities with a strongly focused visit of vice-chancellors and then deans to an American university; significant changes were documented in the follow-up period back in Sweden. In another example, the Conference of European Rectors has used a 'live case study' approach wherein a university hosts a seminar and at the same time invites the participants 'to act as consultants on a management issue or project that the university wishes to tackle' (Middlehurst 1995: 111–12).

An approach to formal individual development has been described by Brown-Parker (1996: 3–4). Seven Australian universities in the state of Victoria formed a consortium with a special grant to 'establish a variety of non-formal learning schemes' for 'academic and general staff holding a senior leadership and management position'. The seven selected schemes are mentoring, shadowing, special projects, job exchanges, structured placements, networks and action learning groups.

Boud (1995: 209) has listed developments in learning theory with implications for staff development:

- learning occurs whether or not there is formal instruction;
- learning is relational;
- learning which occurs away from the workplace may be necessary, but it is intrinsically limited;
- learning in organisations is typically problem-orientated;
- learning in the workplace is a social activity which is influenced by the norms and values of the workplace;
- learners' expectations are a function of their prior experience; and
- learning from experience requires attention to reflection and processing of experience.

Judged against this list, we suggest that non-formal development activities in a work context and problem-based programmes in real work settings will have greater value than formal short courses in enabling executives, leaders, planners and decision-makers to develop and manage new paradigms and modes of higher education.

Learning within the university

Scott (1995: 69–70) sees a shift in large institutions in mass higher education systems from a managerial to a strategic culture, claiming that: 'outwardly stratified . . . and inwardly differentiated . . . these new universities may become 'unmanageable' – but with creative rather than destructive consequences. Flexibility, synergy and volatility will be the dominant modes of these new organisations. Flat hierarchies and loosely coupled networks will abound.' According to Scott, this shift from managerial to strategic culture is characterised by reflexivity, wherein 'individuals, and social institutions, are freed from the givens, the fixities of tradition. Their norms ... must be constructed, and frequently reconstructed, in the light of interaction between abstract systems and actual environments. In other words, they become reflexive' (p. 116).

Scott's premise adds strength to the argument that leadership development for open and flexible learning should be integrated into working life. Middlehurst (1993: 182) described her vision for organisational development thus:

> Within interactive arenas (from committee meetings to appraisals), learning could be a reciprocal process, although the individual outcomes of learning will be different. The idea of 'learning leadership' builds on this reciprocity of influence between leaders and colleagues by emphasising mutual responsibilities. Nurturing such an ethos within a university depends on creating a continuing and open dialogue about the institution's purposes and outcomes, the means of achieving them and the contributions of individuals and groups to the whole; and in reverse, it depends on demonstrating the university's contribution to individual and group learning and creativity. Both aims can be achieved by actively welcoming and encouraging individual and team initiative and ideas in all areas of the institution.

What does this imply for the work of open and flexible learning professionals? Will our leaders, planners and decision-makers learn best and most about open and flexible learning and all that it involves in our institutions by attending showcase events, going on short courses and taking packaged tours of 'best practice'? The literature suggests that these sorts of events might be useful to create an initial level of awareness. In our analysis, however, *everyone* in our universities should be aware of, and learning about, new developments and changing directions all the time. This requires a culture that fosters collaborative development.

What is needed from the experts in open and flexible learning is creative energy to raise issues, generate discussion and put forward solutions. Examples that come to mind are Beaty's (1995) 'ginger group' of senior people who undertake voluntarily to discuss and raise policy issues in the wider university, or Latchem and Parker's (1996) teaching and learning strategic planning exercise that engaged the university at different stages of defining goals and directions.

In the *learning university*, 'staff and career development come to be seen in their multifarious forms (training courses being but one minor element) as the means whereby the whole institution continuously learns and adapts towards purposes agreed and valued by its members' (Duke 1992: 108–9).

References

Beaty, E. (1995) 'Working across the hierarchy', in A. Brew (ed.), *Directions in Staff Development*, Buckingham: The Society for Research into Higher Education and Open University Press, pp. 146–57.

Bok, D. (1986) *Higher Learning*, Cambridge, MA: Harvard University Press.

Bottomley, J. (1995) 'Distance education, open learning and the regional problem', in D. Sewart (ed.), *One World Many Voices: Quality in Open and Distance Learning*, collected papers from the 17th ICDE World Conference of Distance Education, vol. 1, Oslo and Milton Keynes: International Council for Distance Education and Open University, pp. 224–7.

Boud, D. (1995) 'Meeting the challenges', in A. Brew (ed.), *Directions in Staff Development*, Bristol, PA, and Buckingham: The Society for Research into Higher Education and Open University Press, pp. 203–13.

Brown-Parker, J. (1996) 'Non-formal leadership and management development: making the practice reflect the theory', paper presented at the 1996 HERDSA Conference, Perth, University of Western Australia.

Davies, J.L. (1995) 'The training of academic heads of departments', in A. Brew (ed.), *Directions in Staff Development*, Bristol, PA, and Buckingham: The Society for Research into Higher Education and Open University Press, pp. 118–32.

Dolence, M.G. and Norris, D.M. (1995) *Transforming Higher Education: A Vision for Learning in the 21st Century*, Ann Arbor, MI: Society for College and University Planning.

Duke, C. (1992) *The Learning University: Towards a New Paradigm*, Milton Keynes: Open University Press.

Higher Education Management Review Committee (Australia) (1995) *Report of the Committee of Inquiry/Higher Education Management Review*, Canberra, Australian Government Publishing Service.

Latchem, C. and Parker, L. (1996) 'Developing a teaching and learning strategic plan: a case study', RMIT, ultiBASE, http://ultibase.rmit.edu.au/Articles/latchem.html.

Le Grew, D. (1995) 'Global knowledge: superhighway or super gridlock', paper presented at Symposium – Media and Higher Education, National Institute of Multimedia Education, Japan (Nov.).

Middlehurst, R. (1993) *Leading Academics*, Buckingham: The Society for Research into Higher Education and Open University Press.

—— (1995) 'Top training: development for institutional managers', in A. Brew (ed.), *Directions in Staff Development*, Bristol, PA, and Buckingham: The Society for Research into Higher Education and Open University Press, pp. 98–117.

Rumble, G. (1992) 'The competitive vulnerability of distance teaching universities', *Open Learning*, 7(2): 31–45.

Scott, P. (1991) 'The idea of mass higher education 3: confusion as evidence of health', *The Times Higher* (23 Aug.), p. 12.

—— (1995) *The Meanings of Mass Higher Education*, Buckingham: The Society for Research into Higher Education and Open University Press.

Slee, P. (1990) 'Apocalypse now? Where will higher education go in the twenty-first century?', in P.W.G. Wright (ed.), *Industry and Higher Education: Collaboration to Improve Students' Learning and Training*, Buckingham: The Society for Research into Higher Education and Open University Press, pp. 88–91.

Steeples, D.H. (1990) *Managing Change in Higher Education*, San Francisco: Jossey Bass.

Webber, M. M. (1963) 'Order in diversity: community without propinquity', in L. Wingo (ed.), *Cities and Space*, Baltimore, MD: Johns Hopkins University Press, pp. 23–56.

2

INFORMING GOVERNMENT AND INSTITUTIONAL LEADERS ABOUT THE POTENTIALS AND PITFALLS OF OPEN LEARNING

Ross Paul

Increasingly, efforts to promote educational opportunity and lifelong learning are confronted by high costs and the need for new efficiencies in education and training. The optimism that characterised massive investments in education in recent decades has gradually been displaced by the political will to control spending as deficits rise and by disillusionment with what are often perceived as unresponsive educational institutions. In this climate, politicians and institutional leaders are seeking new structures and new techniques, spurred on by rapid developments in communications technologies which seem to promise rosy new horizons for the future.

Given the widespread acceptance of 'knowledge' as the new currency of power, one would expect the university to be viewed as the pre-eminent institution in the development of a new society. However, its elitist roots, academic culture and collegial governance model are widely misunderstood and questioned by political leaders seeking quick fixes, rapid responses and cost-efficient higher education for the masses.

In its flexibility, openness and provision for the needs of individual learners, distance learning may be viewed as responsive to criticisms of the more traditional academic approaches. However, most experienced practitioners of distance education and open learning are still outside the mainstream and most breakthroughs in educational technology are coming from campus-based institutions (Paul 1995: 132–3). Hence, those in the best position to advise on the suitability of distance learning systems are relatively marginalised and there is a danger that educational innovation over the next decade or two will largely ignore recent experiences with distance education.

In this chapter, it is argued that much better understanding of the hard lessons of open learning is a prerequisite to the ability of political and educational leaders to realise the high expectations they hold for it.

What politicians want from educational systems

While the details will vary from country to country, there is remarkable international consensus about what political leaders want from higher education institutions in today's tight fiscal climate. The following speech from a slightly caricatured minister of education should sound familiar to readers in many countries:

> My fellow citizens. As Minister of Education, I am launching today a major inquiry into the future of our educational system. Ours is a knowledge-based society where international communications have shrunk the world. We cannot afford to enter the new millennium with the institutions and practices of the old, nor can we afford to carry their corresponding debts and deficits. The burgeoning costs of education, health care and other vital services have led to such large debt loads that the costs of servicing them are greater than the budgets of some government departments! We are thus forced to re-examine not only the relative priorities among services but how moneys are deployed within them and what relationship expenditures have to the quality of product.
>
> We have invested heavily in schools, colleges and universities and yet they are resistant to change, they don't interact effectively with each other and too many students drop out. We need a much more entrepreneurial system, one that is responsive, cost efficient and accountable, accountable to the taxpayer, the parent and the student. We must equip the citizens of today with the tools of tomorrow. Only in this way can we reinvent our future!

If the rhetoric is at all familiar, the following specific outcomes will be recognised as those most frequently sought by local political leaders.

Cost efficiency

This primary requirement covers a series of concerns common to all ministries of education and the corporate jargon used is remarkably similar across national contexts:

- the proportion of expenditures on the 'core' business must be maximised – this usually means 'teaching' in a university, with the research agenda being a much harder sell among most politicians;
- there is need to review the amount spent on salaries in general but especially on administration;
- there is need to develop a more integrated system among schools, colleges, polytechnics and universities through collaboration and articulation agreements which reduce duplication and rigid boundaries across institutions; and

14

- there is need to reduce programme duplication among competing institutions. (However, political considerations usually result in fewer interventions in this domain than is envisaged at the outset.)

Accountability and productivity

Given the huge investment of 'inputs', there is growing concern for the 'outputs' of the educational system, especially those that are measurable. Calls for such performance indicators as cost per student, graduation rates, comparative scores on international tests and job placement successes are universal. Few ministries pay more than lip-service to the legitimate concern that what is quantifiable and measurable may not be the best measure of the long-term impact of the educational system. Unfortunately, while higher education is about the long term, politics are about the immediate.

Cost sharing and new sources of revenue

If the taxpayer cannot or will not pay for more and better educational services, other sources of revenue and support must be found. The two most popular of these are tuition fees and the private sector.

Students are asked to pay an increasingly greater share of the costs of their tuition, which further strains government-subsidised loan schemes. Income contingent repayment plans are supposed to reflect the investment value of higher education to the individual, but these are controversial when even a university degree does not guarantee immediate access to the job market.

The private sector, a presumed beneficiary of the products of the educational system, is also expected to contribute more to its funding. There is consequent tremendous interest in partnerships, collaboration, outsourcing and privatising all sorts of programmes and services, interest that far exceeds the effective actions taken in this regard. Even where there is increased private support for research and capital investment, it almost never replaces reduced government funding for programming or on-going operations of the institutions.

Internationalism and world standards

Politicians dream of the global village in which national boundaries are of diminishing importance as students connect across cultures, and where local products and services are exported to other nations. One of the most overused adjectives of the nineties is 'world-class' whereby local leaders envisage their town or country as a global leader in a given field. With its professional expertise and international linkages, the local university may be seen as the best avenue to this competitive position, but its often slow and bureaucratic decision-making processes may also counter this expectation.

Flexibility

There is growing recognition that traditional, lock-step, kindergarten to university full-time education may no longer be sufficient in the knowledge society. As education is recognised as a lifelong process, more flexible learning systems are demanded to cater to the idiosyncratic needs of individuals to study at their own rate and in their own place. A focus on educational outcomes has also spurred interest in prior learning assessment and competency-based challenge examinations.

This search for flexibility ties in with concerns about the resistance to change that is apparently built into so many of our established institutions and hence there is a search for more free-wheeling and flexible systems that can adapt quickly to the fast-changing information needs of modern society. The quest for quick response is linked to computers, graphics and the Internet, while classroom lecturing and textbooks are associated with older and less responsive university models.

Consumer-driven provision

Much of the criticism of current practice emanates from concerns that institutions are limited by faculty who teach what they want to teach rather than what others think should be taught. Centuries of faculty control are being challenged by those who want students and taxpayers to have greater say in curriculum and its presentation. The notion of student as 'customer' is a direct challenge to the prevailing academic culture, especially to the extent that it ignores the responsibilities of individual students for their own learning.

These factors combine to support a more utilitarian and shorter-term view of the university which blurs its distinctiveness from community colleges and other more flexible training institutions. They also increase the status of the 'harder' disciplines (science and professional programmes) and of cooperative and work-study arrangements, often at the expense of the arts and the humanities.

Overcoming distance in traditional classrooms

The problems of distance education are so obvious (distance, time, asynchronous communications) that they draw attention to the same concerns that exist in more subtle ways in traditional classrooms. Especially as university classes get larger and larger in these days of fiscal constraint, there may be as much distance between student and professor as there is in a distance education programme. In fact, the latter may provide for more interaction between student and tutor than is ever experienced in a huge first-year class on campus.

Why politicians are interested in distance education

Given the above visions, it is not difficult to understand why there is suddenly so much interest in distance education and open learning. The irony is that those less familiar with these concepts are among their strongest advocates, while experienced practitioners are often more cautious. Consider the following not atypical example of a minister's view of distance learning:

> We are very excited about the contributions that distance learning can make to our national requirements. We envisage a world where students take responsibility for their own learning, where they are plugged instantly into the Internet and can communicate directly with the best experts in a given field in their own time and in their own place. We must have a computer on every desk, a modem in every house and the necessary software to permit every student to access the Internet at any time of the day or night. We need students who take much more responsibility for their own learning – let's take the distance out of distance education and put the 'you' back in university!

A primary but often unstated motive for interest in distance education is the seductive vision of a brave new world of technology and communications. Even those who have never had access to the World Wide Web portray it as a panacea for all of the ills of our current educational system. They dream of 'virtual campuses' (no costly capital or maintenance expenditures) where every citizen learns at his or her own time, pace and place and where learning is exciting, entertaining and stimulating.

At first glance, distance education can be adapted effectively to meet each of the needs outlined above – cost efficiency, accountability, collaboration, international communications, flexibility, learner-centredness and improving interaction. Politicians thus have some grounds for their visions of virtual universities built around modern technology, but how well does this vision match the realities of the practice of distance education and open learning over the past three decades?

Some hard lessons from distance education

The hypothetical minister of education quoted in the above two excerpts might be disappointed with the following lessons from the recent practice of distance education and open learning.

The key role of open admissions

The overemphasis on technology by advocates of distance education overlooks the critical role that open admissions has played in the success of open universities around the world. The UK Open University has been a great success – but not because it attracted many more students from the lower social strata as had been its original intention. The success of most open universities has been the high performance of *already self-actualised* learners previously denied access to university who would have performed well in any system of higher education (Paul 1990: 83).

This may be a key reason why distance education is such a different concept in the USA. Open learning has had a major impact in Europe where, until recently, only a small percentage of the population attended university. This contrasts with the USA where, with such a variety of institutions and standards, there has not been the same need for new concepts to ensure access. American 'distance education' usually refers to the use and potential of new communications technologies rather than open admissions, course teams or regional student services.

High front-end costs

While the field badly needs up-to-date and sophisticated economic analysis, there is a general consensus that distance education is cost-efficient only when a critical mass has been surpassed (Rumble 1997). Up-front costs tend to be high, whether one is paying for course design and development, the acquisition of expensive technology or the establishment of open learning support systems. The savings are longer term in the marginal costs of course delivery, the comparative lack of reliance on capital investment and the flexibility to the learner that distance education permits.

Low completion rates

With a few exceptions, completion rates in open and distance learning institutions are lower than for traditional on-campus institutions and this cost must be factored into any economic assessment of distance education. While there have been very effective responses to this concern (Woodley 1994), they have usually involved greater investments of funds (such as for staff development, more and better support services, and regional networks) and so the cost efficiency has not necessarily increased.

One-way learning

An important early component of distance education was Instructional Systems Design (ISD) which emanated from the US military. With its emphasis on mastery learning and measurable learning outcomes, this approach was, and is, extremely effective in skills development, but it is also a Fordist industrial model less suited to more complex learning tasks and with little provision for differences among individual learners. A more critical perspective has been adopted in recent literature (see especially, Evans and Nation 1993), but much international distance education, especially in more authoritarian regimes, still involves one-way communication, usually by television or correspondence.

In extolling the virtues of distance education, Cook (1989) has written eloquently about the hidden tyranny of the authority of the teacher in the classroom. For some, the freeing up of the student from the dominance of the teacher is a very attractive feature of distance learning. However, what is often overlooked is that the same tyranny can be replicated in distance education – through top-down course design, or insufficient provision for interaction and critical thinking, or because inadequate student support systems leave isolated students ill-equipped to challenge the pre-packaged learning materials.

Paying attention to the individual learner

Advocates of mass distance education often overlook the importance of assessing the abilities, needs and characteristics of the target student groups involved. As noted above, most successes in distance education have been among highly motivated, often part-time, adult learners. Early ISD tended to assume that all students were the same, focusing more on course design than on the varying needs of learners. It was soon realised that this was a major shortcoming of the ISD approach. For example, the Canadian Athabasca University had far more success with northern First Nations students when it replaced its traditional course package/telephone tutor model with on-site native counsellors and gave local tutors more authority to adapt course materials to the local culture. A recent book based on Australian experiences (Evans 1994) offers insights into the extent to which factors such as gender, age, money and time influence the distance learner.

Many question whether distance education can match the broader benefits of campus life, especially for young full-time undergraduates experiencing the freedom to pursue ideas and socialise in an open atmosphere for the first time in their lives. This is not to deny the tremendous advantages of distance education but simply to recognise that education is much more than an academic endeavour.

The importance of local context and culture

The oft-cited advantage for distance education – that it enables us to use the expertise of the best faculty available, not just those under our own employ – can undervalue the importance of the local context and culture to learning. In fact, the above example of Aboriginal education led Athabasca University to reform its whole interaction with students, recognising that an MBA, whether delivered into a large corporation, as a home-study course or via teleconferencing to a group of professionals, required sensitivity to the particular cultures and circumstances of the respective student groups.

Technology is value-laden

As I have attempted to show elsewhere (Paul 1995), distance education has actually contributed very little to the development of new technologies for learning systems, their management or their leadership. Even though it is obvious that technology is only a means to an end that must not be allowed to become an end in itself, this supposed axiom is frequently belied in educational practice. Instead of starting with the learning needs of students and then trying to find the best combination of learning strategies to meet them, so many 'innovative' programmes start with the technological toys. It is too seldom recognised that introducing a new technology confronts the culture of an institution and often significantly changes it, sometimes in unintended ways. This underlines the need to understand the prevailing culture, to plan for the introduction of change and to be sensitive to its impact on faculty, staff and students.

Not all unintended consequences are negative. Athabasca University recently introduced a 'talk' computer conferencing programme to encourage academic interchanges among isolated students. The students, however, turned this into an electronic 'coffee shop', used more for personal support than for formal learning. As a result, its users feel more engaged, more supported, and are consequently more apt to persist than those lacking access to such informal support.

Heterick (1994) has observed that we tend to overestimate the short-term and underestimate the long-term potential of any given new technology. Our biggest problem with educational technology lies in how we interact with our students, not with the supporting hardware and software. This, not competitive anxiety, must drive technological change in our universities.

The implication of these lessons for educational reform

The central thesis of this chapter is that while it is appropriate for government and institutional leaders to look to distance education and open learning for educational reform, they tend to pay disproportionate attention to the glamour of technology, overlooking the real lessons of three decades of experience. Opinion and policy-makers, leaders and managers need to be helped to appreciate that distance education has its appropriate place – for the right tasks, for the right learners and with the right support – that it is not the *whole* answer, but that it can increasingly be *part of* the answer.

Paul and Brindley (1996) suggest several reform strategies that take account of recent practice. Among the most important are adopting a critical perspective, recognising and managing the cultural implications of the introduction of new technologies into an organisation, and providing strong and flexible student support systems. Course delivery methods should be dependent upon a wide range of factors, including the academic discipline and the circumstances of the learners involved.

Another aspect of distance education that deserves more attention is how readily it lends itself to inter-institutional collaboration. For example, several

Ontario universities serve a minority and widely dispersed Franco-Ontarian culture by offering a comprehensive range of university programmes in the French language. The universities plan the overall programming together to minimise duplication and deliver many of the key courses at a distance. This network, which permits Francophones anywhere in this vast province to gain access to the courses they need, is a model of efficiency for the much larger English provincial system to emulate.

Distance education and open learning are thriving because they are addressing important shortfalls in more traditional learning systems. They have provided opportunities to new categories of student, provided flexibility and support to non-traditional learners in their own time and place, and, most importantly, have helped demonstrate that a much greater proportion of the populace can contribute to, and benefit from, higher education than was ever previously anticipated.

These concepts and practices have much to offer the evolution of our formal educational system. If we are really to benefit from the experience of distance learning, however, we must pay more attention to the lessons of its practical experience. This means that distance education practitioners must participate more fully in debates about the reform of traditional education. In response to the shiny dreams of politicians, we must offer optimistic but well-informed and realistic perspectives that will ensure that the lessons we have learned in the narrower field of open learning will soon be applied to all formal learning systems.

The danger, both for education in general and the field of distance education in particular, is that those most enamoured with new technology, who come almost exclusively from outside the domain of open learning, will dominate educational developments over the next decade – and that those who have so much to contribute, the distance education practitioners, will be passed over once again. Those of us in the latter category must ensure that this does not happen.

References

Cook, J. (1989) 'The liberation of distance: teaching women's studies from China', in D. Nation and T. Evans (eds), *Critical Reflections on Distance Education*, Lewes: The Falmer Press, pp. 23–38.

Evans, T.D. (1994) *Understanding Learners in Open and Distance Education*, London: Kogan Page.

Evans, T. and Nation, D. (eds) (1993) *Reforming Open and Distance Education: Critical Reflections from Practice*, London: Kogan Page.

Heterick, R. (1994) 'Technological change and higher education policy', in *AGB Priorities* I: 1.

Paul, R. (1990) *Open Learning and Open Management: Leadership and Integrity in Distance Education*, London: Kogan Page.

—— (1995) 'Virtual realities or fantasies? Technology and the future of distance education', in J. Roberts and E. Keough (eds), *Why the Information Highway? Lessons from Open and Distance Learning*, Toronto: Trifolium Books Inc., pp. 126–45.

Paul, R. and Brindley, J. (1996) 'Lessons from distance education for the university of the future', in R. Mills and A. Tait (eds), *Supporting the Learner in Open and Distance Learning*, London: Pitman Publishing, pp. 43–58.

Rumble, G. (1997) *Costs and Economics of Open and Distance Learning*, London: Kogan Page.

Woodley, A. (1994) 'Drop out – it may be inevitable but is it predictable?', in M. Thorpe and D. Grugen (eds), *Open Learning in the Mainstream*, London: Longman.

3

STAFF DEVELOPMENT IN CONVENTIONAL INSTITUTIONS MOVING TOWARDS OPEN LEARNING

Roger Lewis

Many 'conventional' educational institutions are now seeking to implement open learning because pressures in their current environments require them to widen student access and increase students' responsibility for their own learning. In this process, changes will be required in the ways in which providers operate:

- in the development of the curriculum;
- in the application of technology;
- in the use of learning materials; and not at least
- in defining and supporting the role of the student.

These changes require staff to operate in new ways, yet this is at a time of relatively low morale. Institutional managers have to empower staff and create a situation in which energy and imagination are released. Staff development has an important role in this, but can be only one part of a multifaceted strategy.

The challenges

The challenges facing education are well known and documented. Hence this introductory section offers only the briefest of overviews. Higher education in the UK is used as the example, but the points made throughout this chapter also apply, with relevant modification, to other levels of educational provision, such as schools and further education, and to other countries. These challenges – which many in the UK higher education see as imposed – include:

- maintaining standards of quality with increasing student numbers (in the UK numbers in higher education grew by 44 per cent between 1988–89 and 1992–93), on campuses that are often already over-crowded and under-resourced;

- offering guidance to, and subsequent support for, increasingly diverse students – diverse in terms of social, cultural and educational backgrounds, age and aspirations;
- meeting the expectations of the students and other stakeholders (for example employers) that the educational service will operate flexibly in terms of time and place, supporting students as they learn in the home, workplace and community;
- helping students to acquire not only subject-specific skills but also the capabilities needed for employment (for example, communication skills and working in teams); this imperative is reinforced by student expectations, as they increasingly have to finance their university studies through concurrent and subsequent earnings; and
- responding to all of the above in the context of declining state funding (in the UK funding per higher education student declined by 20 per cent between 1989–90 and 1993–94, and by a further 10 per cent between 1994–95 and 1996–97).

In such circumstances, 'the need to review the nature of the delivery of teaching and learning is clear' (Davies 1994: not numbered). In the UK, some commentators are looking for 'massive innovation' using new technology and ideas, paralleling the creation of the Open University in the 1960s and 1970s (Williams and Fry 1994: 39).

These pressures translate into challenging criteria for a new learning environment – one which must meet the needs of mass education cost-effectively, provide learning experiences of perceived quality for a disparate student group, develop generic skills as well as subject-specific knowledge, and foster a culture of lifelong learning.

Responses to the challenge

These challenges can be met by following two major strategies: increasing access to education, and helping students to assume greater responsibility for their own learning. These will be familiar to readers as the two main thrusts of open learning.

Increasing access to education

The first strategy – increasing access to education – is often perceived as largely a question of creating opportunities for students who would otherwise be debarred from study by geographical distance or time constraint. The oft-repeated dictum is of opening up time, place and pace. Open universities and correspondence colleges have succeeded in widening options in these ways for countless students over the years, using packaged materials and flexible delivery methods. Related to this has been the freeing up of fixed curriculum structures. The curriculum has been broken into shorter chunks, often self-contained and credit-rated, making it easier for students to accommodate formal learning within their lives. In the UK, this was an early achievement of the Open University. In another arena, the system of national vocational qualifications has created comparable flexibility.

But physical access to learning is only part of the requirement. Access also has a psychological dimension. Education providers thus have to attend to such matters as

- the attractiveness of the curriculum and its delivery;
- the clarity of the curriculum, especially in terms of its intended outcomes and the methods by which these will be assessed; and
- the quality of support for the students.

The extent of psychological access is related to the choices available to students once they have gained physical access to learning. The attractiveness of the learning environment to students is likely to depend on the number of areas in which choice is available, and the extent of choice in each area. Some providers put all their energies into enabling physical access, but once in, the students then experience a closed curriculum. Choices may thus be needed not only in the time and place of study but also in regard to the available learning methods, media, assessment, content and tutors.

Helping students assume greater responsibility for their own learning

The second strategy – helping students to assume greater responsibility for their own learning – is often espoused by open learning providers. The link with the earlier discussion is student choice. It is through exercising choice, assessing the consequences, and choosing accordingly next time, that we become more responsible, not only for our learning, but also for other aspects of our lives.

There are at least three good reasons for stressing the importance of choice. These relate directly to the challenges set out at the start of this chapter. First, if education is to meet the requirements placed on it by society, it must become ever more cost-effective. The reasons for this are set out elsewhere (Daniel 1996). Technology is often advocated as a way of achieving cost-effectiveness, but another major consideration is that the more self-directed and self-reliant students become, the more selective and strategic will be their demands on the tutors and facilities. Thus more independent learning makes excellent economic sense.

But the economic argument is by no means the only one. The second thrust behind increased student responsibility is educational. The argument that good educational provision frees students to go on to learn independently is scarcely new. Teachers have always expressed the hope that their students will acquire a love of learning and capacities to study independently, outside and beyond formal provision. Thus the economic argument is supported by a strong and respectable educational rationale, one which has recently gained far greater prominence.

Implicit in this is the third reason for increasing student responsibility; namely, that through exercising choice students become better equipped, not only to go on learning, but also to face the challenges of other life roles in the twenty-first century. Individuals are now required to make choices over all aspects of their lives, to an extent that would not have been predicted even twenty years ago. To survive as a parent, an employee, or a member of a local community now demands the capacities of the lifetime learner.

Changes to the learning environment

Increased access and development of greater student independence will involve changes in the learning environment:

- in the development of the curriculum;
- in the application of technology;
- in the use of learning materials; and not least
- in defining and supporting the role of the student.

Development of the curriculum

The importance of this dimension was highlighted in a project on Quality in Higher Education, carried out in the UK. Key quality criteria were identified across eight groups of stakeholders (Harvey 1994). Eight of the ten items related to curriculum development:

- programme explicitness (two items);
- assessment and feedback (four items);
- transferable skills/independent learning (two items).

The other two items related to the adequate provision of physical and human resources.

Although the structures of the curriculum may have been relaxed, much has still to be achieved in the three areas listed above, and particularly in regard to

- balancing subject content with skills development;
- harmonising learning outcomes, assessment methods and learning methods;
- designing appropriate assessment methods; and
- generating full, frequent and regular feedback to students on their performance.

Application of technology

Technology is frequently advanced as the means by which education will meet current challenges. But a recent survey suggests that progress in this area has been patchy to date (Lewis and Merton 1996). Daniel (1996) also subjects the claims of technology to scrutiny. If it is to be used to widen access and develop greater student independence, technology has to be used strategically within institutions, and systematically across all learning functions. Lewis and Merton (1996) summarise some of the main ways in which technology can support students. It can provide:

- information on the curriculum;
- recognition for existing achievement and advice on appropriate learning routes;
- flexible access to resources, facilities, and programme content;
- tutorial guidance, including assessment and feedback; and
- opportunities to practise and apply learning.

Particularly important will be uses of technology to maintain contact between students and tutors who may be geographically dispersed or otherwise remote from each other (even on campus).

Technology can thus help teachers manage an environment that is adapted to individual needs, and perceived by students as attractive. But this can only be achieved through the vision, energy and expertise of staff.

The use of learning materials

Learning materials help educators achieve the dual objectives of access and independence. They open up choice over the learning process – for example, by providing explicit statements of outcomes; facilities whereby students can check their understanding and apply their learning; feedback on students' responses; clarity, attractiveness and consistency in the presentation of content; and a transparent structure, with good signposting. Such features make it possible for the student to learn without constant recourse to a tutor; the tutor is, to some extent, present within the materials.

Materials can help providers respond to the pressures identified earlier in this chapter. One can, for example, envisage a situation in which many disparate student groups, on and off campus, learn a particular discipline through an identical set of core materials, customised as necessary by additional components such as study and assessment guides, and supported by tutors in a variety of ways: face-to-face, telephonically and/or electronically.

Sharing of learning materials between institutions is advocated by the MacFarlane Report (Committee of Scottish University Principals 1992: 42); this is increasingly likely to occur on an international basis.

Defining and supporting the role of the student

In this environment, students will need the three capabilities of the independent learner: motivation, self-management and the ability to reflect on their learning (Lewis and Allan 1996). Many will not find this easy. As the MacFarlane Report points out: 'it will be essential that students are carefully prepared for that independence. Many students are unsure how to handle the amount of freedom they are given in higher education' (Committee of Scottish University Principals 1992: 10). Several recent accounts show that students resist the challenge of taking decisions about their learning (Lisewski 1994; Wade *et al.* 1994; Harris and Stoney 1996). In the new environment, students are required to be 'more than customers'; they should become active participants, 'members of the team that "produces" their learning system' (Elton 1994: 11), a line of argument which is also developed in Fitzgerald (1996). Elton points out that students traditionally play active roles in shaping their social and sporting activities, but not in designing their learning environments. McDowell (1994) argues that this is largely because of the ways in which students are disempowered by current arrangements: poor feedback, vagueness over outcomes, lack of choice, lack of lecturer interest in learning, and undervaluing of experiences outside the institution (McDowell 1994).

The need for strategic change

Changes have been made in all of these regards, but the approach has been piecemeal. For example, the use of open learning materials in conventional institutions tends to be confined to special groups such as MBA students, whose high fees are paid by their employers but whose work routines preclude attendance on a traditional campus. Or such materials are used only to enrich conventional delivery, which proceeds unchanged.

A step change is needed. As Heseltine (1994: v) says: 'We are still trying to map these changes onto the old landscape of teaching. . . . We need to construct a new teaching and learning environment. That must be the starting point, not the question of how to adapt what we have now to a higher level of demand.'

Staff roles and staff development

These changes require a major adjustment in the roles of staff. The traditional role of the teacher consists of:

- transmitting subject content;
- managing a group learning environment (the lecture theatre or the classroom); and
- assessing students.

In this, each teacher acts largely alone, rather than as a member of a team.

Various initiatives have shifted the focus, for example towards giving detailed feedback to students, using technology, and helping students learn from one another. Examples in the UK are the Enterprise in Higher Education programme, and (in schools) the Technical and Vocational Education Initiative.

In the learning environment described above, the 'teaching' role will continue to shift towards supporting individual students as they acquire independence. Staff will help individuals to manage their learning, formulate objectives, monitor their own progress, and chart their paths through an increasingly complex curriculum. Greater specialisation is also likely to occur. Different staff will develop particular aspects of the learning environment, engaging in, for example:

- curriculum design and development;
- the adaptation and creation of learning materials;
- the development of new technological applications;
- networking with industry and other stakeholders;
- action research;
- policy-making and developing improved procedures; and
- the design and management of learning environments.

Williams and Fry (1994: 48) describe other likely developments: a smaller group of core staff supported by networks of part-time staff; more flexible terms and conditions of employment; greater mobility; more shared posts with industry; and a further erosion of the distinction between 'academic' and other staff.

Change in the current climate

In some ways, the current climate is a difficult one in which to seek such changes. In 1994, one UK university consulted on its future learning environment with a wide range of its staff. More than 320 staff took part in the thirty-eight hours of discussion. Although the concept of a student-centred learning environment was attractive to some staff, many reservations were expressed. The report arising from this consultation exercise describes 'a generally lukewarm and cautionary approach to the use of technology . . . a lack of enthusiasm for the topic . . . [and] little awareness of how technology is regularly used in open and distance learning' (Lewis 1995a: 8). The motivation for change was questioned: was this merely an attempt to save money, especially at the expense of staff jobs? A proportion of those consulted predicted 'a [second-class] distance system, in which students are isolated and unsupported . . . an imposed, prescriptive and standardised approach, driven by formulae, stifling innovation and leading to a reduction in the range of available learning methods'. Instead of identifying the positive aspects of their likely future roles, the staff feared the removal of 'the skilled teacher from the centre of a university education' (1995a: 4).

The major challenge to institutional managers is thus to bring about change in an environment currently characterised by low trust and low energy. For the key resource in energising students towards greater independence is undoubtedly staff, especially given the suspicion that many students feel towards uses of learning methods with which they are unfamiliar. Mandated change cannot create a new learning environment. Staff energies and imagination will be released only if they are working towards a future to which they too aspire. For this reason, a number of institutions are now systematically involving staff in 'envisioning workshops', wherein compelling and detailed pictures are built of the learning environment which different areas wish to create (Healey 1995).

Staff development

It is tempting to turn to staff development as an answer. In education, this has the status of panacea or totem. But, in achieving change, staff development can be only one strand of a strategy. We must, for example, remember the importance of the non-people elements: systems, equipment, buildings and IT networks. Some of these have been mentioned earlier in this chapter. When it comes to staff, the context includes not only their development but also

- agreement on roles and responsibilities – who will do what in the new learning environment?
- recruitment;
- appraisal/feedback on performance;
- recognition and rewards; and
- arrangements for career development. (A fuller list is given in Lewis 1995b.)

Staff development fits into this more complex picture but it makes sense only when a clear need has been identified. Staff development can stem, for example, from

- the acceptance of a new appointment;
- the acceptance of a newly defined or redefined post (the boundaries between 'academic' and 'library and learning resource' staff are particularly volatile at the time of writing);
- feedback on performance via appraisal, leading to agreement on a personal and/or professional development plan;
- preparation for a likely future responsibility and/or career development; and
- preparation for redundancy or retirement.

Much has still to be achieved in managing these processes in our schools, colleges and universities. The education sector has, for many years, chosen to leave important issues undebated. Many practices have operated with tacit agreement, and, given resource constraints and the rapidity of change, the resulting problems are becoming apparent. Staff development opportunities, for example, have often been unrelated to need and staff development has sometimes been perceived as a perk, a reward for long service, or time spent away in more comfortable surroundings. It has rarely been linked to any organisational strategy. Boundaries between different staff groups have been ill defined, leading to the exploitation of vulnerable groups of staff – for example, those working in support roles or as junior academics. Staff could teach for years without seeking any information on their performance – perhaps comfortable in the belief that, as professionals, they had no need for feedback from their managers, colleagues or students.

This situation has changed in some institutions – but not necessarily for the better. With the insensitive importation of practices from industry have come target-setting or appraisal systems that fail to respect the educational context. Some of these appraisal processes have become so complex that staff are still denied the benefits of shared clarity over their roles, detailed and timely feedback on their performance, and opportunities to plan for an agreed future.

Staff development needs to be embedded in the broader strategic approach outlined earlier. Only then are we likely to create an environment in which 'personal purpose' is seen as 'the route to *organisational* change' (Fullan 1993: 14, original emphasis). Without this, we shall end up, not with a new learning environment but with the familiar 'continual stream of fragmented surface, ephemeral innovations' (Fullan 1993) described so well by Gibbs (1995). What is needed is not adaptive but generative learning, and this occurs only when people are striving to achieve something that matters deeply to them (Senge 1990).

This returns us to the starting point. If students are to take charge of their own learning environment, then so too must their teachers. The *learning organisation* offers this opportunity to both. Successful organisations will energise their students and staff to work collaboratively to this end.

References

Committee of Scottish University Principals (CSUP) (1992) *Teaching and Learning in an Expanding Higher Education System* ('The MacFarlane Report'), Edinburgh: Committee of Scottish University Principals.

Daniel, J. (1996) *The Mega-universities and the Knowledge Media*, London: Kogan Page.

Davies, G. (1994) 'Teaching and learning in the changing higher education environment', paper presented at *Teaching and Learning: Making Change Work in Higher Education*, Careers Research and Advisory Centre, Regent's College, London (20 Oct.).

Elton, L. (1994) 'Enterprise in higher education: an agent for change', in P.T. Knight (ed.), *University-wide Change, Staff and Curriculum Development*, Staff and Educational Development Association (SEDA) Paper 83, SEDA.

Fitzgerald, M. (1996) 'No mark for effort skews assessment', *The Times Higher* (5 April), p. 12.

Fullan, M. (1993) *Change Forces: Probing the Depths of Educational Reform*, Lewes: The Falmer Press.

Gibbs, G. (1995) 'Changing lecturers' conceptions of teaching and learning through action research', in A. Brew (ed.), *Directions in Staff Development*, Bristol, PA, and Buckingham, UK: The Society for Research into Higher Education and Open University Press.

Harris, V. and Stoney, C. (1996) *An Independent Learning Project in Hospitality Management*, Open Learning Foundation (OLF) case study series, London: OLF.

Harvey, L. (1994) 'Continuous quality improvement: a system-wide view of quality in higher education', in P.T. Knight (ed.), *University-wide Change, Staff and Curriculum Development*, Staff and Educational Development Association (SEDA) Paper 83, SEDA.

Healey, M. (1995) *Prospero's Enchanted Isle*, Hull: University of Humberside.

Heseltine, R. (1994) 'Vices and virtues in the virtual library', *The Times Higher* (14 Oct.), multimedia insert, pp. iv–v.

Lewis, R. (1995a) *Consultations on the New Learning Environment*, The Learning Development Unit, University of Humberside, Hull.

—— (1995b) 'The role of national standards for human resource development in open learning', in *One World, Many Voices: Quality in Open and Distance Learning*, collected papers of the 17th ICDE World Conference for Distance Education, Oslo and Milton Keynes: International Council for Distance Education, vol. 2, pp. 125–8.

Lewis, R. and Allan, B. (1996) *The Independent Learner: An Overview*, The Learning Exchange/University of Humberside, Hull.

Lewis, R. and Merton, B. (1996) *Technology for Learning: Where Are We Going?* A position paper, BP/University of Lincolnshire and Humberside, Hull.

Lisewski, B. (1994) *A Pilot Project at the Liverpool Business School*, Open Learning Foundation (OLF) case study series, London: OLF.

McDowell, L. (1994) 'Learner-centred change: some outcomes and possibilities', in P. T. Knight (ed.), *University-wide Change, Staff and Curriculum Development*, Staff and Educational Development Association (SEDA) Paper 83, SEDA.

Senge, P. (1990) *The Fifth Discipline*, New York: Doubleday.

Wade, W., Hodgkinson, K., Smith, A. and Arfield, J. (eds) (1994) *Flexible Learning in Higher Education*, London: Kogan Page.

Williams, G. and Fry, H. (1994) *Longer Term Prospects for British Higher Education: A Report to the Committee of Vice-Chancellors and Principals*, Centre for Higher Education Studies, Institute of Education, University of London.

4

A STRATEGIC PERSPECTIVE ON STAFF DEVELOPMENT FOR OPEN AND DISTANCE LEARNING

Bernadette Robinson

Staff development for open and distance learning is still largely seen by organisations as a cost, not an investment. It is often given low priority in organisational plans and funding allocations. Provision tends to be unsystematic, piecemeal or minimal, and staff may often be left to pick up what knowledge and skills they can from doing the job. Even when staff development is provided, organisations are not always ready enough to utilise the new learning. This results in lost opportunities for capacity building and wastes resources. Organisations need to adopt a more strategic perspective on staff development. This chapter suggests how this might be done.

A strategic perspective on staff development

A *strategy* is the means by which an organisation chooses to reach its objectives, typically through a plan of action or formulated policy. It can also mean the stance an organisation adopts in regard to its structure, staff, operations, competitors, learners, learning processes, the public, the wider world of education and training – and itself. *Strategic decisions* are those which significantly affect the organisation's ability to achieve its objectives. *Strategic management* is the process of managing change to reach an organisation's objectives (Bowman and Asch 1987).

In educational contexts, staff development is usually seen in terms of benefits to individuals or as their own professional responsibility. Viewed in these terms, staff development provision may lack coherence, be a series of *ad hoc* events, and assist some individuals while others miss out on any share of the resource and underperform. Furthermore, minimum standards of provision and entitlement across the organisation as a whole will be impossible to achieve. To take a more strategic perspective, staff development needs to be

- aligned to organisational as well as to individual goals;
- a systematic process with planning and control (not just chance learning from experience); and
- directed at improving knowledge, skills, attitudes and performance at the levels of the individual, the work group and the organisation.

Improvements in individual skills and work performance cannot easily be divorced from the organisational context in which the individual works. In my experience as a staff developer and facilitator, organisational issues surface fast when staff development involves the transfer of training to 'real-work' contexts. Procedures, role boundaries, communication routes, systems and other people are often affected by, or impact on, changes in individual work practices. All of these can provide obstacles to the application of new learning. Putting an individual's new skills and learning to use involves other people and possibly, additional resources. It needs the support of a receptive and well-prepared organisation.

Staff development as organisational change

The planning of staff development sometimes starts with the wrong set of questions, largely about the training event(s) to be provided. It needs to start with a set of organisational questions, directed to all of those involved, about the organisational goals (short- and long-term) and priorities. These goals, and the standards for their achievement, should determine the main training provision, especially where resources are scarce.

Senior managers therefore have a critical role in aligning staff development with strategic goals; they are responsible for ensuring that

- staff development is directed towards the goals of the organisation as a whole;
- learning needs are systematically analysed and prioritised within the institutional plan;
- the activities have explicit purpose, and policies and plans;
- the activities have status and are resourced adequately; and
- the investment of time, effort and resources are carefully evaluated and used as a basis for decision-making.

Furthermore, the senior and middle managers have an important role before, during and after staff development events, in regard to the following tasks (this list is not exclusive):

Pre-training preparation

- clarifying the precise objectives of the programme(s) and intended use of participants' learning after the event(s);

34

- selecting appropriate participants according to clear criteria;
- preparing the ground and building positive expectations and motivation in participants; and
- planning for any changes that improved performance will need (such as organisational or equipment re-arrangements).

During training

- protecting participants from job demands and providing adequate cover for participants' work and responsibilities during the training period;
- showing an interest in, and possibly contributing to, training events if provided 'in-house', and maintaining contact with staff on long off-the-job programmes; and
- ensuring adequate facilities for the event (if 'in-house').

Post-training support

- providing opportunities for participants to discuss the training experience with others in their work group and identify ways in which it could contribute to work practices; and
- ensuring a breathing space for re-entry (not leaving returnees with an overwhelming backlog of work awaiting their attention).

Such an approach to staff development embeds it within the organisation and work context.

The checklist in Table 4.1 can be used to identify gaps and weak links between the organisational and strategic goals and staff development provisions.

Developing a staff development strategy

The starting point for any staff development strategy is the support of senior management, followed by the definition of a purpose, policy and plan. The *purpose* expresses the general reason for such an approach. The *policy* provides the guidelines for the planning activities and clarifies the responsibilities, types of staff development, resources and goals. The *plan* details what will be done to translate the purpose and policy into action. The defined purpose and policy together set the framework for the development of a staff development plan. Ideally, this needs to come after, and be informed by, an audit of specific training needs, but sometimes it is necessary to construct a plan in a general way, before an audit. Staff development may sometimes be needed at short notice, as an immediate response to major problems or changes. In these circumstances a 'problem-centred' strategy can be used; its purposes and policy need to be agreed and plans made on a rolling and short-term basis (and reviewed frequently)

Table 4.1 Checklist: how far is staff development linked to the strategic goals for open and distance learning within the organisation?

- Is there a staff development policy? Is it widely known? Does it cover all categories of staff (full- and part-time, central and regional, on-site and off-site?)
- What are the implications for your staff development policy of 'contracted in' or 'outsourced' services and the people who provide them? Where do your boundaries of provision lie?
- How are decisions made about staff development provision? Who decides? Who is consulted?
- What methods are used to identify staff development needs:
  – at the organisational level?
  – at the job level?
  – at the personal/individual level?
- How well are these levels integrated? Which dominates? Why? Which level is neglected?
- In your view, in what direction does the balance need to change?
- How are the priorities decided? On what basis?
- What is the effect of this on staff development provision?
- In what ways is staff development provision linked to organisational objectives?
- How well is it linked? What areas of weakness are there? How could it be strengthened?
- Who is responsible for this? Who, in your view, should be responsible at the different levels?
- Do training objectives and programmes change as soon as there is a change in the organisation's strategic decision? What time-lags have you observed?
- When did a major strategic change last happen in your organisation? What was the effect on your work group or department? What staff development was provided to meet these changes? What was the outcome?

---

instead of working to a longer-term time span. The initial stage is similar in both approaches: discussion and agreement with managers and other stakeholders about the explicit purpose and policy needed to guide action and the use of resources.

Implementing a staff development strategy

Whichever approach is taken, the same steps are needed in implementing the plan as shown in Table 4.2.

This sequence provides a framework for a systematic approach, a cyclical process of review and improvement over time. The last step, evaluation to inform future planning, starts the cycle anew. Of course, this process may not always be so clear-cut in practice. Gaining agreement on what is needed is likely to involve wide consultation and result in differing degrees of cooperation, the confrontation of vested interests and competing claims for scarce resources.

Table 4.2 Steps in implementing a staff development plan

- Define and agree within the organisation the general and particular needs for training (based on a systematic needs analysis).
- Review possible ways of meeting needs and the availability of (financial) resources.
- Establish the priorities.
- Select appropriate staff development events, staff categories and participants.
- Construct a coherent staff development plan in the light of available financial resources and in consultation with the other stakeholders.
- Communicate the plan to all concerned and build a positive climate towards it.
- Prepare an evaluation plan.
- Use the evaluation data to assess impact, improve staff development provision and inform future planning.

Identifying staff development needs

Identifying needs is an important element in providing appropriate staff development. Unfortunately, this is all too often sketchily done and may concentrate only on the individual, linking too little to priorities within the organisation as a whole.

Training need refers to an observable gap between the individual's or group's present knowledge or competence and the standards identified as necessary to do the job effectively. It should not be defined only in terms of an individual's or group's expression of preference for a particular training event or opportunity. Of course, individual and group interests and preferences have to be taken into account in negotiating, developing and providing the programmes – but a heavy reliance on a needs analysis which is *only* based on expressions of job-holders' wishes is likely to lead to provision which is not well aligned to organisational goals or needs and to an unfair allocation of resources. However, the priorities identified at individual, job and organisational levels may often coincide.

Needs analysis refers to the systematic processes of identifying the standards of skills, knowledge and attitudes required in a job and auditing existing levels to establish where and in what respects these need improvement. It is important to note that a gap in knowledge or performance may not be bridged by providing training: other factors may be responsible – for example, the organisational structure, systems, culture or reward systems. Staff development by itself is unlikely to resolve these problems.

McGehee and Thayer (1961) suggest that needs analysis for staff development should be undertaken at three levels: that of the organisation, the job and the individual. The focus on analysis and the sources of data for these three levels are shown in Table 4.3. Analysis is all too often narrowly restricted to Level 3, the individual needs. A more effective strategy is to start at Level 1, the organisational need, and work through Level 2 towards the individual needs. However, this may prove to be difficult, especially in large organisations. Diagnosis of training needs at the organisational level requires quite

Table 4.3 Levels of training needs analysis

Level of analysis	Focus of analysis	Sources of data
Level 1 *Organisational needs*	Whole organisation's objectives	Staffing plan and projections
	Pool and pattern of skills and expertise available in staff	Audit of skills and knowledge of staff; identification of any shortages in future plans for new systems or developments
	Indices of effectiveness	Efficiency indicators, organisational output and results
	Organisational climate	Organisational climate surveys
		Monitoring data from quality systems
		Requests from departments and group managers and staff
		Data and feedback from users or clients such as satisfaction surveys, analysis of complaints, learner performance and problems
Level 2 *Job needs*	Particular job or group of jobs	Job descriptions and specifications
	Tasks, skills and standards needed	Objectives, standards and targets set and priorities identified
	Knowledge, skills and attitudes needed to achieve standards and output	Work sampling or job observation
		Asking the job holder and head of unit about the work or job
		Data and feedback from users (as per Level 1)
Level 3 *Individual needs*	Person analysis in terms of skills, expertise and competence	Performance appraisal and identification of development needs
	Standards of performance at job tasks	Observation and work sampling
		Interviews and questionnaires
		Asking the job holder and head of unit
		Data and feedback from users or clients (as per Level 1)

sophisticated skills of analysis, evaluation and diagnosis as well as access to information and people.

Managers and providers need to decide if a comprehensive needs analysis is necessary in every context. It can be costly, generate a large amount of data and raise expectations which cannot then be met. An alternative approach is to identify 'priority problems' which can be assisted through training, and concentrate on these. In arriving at decisions about the alternative modes of staff development (external courses, in-house seminars and so on), the costs need to be weighed against anticipated benefits, and such cost-benefit analysis may lead to the use of open and flexible learning itself for staff development in distance and open learning.

Why does staff development sometimes fail?

Staff development can fail to achieve its purpose because of

- trainers' inadequate knowledge and skills;
- poor preparation by the organisers or leaders;
- inappropriate content or learning material;
- the wrong people being selected to participate;
- the inappropriate duration of the event for the intended objectives (for example, expecting skills to develop in workshops which are too short to provide practice and feedback);
- erratic attendance by participants (especially when workshops are provided on-site and work demands interfere);
- too long a time-lag before applying new learning to 'real work';
- training content being too remote from 'real-work' needs or organisational realities;
- too little embedding of the learning in the organisational context (lack of preparation and follow-up).

For these reasons, some staff development has little impact on, or transfer to, the 'real-work' situations, even if needs have been soundly analysed. So, how can better transfer of learning be achieved?

Transfer of training to 'real-work' situations

Some training approaches are likely to result in better transfer than others. The 'trainer-centred' approach isolates training from the organisational context. It sees the acquisition of relevant knowledge as sufficient in itself for change, leading inevitably to its application in 'real-work' contexts and ensuring competent performance of skills, even without practice and feedback. Here, the responsibility for training is seen as belonging wholly to the training provider and beginning and ending with the training event.

A more 'holistic' view of training sees it as the shared responsibility of three partners: the organisation; the staff developer or training provider; and the learner or job holder. Learning and improvement on the job are seen as dependent upon such factors as the motivation and capability of individuals; the norms of the training and work groups; the training methods and skills of the trainers; the organisational climate; the support given by the organisational context and individuals with mentoring or support roles; the perceived value of the training, the opportunities for practice and feedback; and an integration of the elements of training into a system which is meaningful to the individual or the group and the organisation.

The transfer to training from events such as workshops to 'real-work' situations is a complex process. Unused, learning acquired through training is often forgotten or becomes a source of frustration on the part of the learner, or both. A strategic perspective requires training (whether in-house, on-site or off-site, or outsourced, on-site or off-site, in-country or overseas), to be set within arrangements for its utilisation. Essential to this is communication between staff developers, learners, and managers of departments and staff, the sharing of information and the development of joint plans.

Evaluating staff development

Evaluation plays a key role in developing a strategic perspective on, assessing, and improving staff development and training. Unfortunately, evaluation tends to be neglected in staff development provision or restricted to a limited part of the outcomes and not closely linked to the wider, longer-term impact of training on 'real-work' situations.

The purpose of evaluating staff development is to gain feedback on

- the effectiveness of the training methods and approaches;
- the extent of the achievement of the objectives set by the trainers and participants;
- the extent to which the needs identified at both the organisational and individual levels were met and reflected in improved practice.

The key questions to ask about staff development and training are:

- Was it efficient? Has it achieved its objectives at acceptable costs?
- Was it effective? Was it well done and worth providing? What did it contribute to the achievement of the organisational goals?
- Was it cost-effective? Did it achieve most of its objectives in a reasonably economic way? Did it represent value for money to the participants and the providers, or were there better alternatives?

Staff development is most frequently evaluated in terms of participant satisfaction with a workshop or course. However, other sources of data are equally important in evaluating changes in individual performance and/or work-group effectiveness in 'real-work' settings or in their contributions to the organisational goals. To evaluate only the training event is to evaluate within a closed loop which only contains the objectives for the event. Objectives are also to be found outside the event, in the work and organisational contexts which gave rise to the staff development or training activity.

The Contexts–Inputs–Reactions–Outcomes (or CIRO) model (based on Warr et al. 1970) provides a useful model for evaluating staff development (Table 4.4). In this model, the questions are not restricted to gauging the reactions of the participants to the event. They also refer to the outcomes, long-term impact and 'real-work' changes. So, what kinds of outcomes should we evaluate?

Outcomes to be evaluated in staff development

One useful framework proposes five levels of outcomes for evaluation (Hamblin 1974). It moves from the level of individual reaction to the training given to change in practice in the individual, the work group and the organisation. It assesses the impact of training over different periods of time, short- and long-term. And the different levels of outcome are linked together in a cause-and-effect chain, each dependent on the success of the previous one.

The objectives to be measured at each level of outcomes are shown in Table 4.5. Staff developers can make these more specific to particular contexts by adding a third column to this. It becomes more difficult and time-consuming to evaluate the outcomes as you move down through these levels – one reason, perhaps, why most evaluation only focuses on the Level 1 outcomes, 'reactions'. Another difficulty lies in demonstrating changes in complex areas of skills development which need to take place over time. However, difficulty is not an argument for restricting evaluation to reactions. Evaluation should be carried out on a regular but selective basis, and for staff development activities as a whole as well as for individual components. Evaluation itself is an aspect of staff development needing more research and development.

Conclusion

Recognition of the value of staff development is growing, especially in quality improvement approaches such as 'Investors in People', but it is still a marginal activity in many organisations providing open and distance learning around the globe. Actions needed to promote a more strategic perspective in training and staff development for open and distance learning include:

- negotiating organisational support, particularly at senior management level, and adequate resources;
- developing a purpose, policy and plan at an organisational level;
- aligning staff development effort with organisational goals;

Table 4.4 The CIRO model for evaluating staff development (based on Warr *et al.* 1970)

Contexts in which the learning event takes place:

- How accurately were the needs initially diagnosed?
- What information was used and how was it analysed to establish these needs?
- Was the training an appropriate solution to the problem?
- Why was this particular kind of training provision chosen?
- How were the learning objectives selected?
- What learning objectives were set? Which level of outcomes did they relate to (e.g., individual learning, performance on the job, departmental change, organisational change)?
- How does this learning event link to others in the participant's experience, and to other training provided? Does it fit with an organisational plan for staff development? If so, how?

Inputs to the training event:

- What resources were available for the training event?
- What resources were actually used (e.g., personnel, physical, financial, time)?
- Was the selection of participants appropriate?
- Did these participants attend the event provided? What was the take-up or participation rate?
- What learning structure, content, media and methods were used? Did these incorporate sound principles of learning? How do you know?
- What was the final cost?
- Was this the best and most appropriate form of provision? What criteria are you judging it by?

Reactions to the training:

- What reactions to the learning event did the participants and trainers have?
- Was it perceived to have achieved its original objectives?

Outcomes from the training:

- Was it efficient?
- Was it effective?
- Was it cost-effective?
- What remaining or new needs were identified?
- What follow-up plans are there for evaluating impact? On what time-scale? How will this information be used?

- using staff development goals to guide the choice of training strategies;
- developing staff development systems instead of isolated events;
- widening the staff developer's role to engage with the context beyond the training event;
- evaluating staff development provision to assess its impact and effectiveness at several levels and to make improvements; and, in all of this
- leaving room for the individual.

Table 4.5 Five levels of outcome for evaluation

Outcomes	What to measure
Level 1 Reactions	• Satisfaction with the event or course, tutors, materials, etc. • Perceptions of the training's relevance and value
↑↓	
Level 2 Learning	• Changes in specific knowledge, skills and attitudes
↑↓	
Level 3 Change in work performance	• Key aspects and improvements in the individual's work behaviour and job performance
↑↓	
Level 4 Change in the department or work group	• Key aspects and improvements in achievement at the work group, team or department level
↑↓	
Level 5 Effects on the achievement of organisational goals	• Achievements of some overall organisational goal or explicit changes (including changing an organisation's culture or values)

Staff development has its limitations too. While particular training activities and events may in themselves be effective, their impact can also depend for success on factors outside the control of staff developers – for example, on reward structures for work performance, relationships between people and role holders in personal and power terms, and the values, norms and focus of the organisations or groups within which the staff development occurs. The effectiveness of training is inevitably linked to the particular context, that of the organisation and its culture.

References

Bowman, C. and Asch, D. (1987) *Strategic Management*, Basingstoke: Macmillan Education Ltd.

Hamblin, A.C. (1974) *Evaluation and Control of Training*, Maidenhead: McGraw-Hill.

McGehee, W. and Thayer, P.W. (1961) *Training in Business and Industry*, New York: Wiley.

Warr, P.B., Bird, M. and Rackham, N. (1970) *Evaluation of Management Training*, Aldershot: Gower.

5

RESEARCH AND STAFF DEVELOPMENT IN OPEN AND DISTANCE EDUCATION

Terry Evans and Daryl Nation

This chapter emerges from our experiences as researchers and teachers in open and distance education, and from our various contributions to forms of staff development within our organisations. Staff development is a crucial aspect in the creation and implementation of new approaches to teaching and learning, especially in the context of rapid cultural, economic, social and technological change. Effective staff development deals reflexively and creatively with the needs of staff in their work context. Research has a fundamental role in critically reflective educational practice and the chapter examines how this can be fostered in open and distance education.

The discussion adopts a broad understanding of staff development and incorporates a perspective which attempts to foster 'critically reflective practice' among all those involved in educational projects, including staff developers, teachers, students, managers and support staff. This perspective rejects approaches which view staff development as 'done to' or 'done for' members of an organisation. Staff should be encouraged to engage in a constant examination and improvement of their professional performance assisted by resources provided by their organisations and in conjunction with their own involvement with professional and other bodies on the widest possible basis. The recent enthusiasm of practitioners and policy-makers for 'lifelong learning' embraces staff development as the process within which members of organisations are given the encouragement, resources and rewards necessary to develop their intellect and professional skills on a continuing basis (Evans and Nation 1996: 169–75).

Practice, research and theory

In our publications we have often used the trichotomy 'practice, research and theory' when justifying the relevance of our own research and theoretical work for practitioners. These should be regarded as related activities, even in contexts where one may be given particular emphasis. For example, the theoretical work we have engaged in since the mid-1980s was engendered by the challenges of the practicalities of our work as teachers in universities teaching on-campus and off-campus students.

In adopting a broad definition of staff development we recognise the importance of specialists in the field. Institutions involved in open and distance education generally have a sound record in the employment of staff whose main task is providing expertise which assists teaching, production and administrative staff to improve their performance. These specialists are termed variously educational developers, instructional designers, educational technologists and course developers. Commonly these specialist staff are located in a central unit, often associated with the administrative and production services which are crucially important for teaching. Many institutions which are not involved in open and distance education have also appointed specialists with similar academic and professional backgrounds – although, it is fair to observe that conventional institutions generally have not valued these experts as highly as those engaged in open and distance education.

The fundamental staff development problem for those interested in assisting teachers to become effective facilitators of open and flexible learning remains: 'converting' people who have been reared as learners and teachers in classroom contexts to different forms of practice. Our experiences in classrooms, as learners and teachers, and our favoured educational theories convince us that small group activity and discussion is one of the most effective methods for fostering critical and independent learners. However, ill-informed critics of distance education have long used a mythical construction of classroom education to prosecute their own uncritical acceptance of forms of face-to-face teaching (even the mass lecture) and to reject those who show any interest in constructing alternative means of teaching and learning. These rejections can be very effective, especially when directed to those with some positive experiences in classrooms but with no experience of effective forms of teaching and learning outside classrooms. They can pose enormous challenges for those involved with staff development and educational change. Research is not the panacea for such ills, but research-based staff and educational development have the capacities to inform critiques of both on- and off-campus teaching and enable the reform and strengthening of both.

Research and reflective practice

The key to effective individual and institutional performance is a commitment to partnership and a mutual valuing of expertise by academics, administrators, educational developers and production staff. Fundamental to these processes is expertise in staff development: knowledge and skills about the processes which encourage staff to improve their professional performance individually and corporately. This theoretical and practical expertise has to be continually regenerated and this requires staff developers to engage in research relating to their practice and to encourage research by others involved in open and distance education.

Research in open and distance education has developed substantially in recent decades. A growing number of researchers, with increasing institutional and grant-funded support, are undertaking a broad range of projects employing a variety of theoretical and methodological approaches. Perhaps more so than specialist staff developers, researchers often regard themselves, and are regarded by others, as independent from the professional worlds of the practitioners whose work they are studying. Coldeway (1988) has advocated this approach, but this is countered by Calvert (1989) who advances a case for partnership between practitioners and researchers. This chapter proceeds from a radical version of the latter perspective (Nation 1990).

Research is founded on the belief that the systematic gathering of facts, and a careful analysis of these in the light of existing knowledge from previous research and relevant theories, will provide the best basis for understanding the social world and making changes to it. The techniques of research are available to all and can be practised by specialists with other professional callings, given that they have the interest and resources to acquire these. This is best done on the partnership basis described above; a research culture allows for these partnerships to occur on a public basis and engagement in publication ensures that others can share in the results.

Evaluation studies are of particular importance in the process of professional improvement. Unfortunately some researchers are not prepared to accept evaluation research as a legitimate form of research (Coldeway 1988: 46–9). From this perspective, evaluation studies are focused essentially on the measurement of outcomes of specific projects, are not well connected to relevant research literature and are often undertaken by people without adequate research training. Of course there are instances of poor-quality evaluation research, but this view is based on an inadequate understanding of the field generally and the excellent work which has been done in open and distance education specifically (Nation 1990: 86–93).

Evaluation research in the field has been very effectively connected to theoretical and methodological developments in the social sciences (Morgan 1990; 1997). A project by the Study Methods Group at the UK Open University illustrates the practical value of this type of research. The course team for a first-year social sciences subject wished to test whether the pedagogy they had devised for teaching important basic concepts had enabled students to develop an effective understanding of them. The team, which included members of the Study Methods Group, created the questions for in-depth interviews with a sample of students. The results confirmed that some concepts had been well understood but others had not (Morgan 1993: 115–17). Evidence such as this can have a powerful effect on professional practice, especially when combined with feedback from tutors and when interpreted by team members with a thorough knowledge of relevant theory and research. Evaluation research works very effectively with a team approach and, provided some members of the team have substantial knowledge of relevant theory and methodology, it allows the team to resolve practical problems by using solid evidence and diverse ideas. By publishing accounts of their research, teams can share their evidence, methodologies and interpretations with colleagues on a broader basis.

Publishers have been prepared to support those interested in promoting improvement in professional practice in open and distance education on the basis of research and theoretical work. The two collections *Critical Reflections on Distance Education* and *Reforming Open and Distance Education: Critical Reflections from Practice* are part of our attempts in this regard (Evans and Nation 1989; 1993a). Fundamental to the processes which engendered these books is the creation of critical communities whose members are prepared to review one another's professional activities in the light of relevant practice, research and theory. In each project participants were invited on the basis of a breadth of professional experience, ranging over administration and management, educational development, teaching and research.

In accepting membership in each project participants expressed general support for 'critical reflection' as the basis for the project, where it was defined as 'the process through which human beings use their analytical powers to assess elements of their lives against their explanatory frameworks [theories]' (Evans and Nation 1989: 10). Members were willing to expose their professional lives orally and in writing and to participate in vigorous debate. These exchanges allowed contributors to sharpen and revise their understandings of their own situations and to develop knowledge of others' professional problems.

The publications arising from each project are a consequence of many revisions to the papers produced for debate. The published versions represent the processes as well as the results of these debates. They provide others with a basis for organising similar forms of staff development. It is not essential or possible, given scarce resources, for every such project to produce a publication, although, if more of these activities can be pushed through to publication, it compounds the likelihood of other partnerships developing and should assist their execution.

All research proceeds from a theoretical perspective, even if this is only acknowledged tacitly. We have been interested in publicly declaring our theoretical views as they have developed. The books discussed above offer examples and references to relevant work, as does our recent publication, *Opening Education: Policies and Practices from Open and Distance Education* (Evans and Nation 1996). These ideas have influenced the work of colleagues interested in applying the results of research to professional practice.

In *Improving Your Students' Learning* Alistair Morgan aims to demonstrate 'that understanding learning from the learners' perspective is the crucial starting point of our work as teachers, trainers and course designers in improving student learning, in distance and open learning (1993: 11). As part of his analysis he adopts our suggestion that '"dialogue" should be placed at the centre of the teaching-learning process' (1993: 83). Morgan has been one of the key practitioners of research dealing with how students actually use teaching materials. After a review of this research he concludes that 'the challenge is to design learning activities which actively engage students in dialogue, and also involve them in taking some degree of control and responsibility for their learning' (1993: 132).

Morgan's conclusions are particularly pertinent when the breadth of his professional experience is considered. He has combined educational development, research and teaching. The research undertaken with colleagues in the Institute of Educational Technology at the Open University was designed to understand the effectiveness of the teaching materials that had been developed by course teams with which they had worked as educational developers. He has also had the opportunity to create teaching materials which implement the principles he advocates. His book reflects the breadth of these experiences and it is a useful starting point for those seeking assistance in relating practice, research and theory.

Understanding Learners in Open and Distance Education is based on research which attempts to appreciate how learners' social contexts affect their engagement with distance education at university level (Evans 1994). On the basis of interview transcripts, a substantial proportion of the book has individual students reporting and analysing their experiences of study. The project is founded on the premise that individuals engaged in teaching at a distance will all ask: 'Who are my students?' (Evans 1994: 123). It challenges professionals involved in open and distance education to include students' perspectives, and the means of ensuring that we can understand them, in all aspects of our practice.

There has recently been a growing interest in applying the fruits of research to critically reflective practice in open and distance education. This work needs to be extended, and a useful basis for this is the continuation of the intellectual partnership between the variety of specialists who work together in this professional field. Further development will be enhanced by a continuing commitment to public sharing of these reflective practices.

Research and organisational practice

An important aspect of staff development, which is too often ignored, is the development of a critical understanding of the policy and political environments in which educational practice occurs. It is perhaps understandable that persons who are employed as staff developers respond to particular immediate aspects of their organisation's needs and then tend to focus quite specifically and inwardly to these ends. Staff are (seemingly) oblivious to the broader contexts and needs for change which surround their work and this impedes or prevents the change which circumstances suggest may well be inevitable. However, in order to work effectively as a teacher, researcher and/or manager, it is necessary to understand the broader contexts of one's work, and to have reflected critically on one's own position in this regard. Engaging in research into organisations and their policies is a powerful way to achieve this end. This is not to suggest that such an understanding will necessarily lead to a better implementation of the particular aspects which are the objects of staff development; indeed, a greater understanding might lead to resistance and rejection of some aspects, or a reshaping of practices, conditions or purposes.

In order to be in a position to think and act in terms of broader institutional (and government) policies, it is necessary to develop the appropriate research skills and understandings of staff. Moodie and Nation (1993) exemplify how historical and policy analysis skills can be marshalled in this fashion, to understand the needs for, and contexts and processes of, change in distance education. Working with colleagues who teach such forms of research (or the outcomes of it), in other disciplinary contexts, may well serve to enhance staff development in the field. The capacity exists to link staff development of such research skills to critically reflective policy development and implementation within an organisation. Thus, for example, a broad research-based staff development approach to change within an organisation could involve establishing a team to work on the development of new or revised policy and its implementation. Research on the broader and external policy environment, perhaps including small case studies of how other organisations are managing the change, is likely to produce an outcome where, not only have the staff been 'developed' in terms of their research skills, but also the knowledge gained should lead to a more informed and well-grounded policy for the organisation together with a strong implementation plan.

Such an approach can be adapted to other forms of institutional reform, development or change. Hence, reform, development or change to aspects such as assessment, evaluation, student support, curriculum development or educational technology could all be facilitated through forms of research-based staff development which use the existing research strengths of staff, adapted to the current 'problem', and which lead to well-informed and well-grounded new practices.

Research and developing educational technologies

Fundamental to our recent work has been a recognition of technologies as integral to educational endeavours rather than as adjuncts, and also a conceptualisation of the term 'technology' which is much more embracing than is commonly understood (Evans and Nation 1993b). Such an understanding is important for considering the place of research in, and for, staff development for the 'new educational technologies' – the contemporary digital, computer and communications-based educational technologies.

The broader definition of technology foregrounds the science or understanding behind technical equipment. Popularly, technology is narrowed to mean the tool or piece of equipment itself; hence, educational technology becomes a tool used for education. Recognising that educational technology is actually about understanding the educational principles, processes and capacities of particular tools enables staff development to be understood as more than just learning how to 'purchase, plug-in and turn-on' unfamiliar pieces of equipment. Rather, staff development should include developing capacities for enquiry and research into the educational processes and possibilities which new educational technologies afford. In particular, the shifts in educational technology which are being promoted internationally cannot be achieved locally without forms of staff development which enable the people involved to research and (re)create the educational technologies in their local contexts.

In these ways, staff development becomes less about offering workshops on 'how to' in relation to any particular pieces of equipment, and more about an holistic approach which encourages a critically reflective community in which new educational technologies are created to improve or enhance practice. Staff development under such conditions is more likely to occur as a form of action-orientated critical reflection and participatory enquiry and evaluation, or as a form of collaboration or dialogue between practitioners. In this way any particular educational 'community' (a course-team, project group or department, for example) is able to explore the potential of a particular educational technology for incorporation into its own work. Wood's action-research-orientated staff development for computer-mediated communications (CMC) demonstrates this. A learning–teaching dialogue is fostered through Wood's facilitation, not only of the CMC staff development itself, but also of the action research in which her colleagues participate (Wood and Rahman 1995). Wood takes the whole task a stage further, and is using the research and development project as the basis for her own doctoral thesis.

The adoption of personal computers and the Internet within universities has caused substantial changes in administrative and scholarly work, and has provided a strong focus for staff development activities. The foundation stones of some 'virtual universities' have been laid, but most of the educational design and construction is still to be done. A review of the journals which cover open and distance education, as well as educational publishers' catalogues, illustrates how the use of the new educational technologies has increased their influence in the field. Likewise, a review of the collections published as a result of the *Research in Distance Education* conferences at Deakin University shows a similar strong and rising trend over the past eight years among those undertaking research and scholarship in the field (Evans 1990; Evans and Juler 1992; Evans and Murphy 1994; Evans *et al.* 1997). Like ourselves, some of these contributors would see themselves as engaged in staff development for at least part of their activities, and that the research informs (and is probably informed by) their staff development work.

With the increasing technological complexity of teaching and learning processes it seems important to ensure that forms of staff development are not based on the 'purchase, plug-in and turn-on' approach, but rather on more creative practitioner action research approaches, perhaps on approaches which, where appropriate, draw the technologies into the staff development practices as Wood has done. The goal needs to be to develop educators who are capable of constructing new, efficient and worthwhile experiences for their students; and of recognising and culling a white elephant when they see one!

Concluding comment: research and critical reflection

Many involved in research and staff development in open and distance education have demonstrated an interest in academic and professional activity which creates and maintains mutual support between the two fields. They are united in a quest to create knowledge and techniques which encourage and allow organisations and their members to examine and improve their performance. These endeavours value the expertise of specialists, but emphasise the need to create and maintain organisational, academic and professional processes which foster sharing of the means to define problems, seek relevant knowledge and create solutions.

Our own approach has endeavoured to explore the relationships between practice, research and theory and to value each of these aspects equally. We proceed from a perspective which values critical reflection fundamentally (Evans and Nation 1989; 1993a; 1996). Critical reflection on one's own practice in the light of that of fellow practitioners and relevant theories and research ensures that individuals are engaged actively in their own professional development. This is not to be taken as an individualist argument, because collectively such practitioners are more likely to be able to sustain dialogue in conditions of mutual risk and benefit than those who never consider or research the problems of their own practice.

References

Calvert, J. (1989) 'Distance education research: the rocky courtship of scholarship and practice', *International Council of Distance Education Bulletin* 19: 37–47.

Coldeway, D.O. (1988) 'Methodological issues in distance educational research', *American Journal of Distance Education* 2 (3): 45–54.

Evans, T.D. (ed.) (1990) *Research in Distance Education 1*, Geelong: Institute of Distance Education, Deakin University.

—— (1994) *Understanding Learners in Open and Distance Education*, London: Kogan Page.

Evans, T.D., Jakupec, V. and Thompson, D. (eds) (1997) *Research in Distance Education 4*, Geelong: Deakin University Press.

Evans, T.D. and Juler, P.A. (eds) (1992) *Research in Distance Education 2*, Geelong: Deakin University Press.

Evans, T.D. and Murphy, D. (eds) (1994) *Research in Distance Education 3*, Geelong: Deakin University Press.

Evans, T.D. and Nation, D.E. (eds) (1989) *Critical Reflections on Distance Education*, London: Falmer Press.

—— (eds) (1993a) *Reforming Open and Distance Education*, London: Kogan Page.

—— (1993b) 'Educational technologies: reforming open and distance education', in T.D. Evans and D.E. Nation (eds), *Reforming Open and Distance Education*, London: Kogan Page, pp. 196–214.

—— (1996) 'Educational futures: globalisation, educational technology and lifelong learning', in T.D. Evans and D.E. Nation (eds), *Opening Education: Policies and Practices from Open and Distance Education*, London: Routledge, pp. 162–76.

Moodie, G. and Nation, D.E. (1993) 'Reforming a system of distance education', in T.D. Evans and D.E. Nation (eds), *Reforming Open and Distance Education*, London: Kogan Page, pp. 130–49.

Morgan, A.R. (1990) 'Whatever happened to the silent revolution? Research, theory and practice in distance education', in T.D. Evans (ed.), *Research in Distance Education 1*, Geelong: Institute of Distance Education, Deakin University, pp. 9–20.

—— (1993) *Improving Your Students' Learning: Reflections on the Experience of Study*, London: Kogan Page.

—— (1997) 'Still seeking the silent revolution? Research, theory and practice in open and distance education', in T.D. Evans, V. Jakupec and D. Thompson (eds), *Research in Distance Education 4*, Geelong: Deakin University Press.

Nation, D.E. (1990) 'Reporting research in distance education', in T.D. Evans (ed.), *Research in Distance Education 1*, Geelong: Institute of Distance Education, Deakin University, pp. 83–107.

Wood, J. and Rahman, S.M. (1995) 'Towards a quantitative understanding of online teachers' workloads', in F. Nouwens (ed.), *Distance Education: Crossing Frontiers*, proceedings of the 12th Biennial Forum of the Open and Distance Learning Association of Australia, Vanuatu (Sept.), Rockhampton: Central Queensland University, pp. 316–19.

6

STAFF DEVELOPMENT FOR OPEN AND DISTANCE EDUCATION

The case of the Commonwealth of Learning

Patricia McWilliams and Ian Mugridge

The issue of staff development for the planning, design, development and management of distance and open programmes and appropriate applications of technology are crucial in developing countries. In developed countries, such staff development can readily draw upon existing exemplars, knowledge and skills but, in many countries around the globe, open and distance education are unfamiliar forms of delivery and there is little infrastructure or support for staff development activities in the many new or existing institutions that are now expected to provide these services. The Commonwealth of Learning (COL) has sought to assist this process in developing Commonwealth countries and this chapter describes the process and progress to date.

Reviewing the needs and strategies

The Commonwealth of Learning (COL) was established at the biennial meeting of the Commonwealth Heads of Government (CHOGM) held in Vancouver, British Columbia, in 1988. The governments signed a Memorandum of Understanding that prescribed the purposes, terms of reference and form of governance for this new agency which was to cooperate with Commonwealth educational institutions and assist in increasing access to education and training at all levels in member countries using distance education and communication technologies. COL began its activities in early 1989.

The Memorandum of Understanding enjoined COL to undertake and support staff development and training in the techniques and management of open and distance education and this was confirmed as a widespread need by an initial review undertaken by COL in 1989. Accordingly, COL set out to consult widely on the specifics of the training needs in both new and existing distance teaching institutions. Early in 1990, COL organised a Round Table with the following objectives:

- to identify the training needs of distance education institutions in the Commonwealth countries;
- to discuss and recommend strategies to meet these training needs;
- to examine the efficacy of the various types and levels of training; and
- to evolve an approach for effective cooperation among various institutions, agencies and countries and COL's role in it.

(Commonwealth of Learning 1990)

The Round Table identified at least four levels at which staff development of distance educators was required: induction/orientation; general basic training; specialist training; and professional training (see Figure 6.1). It was concluded that general orientation was important because so many staff in distance teaching institutions or programmes came to these by way of non-distance institutions or activities. General orientation needed to cover: distance education (philosophical issues); socio-economic considerations; cost-benefit considerations; major models and institutional systems; teaching and learning at a distance; media options; developments world-wide; and COL and its agenda. The Round Table identified the priority training needs for professional and technical staff as being in distance education policy, planning and management; instructional design and course development; and technology in distance education. The Round Table also identified that other important but not primary areas of need were training in student support services; the adaptation and use of materials; research; and the training of trainers.

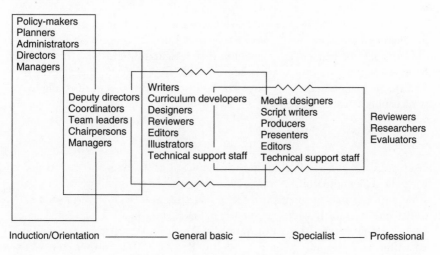

Figure 6.1 A training model of distance educators in different settings

The Round Table deemed four strategies to be appropriate to meeting these needs: the provision of workshops (the assumption was that institutions would prefer in-house, on-the-job training); the development of self-instructional distance education training materials; the establishment of training fellowships (particularly for managers and administrators of distance teaching institutions or programmes); and the development of special training institutions or units. The Round Table concluded that none of these strategies was superior to the others and that the optimal solution to particular training needs should be developed on a case-by-case basis.

The Round Table also identified the constraints on training. It established that the training of staff was beset by a number of internal and external difficulties, the primary obstacle being lack of resources to fund what was clearly, if it was to be effective, a costly activity.

Finally, the Round Table considered COL's potential role in the development and delivery of such programmes throughout the Commonwealth. The group envisaged COL as a facilitator of training, and recommended that COL should:

- organise, or assist other agencies to organise, training workshops on a regional or sub-regional basis;
- collect and evaluate existing training materials, and make such materials available;
- commission training materials to support institutionally based workshops;
- commission case studies of planning and administration;
- develop a register of experts who could assist with training; and
- build up regional pools of expertise by identifying experts and training them as trainers.

(Commonwealth of Learning 1990: 77)

Seven years after this Round Table, the activities of COL in pursuit of its staff development mandate still accord with these objectives. Unfortunately, frequent difficulties, some of them anticipated in these original Round Table discussions, have resulted in the organisation being unable to respond to these needs in a consistent, comprehensive or cohesive fashion. However, several examples of successful practice can be cited.

Responding to the needs

One of COL's early staff development publications, produced in collaboration with the Commonwealth Secretariat, was a comprehensive discussion of the structures and management of distance teaching institutions (Perraton 1991). Other publications have been similarly developed to guide decision-makers on organisational structures, administration, and roles and competencies in distance education (for example, Mugridge 1992; O'Rourke 1993). Further efforts have been directed to providing practitioners with information about existing resources through the exhaustive *Directory of Courses and Materials for Training in Distance Education* (Commonwealth of Learning 1990; 1993; 1995). With funding provided by the British Overseas Development Administration, COL also plans to publish a volume of previously published essays on the training of distance educators with an introduction and conclusion by another contributor to this book, Bernadette Robinson. Through such publications, COL seeks to ensure that essential information and guidance are available throughout the countries of the Commonwealth.

In the early years of COL, the government of British Columbia funded a fellowship scheme designed to send the province's distance educators overseas for training and consulting purposes and, more particularly, to bring managers of Commonwealth distance teaching agencies to Canada. In recent years, this scheme has focused on outgoing fellowship activities designed to meet specific training needs. Over twenty-eight fellowships have been awarded and more than 650 overseas faculty have benefited from these programmes which are organised and supported by COL.

COL has provided or supported a range of off-shore training programmes and workshops. COL-provided programmes have assisted such institutions as eastern Caribbean colleges, the University of Guyana, the Bangladesh Open University and the Solomon Islands College of Higher Education in various distance education practices. COL has also assisted in delivering professional development programmes in Africa, working in collaboration with the West African Distance Education Association, the Distance Education Association of Southern Africa and other national professional associations. Such programmes have covered course and institutional design, the integration and use of various media, educational applications of computers, audioconferencing and broadcasting, student records management and the management of distance education systems. Workshops conducted under the auspices of COL have included preparing competency-based distance education materials for technical and vocational distance training in Papua New Guinea, the potential for training laboratory technicians at a distance in Zambia, and an international workshop to raise awareness on the potential of open schooling for women and girls in Pakistan. Some of these initiatives are taken in collaboration with the Commonwealth Secretariat, UNESCO, UNICEF and other world and Commonwealth agencies.

One major attempt at Commonwealth-wide staff development provision has been the COL Rajiv Gandhi Fellowship Scheme. In 1994, COL reached agreement with the government of India, from the outset one of the major donors to COL, on funding for a scholarship scheme dedicated to the memory of Prime Minister Rajiv Gandhi who had been one of the leaders supporting the establishment of COL at the 1988 CHOGM. This scholarship scheme was conceived to enable distance education staff in developing countries to enrol in the Master's programme in distance education developed and offered by the Indira Gandhi National Open University (IGNOU) in New Delhi, receive local tutorial support within their own countries, and be granted a postgraduate qualification from one of Asia's premier distance teaching universities. The first cohort of 100 students in 1995–96 came from countries representative of all regions of the Commonwealth. This Master's degree is described in greater detail in Badri Koul's chapter elsewhere in this book.

Predictable difficulties have arisen in offering this programme to such a widely dispersed and diverse group of students, and rigorous evaluation procedures are in place to ensure that, if the scheme continues in the latter half of 1997, any necessary changes and improvements will be in place. Plans are also in progress to enable staff in member countries, to take similar advantage of programmes offered by the International Extension College in the UK, Athabasca University in Canada, Deakin University in Australia and other programmes under development.

COL had earlier tried to implement another major strategy suggested by the 1990 Round Table – that of establishing regional and sub-regional training institutions and units. In 1993, the President of COL, visiting IGNOU, proposed a scheme whereby particular institutions or units would be designated by COL as centres of excellence for specific purposes and encouraged to provide training and guidance to other institutions and groups. The first, and so far only, institution to take advantage of this scheme has been IGNOU itself.

Following the visit of two COL consultants in 1994, IGNOU's Staff Training and Research Institute in Distance Education (STRIDE) was mandated to provide training, not only within India, but also throughout the region. COL provided the necessary support and assistance for the training and research activities of STRIDE and thus helped to ensure that the experiences of an institution in which the culture of training had been solidly embedded since its foundation could be disseminated more widely throughout South Asia. COL and STRIDE jointly organised a distance education training needs assessment seminar in Delhi. The participants came from Bangladesh, Pakistan, Maldives, Sri Lanka and (as observers) Nepal and Bhutan, and from the various nodal institutions in India including the National Open School, IGNOU, state open universities and the correspondence institutes of the more traditional universities. This event was designed to guide the training activities of the individual institutions as well as those of STRIDE and COL by establishing training priorities for a three-year period. At the time of writing, a review of the three years of STRIDE as a centre of excellence is under way.

In a second major training initiative focused on South Asia, in 1994 COL established the Commonwealth Educational Media Centre for Asia (CEMCA). This agency, which also draws upon facilities provided by IGNOU, provides training and support for the production of educational media, particularly audiovisual media for distance education, throughout India and South Asia. Circumstances slowed the start of CEMCA, but by late 1996, it was offering its first training workshops and is now moving forward rapidly. Recent participant-paid workshops for associated institutions have included the management of non-print media resources, presentational and interviewing techniques for educational broadcasters, script-writing and the use of multimedia distance learning. It is envisaged that CEMCA will become a major force in providing training in media for open and distance learning throughout the region.

This summarises the extent of the training provision through centres or special units as envisaged by the 1990 Round Table. The establishment of a skilled and mobile group of trainers has to date proved to be impracticable. Training has been primarily provided through local, regional and national workshops. Over-reliance on such methods has been disappointing to some of the staff at COL, as has the concurrent inability to produce the high-quality generic self-instructional training materials as envisaged by the Round Table.

Further reviewing the needs

Evidence of the continuing debate on needs and provision by COL and its clients is seen in the commissioning of a second major review into training needs. Like the 1990 Round Table, the reviewer concluded that the urgency of demand for generic training in distance education theory and practice was increasing and that COL had a key role to play in initiating training materials and in coordinating their global distribution (Forster 1994). This second report argued that COL should practise what it preached and use distance education delivery to meet the large and unmet demand. It defined the materials needed, provided a plan for their development, and suggested ways of ensuring their distribution, utilisation and effectiveness.

As a follow-up to the Forster Report, COL embarked on several initiatives based upon the premise that COL could not meet the widespread demands through total reliance on face-to-face training. COL had grounds for believing that training in instructional design was the greatest need in the majority of its client institutions. In 1994–95, two expert group meetings were held in Vancouver to develop a blueprint for an entry-level, self-instructional course in instructional design. To verify the strength of demand, COL subsequently commissioned a needs assessment survey. The response rate to this survey exceeded 80 per cent, in itself indicative of the level of support for such a project, and the findings clearly indicated that institutions in developing Commonwealth countries would be strongly supportive of such an initiative. It is still the intention of COL, given sufficient resources, to proceed with this vital project.

The second area which COL perceived to be a high priority was staff development in using media and technology in open and distance education. There appeared to be a strong demand, driven in part by the rapid growth in communications and information technology. An expert group meeting was convened in 1995 in collaboration with the Kuala Lumpur-based Asia Pacific Institute for Broadcast Development. Delegates from the Asian region with a strong background in educational media participated in this three-day event and developed blueprints for training materials for three target groups: administrators, planners and policy-makers needing an introduction to applications of media in distance and open learning; academics who needed to explore the potential of media in distance education delivery; and media planners and producers who needed to be trained in production for educational applications. COL proceeded with the development of these training materials during 1996–97 and in collaboration with CEMCA at IGNOU.

Another Round Table held in Vancouver in 1993 was attended by senior women educators from many different countries and organised in response to recommendations from international agencies and Commonwealth countries that the issue of gender sensitivity in distance education be addressed. This initiative resulted in a handbook for educators on producing gender-sensitive learning materials (Commonwealth of Learning 1995), which provides a unique and useful reference for course writers and developers.

A further strategy for envisaging and charting directions and sharing lessons and experiences is exemplified in COL's organising such international conferences as *Educational Technology 2000: A Global Vision for Open and Distance Learning*, held in Singapore in 1996. This event enabled delegates from thirty-eight countries to share and debate the impact of communications and information technologies on distance education. Again, training was identified as a key issue by these delegates. Such forums provide COL with valuable opportunities to network with its client institutions and various experts and gain insights into the issues and concerns facing the global distance education community as it struggles with an ever-changing environment and limited resources.

COL and the Commonwealth Network of Information Technology for Development (COMNET-IT) have recently signed a Memorandum of Understanding to work together in Internet-based distance education, and this collaboration also holds promise for the promotion of awareness and the building of capacities in Commonwealth institutions around the world.

Conclusion

The various initiatives described above confirm the 1990 Round Table's findings that there is an enormous potential and need for training activities in the regions of the Commonwealth and that these can be met through interventions by COL and other agencies. The examples given above show that international and inter-institutional collaboration is part of the answer. IGNOU's STRIDE, CEMCA and the Rajiv Gandhi Fellowship Scheme provide models for addressing these needs.

Unfortunately, to date, COL has been unable to persuade other governments and institutions that such training is central to the effective functioning of distance teaching institutions, that resources are needed, and that staff development is to be regarded as an investment rather than a cost. And regrettably, there is little evidence to convince funding agencies that training is truly an essential element and few research studies to demonstrate the cost benefits or cost-effectiveness of such provision.

Training is therefore sporadic, uneven and uncoordinated and leaves huge gaps that international organisations such as COL are currently quite incapable of filling. However, COL is encouraged by the fact that the Malaysian government, supporting a major shift into distance education by tertiary institutions, has recently commissioned a series of training workshops for staff in these institutions. COL is also encouraged by the commitment to training shown by the Asian Development Bank in its regional technical assistance project for training primary teachers through distance education. This project makes provision for train-the-trainer workshops and, with the assistance of the International Extension College, COL will produce trainers' toolkits for this project. These will be concerned with:

- an overview of distance education;
- designing distance education courses;
- using and integrating media in distance education;
- planning and managing distance education;
- quality assurance in distance education; and
- learner support systems in distance education.

Each trainer's toolkit will comprise a guide suggesting training strategies, overhead transparency masters, handouts, references, a glossary of terms and, where appropriate, audiovisual materials. Such an initiative lays the foundations for the development and distribution of the kinds of generic training material envisaged in the Forster Report. It also serves to show how COL may provide the leadership and support for training distance educators envisaged at its inception.

References

Commonwealth of Learning (1990; 1993; 1995) *Directory of Courses and Materials for Training in Distance Education*, Vancouver: Commonwealth of Learning.

—— (1990) *Perspectives on Distance Education: Report on a Round Table on Training Distance Educators*, Vancouver: Commonwealth of Learning.

—— (1995) *Producing Gender Sensitive Learning Materials: A Handbook for Educators*, Vancouver: Commonwealth of Learning.

Forster, A. (1994) *Training Distance Educators in the Commonwealth: A Distance Education Framework*, Vancouver: Commonwealth of Learning.

Mugridge, I. (ed.) (1992) *Perspectives on Distance Education: Distance Teaching in Single and Dual-mode Universities*, Vancouver: Commonwealth of Learning.

O'Rourke, J. (1993) *Roles and Competencies in Distance Education*, Vancouver: Commonwealth of Learning.

Perraton, H. (1991) *Administrative Structures for Distance Education*, Vancouver and London: Commonwealth of Learning and Commonwealth Secretariat.

Part II

STAFF DEVELOPMENT IN THE ORGANISATION

7

STAFF DEVELOPMENT ISSUES
IN DUAL-MODE INSTITUTIONS
The Australian experience

Colin Latchem and Louise Moran

In Australian universities, even within dual-mode institutions, staff development for improving teaching and learning and support for developing and delivering distance education have typically been distinct activities provided through separate centres and substantially different approaches. Moves to blur the distinctions between on- and off-campus delivery require a re-examination of staff development functions, organisation and practice. The authors suggest that strategic planning and staff development should be linked, that new organisational models and synergies are needed, and that staff developers should be pro-active, involved in policy-shaping and supportive of staff self-management based upon continuous improvement.

The case for a leadership role for staff developers

Australia, a vast land of only 18 million people, cannot afford to regard itself as a resource-rich 'lucky country'. It has to become a 'clever country', its people capable of supporting the growing knowledge-intensive industries and its thirty-eight publicly funded universities internationally competitive.

The Australian universities are experiencing fundamental transformations in their work practices. As elsewhere, the move has been to mass higher education with student numbers trebling in the past twenty-five years. In the past two decades, the Australian higher education system has moved from a British-style state planned model to a North American market system. All students, many of whom are of mature age, are now fee-paying as a consequence of the Higher Education Contribution Scheme (HECS). These students and the other stakeholders are demanding quality and greater accountability. Decreased government funding, decentralisation of labour relations and enterprise agreements, highly managerial modes of organisation, the need for revenue generation, fee-paying international students and technology are having a major impact on the cultures, operations and workloads within the universities. And there is increasingly a perception, as voiced by Professor Steven Schwartz, one of Australia's newer vice-chancellors, that universities must reform and restructure themselves and harness technology or their work will be taken over by others less sympathetic to their traditions (De la Harpe 1996).

There are threats of competition from for-profit, corporate and virtual universities and the global media corporations which control the networks. On the other hand, there is enormous scope for technology-based delivery across national boundaries and through inter-sectoral and international alliances. The environment demands new ventures and new approaches, but as Professor Gordon Stanley, Chair of the Australian Higher Education Council observes, there is a paradox in that universities, established to transform the mind and preserve and extend knowledge, do not always apply intellectual rigour to their own processes of institutional development (Campus Review 1996: 8). He argues for staff development to be at the core of the enterprise, broadly conceived to encompass the creation of cultures supportive of institutional goals and strategic directions, the development of leadership and management capabilities, and the improvement of teaching and curriculum design. He warns that any narrower perspective of staff development will confine it to being marginal, merely concerned with low-level training. Watts (Australian Vice-Chancellors' Committee 1995), noting a growing recognition of the vital link between institutional strategic development and individual professional development, argues for a focus on 'the whole' rather than perceiving staff, performance, leadership and management development as separate issues. Andresen (1991) argues that academic staff developers need to be even more forward-looking than their discipline-based counterparts.

The case for convergence in staff development

A number of Australian universities have for a long time been dual-mode providers, offering students the choice of on- and/or off-campus study. Now, for a variety of socio-economic and educational reasons, distance and open learning are passing from the hands of relatively few proponents to converge with classroom practices and become mainstream educational methodologies in an ever greater number of institutions, generally under the heading of 'flexible learning'.

The federal government has provided significant support for open and flexible learning initiatives aimed at achieving greater access, equity and productivity in on- and off-campus settings and has commissioned major reports on the effectiveness and potential of technology and alternative delivery modes (for example, Taylor *et al.* 1996; Senate Employment, Education and Training References (EETR) Committee 1995; DEET 1994; Tinkler 1994; Jevons and Northcott 1994). Vice-Chancellors and staff, both within campus-based and dual-mode universities, are increasingly recognising the implications and potential of a significantly changing educational environment and resource-based learning, multimedia, the Internet and the Web.

The rhetoric of open and flexible learning, however, currently outstrips practice, and relatively few universities are as yet taking a whole-of-institution approach to all of the following dimensions to flexible delivery:

- providing entry and delivery systems which ensure greater access and equity;
- developing a curriculum which is intellectually and culturally inclusive and sensitive to the needs of Australian and overseas students, both on- and off-campus;
- providing flexible course structures and custom-tailoring content and learning to suit the diverse and individual needs of the learners;
- transforming teaching and learning from a teacher-dominated, transmission-based process to a learner-centred, constructivist process;
- increasing student control over the what, where, when, how and media of learning;
- providing teaching and learner support which positively recognises diversity in the student body;
- using appropriate forms of resource-based learning in classroom and off-campus settings;
- using information and communications technology for enquiry and discourse;
- ensuring that organisational policies, structures and procedures maximise flexibility and quality;
- establishing internal partnerships and external collaboration to improve the range, scope, quality, relevance and cost-effectiveness of teaching and learning; and
- underpinning all of these with concerns for deep learning, lifelong learning, and the purposes and conditions of learning as much as the content.

As institutions and staff increasingly question conventional models of educational delivery and distance learners 'come in from the cold', the traditional divides and tensions between the discrete elements of 'teaching' and 'alternative modes of delivery' begin to lessen. Duning (1990) asks whether we would re-invent our current programmes and services if they and our memories of them vanished and we were then charged with establishing these with all the means currently available. She argues that unless distance educators recast their approach, the profession may be in danger of having captured the hearts of the distance learners while failing to win the minds of potential institutional allies. It is therefore important to consider how staff development, distance and open learning support, and media and information technology services are best organised and managed so as to address the strategic, professional and technological implications of change.

In most institutions, educational development support systems and activities owe more to historical, resource or, in multi-campus institutions, geographical factors than to strategic educational planning. In Australian dual-mode institutions, the same staff teach the same courses on- and off-campus, but the time-honoured arrangement has been for the academic development, distance education, and media and computing services to function quite independently of one another, each with its own values, culture, and approaches to staff development.

Academic staff developers have typically provided induction, helped to develop knowledge and skills in the individual teacher and then withdrawn, respecting the autonomy of the teacher and the classroom. Curriculum and resource material development have been by-products of this process, perceived as the responsibility of discipline-based groups. By comparison, instructional designers in distance education have typically provided on-going support for course and materials design and delivery, and here the development of teaching staff's knowledge and skills in teaching/learning processes has been the by-product.

To generalise these distinctions further, academic staff developers have typically aspired to mid-to-high academic status (some holding professorial positions), held higher degrees (increasingly doctorates), performed scholarly roles and based their advocacy upon research. Instructional designers usually have had lower academic (or general) staff status, have based their advocacy upon educational technology theory or editorial principles, and have adopted a more pragmatic, technology-focused approach to course design and delivery. Media or computing staff developers typically have had even lower academic or general staff status, have based their advocacy upon technical or production expertise, and have been perceived as even more technologically deterministic than the instructional designers. All of these staff developers run the risk of being regarded as out of touch with the realities of the classroom, serving their own interests, marginal – and at times of budgetary constraint, dispensable. Few staff development centres operate with a strategic, unassailable institutional mandate, and staff development has often been seen by managers as a 'quick fix' solution for educational deficiencies or even something that can ultimately be 'outsourced'.

To support flexible learning, a substantially different model of staff development is required, one which converges and goes beyond these approaches and role/status assumptions. A focus on learning and the conditions of learning in various disciplinary and organisational contexts allows staff development to be perceived as the process of improving quality in curriculum design and teaching strategies. Concerns about individual teaching and learning styles, technology applications, curriculum design and content have to be embedded within institutional policies and priorities for academic programmes. The model is predicated upon internal partnerships and external collaboration. Partnerships between content specialists/teachers, staff developers and support staff can focus upon learning processes, and outcomes as well as materials preparation and production and inter-institutional, inter-sectoral and international collaboration can achieve new synergies in the face of globalisation, rapid change and resource constraints (Latchem 1996).

For staff development truly to achieve its potential in institutions engaging in open and flexible delivery, it must operate within the framework of an institutional strategic plan which has explicit goals, values and standards for teaching and learning. It should provide a 'one-stop' academic and technology support service and encouragement and support for all modes of teaching and learning. It should be concerned with far more than teaching competencies, product development or technology mastery. It needs to be concerned with:

- environmental scanning and anticipating and preparing for external and internal change;
- alerting senior and middle managers to trends, opportunities and threats;
- providing leadership and advice for policy development, planning and resourcing infrastructure and processes;
- promoting the development of the 'learning institution';
- encouraging and supporting quality practice and quality assurance in all modes of teaching and learning and technology application;
- providing a span of expertise and support for multiple forms and combinations of face-to-face and mediated teaching and learning in on-campus, off-campus and international settings;
- using a model of staff development based upon the ideas of 'facilitative reflection' (Elton 1995) and the 'reflective practitioner' (Schön 1983);
- engaging in reflective practice, action research and scholarship to advance institutional and faculty understanding and practice in various modes of teaching and learning;
- helping staff to apply for grants and other external sources of funding and encouraging the institution to establish internal teaching development grants;
- helping the institution develop practices which will recognise and reward individual and group initiative and achievement;
- assisting with projects, project management and evaluation;
- managing boundaries and collaborating with internal, external and international agencies in developing and delivering programmes and services; and
- designing and employing criteria, measures and evaluative/quality control techniques to monitor teaching and learning processes and outcomes.

Amalgamated centres: two case studies

At the time of writing both authors (one has since moved on to become a consultant) were heads of centres which resulted from mergers of staff development, distance education and media centres and provided a range of policy-shaping, academic development and technical support services. There are differences of nomenclature, size and function between these two centres, but both support and collaborate with staff in the design and review of the curriculum, teaching and learning, and media applications. In so doing, they blend the classic approaches of academic staff development (emphasising the personal performance and scholarly aspects of teaching and learning) and distance education (emphasising instructional design, self-directed learning and more systematic and learner-focused approaches). Both centres work to a model which involves:

- a focus on the learning and conditions of learning needed to achieve specific attributes in the graduates, including a capacity for lifelong learning and information literacy;
- staff induction and staff development activities – at the University of South Australia, these derive from corporate planning and faculties' priorities for flexible course delivery and the values of student-centred learning as defined in the university's codes of good practice in teaching and assessment; at Curtin University, they derive from the university's strategic plan which emphasises internationalisation, open and flexible learning, technological innovation and community responsiveness in curriculum and pedagogy and the university's teaching and learning plan which includes objectives concerned with self-directed learning and catering for student diversity;
- systems and projects to support inclusive curriculum development, equity and access, on- and off-campus resource-based learning using media, computers and telecommunications, and evaluation of products, processes and services; and
- research, scholarship and supervision of higher degrees.

The Curtin University Teaching Learning Group (TLG) was amalgamated into a single centre in 1991, partly for reasons of resource constraint and partly to achieve the necessary synergy between staff development, course design, development and delivery and materials development. The University of South Australia (USA) created its Flexible Learning Centre (FLC) in 1995 as a consequence of a major policy review and a resolve to take a whole-of-institution approach to student-centred learning and flexible delivery.

From the outset, the FLC was conceived as a university-wide enabling mechanism and integrated into a 'nested' corporate planning framework for the rationalisation and restructuring of courses and curricula, the development of flexible modes of delivery on campus and at a distance, the encouragement of innovative teaching and learning, the integration of technology, and staff and student learning support. The university's Senior Management Group provided the leadership, energy and shared educational philosophy for the development of goals focused on generic graduate attributes, curriculum objectives commensurate with this goal, definitions of intended outcomes and how these were to be accomplished, and the staff development systems to ensure that these occurred (Moran 1996). The FLC has been charged with providing policy advice to the university and faculties across the spectrum of teaching and learning issues and in particular, in regard to staff development, student learning support and the staged implementation of technology change, technology systems specification and delivery systems development. It has played a major role in development of the university's academic planning and priority-setting processes for flexible learning and distance teaching, and is responsible for coordinating other major initiatives such as the development of policy on information technology in teaching and learning.

This policy formation lies at the core part of the Centre's work, tightly coupled with its responsibilities for service provision to help implement the teaching and learning goals of faculties. The most significant development was the linking of staff development to the strategic directions of the university and the faculties. The Centre has provided multiskilled project teams, it has forged internal partnerships – for example, with the Library and Information Technology Unit in relation to staff development for information technology integration; and it has joined with external task groups – for example, to share staff development expertise, resources and programmes focusing on undergraduate and postgraduate teaching and improving the capacities of senior and middle managers across the three South Australian universities and via a jointly developed Web site (the URL for SATURN – the South Australian Three Universities Resource Network – is http://saturn.flinders.edu.au and http://www.129.96.250/SATURN/).

By comparison, Curtin's TLG was initially perceived as a service agency by senior management but assumed a change agent role for itself. It subsequently became the executive arm of the university's Teaching and Learning Advisory Committee. It not only addresses staff development, provides technical services and concerns itself with the issues that affect the everyday working lives of staff, but is also mandated to develop and maintain the university's teaching and learning plan (Latchem *et al.* 1996) and influence and support policy development aimed at achieving quality in, and support for, all forms of teaching and learning. The university's strategic plan defines the overarching mission and goals of the two core activities, teaching and research, and the underpinning values of the university which are internationalisation, technology and community responsiveness. The teaching and learning plan defines the university's expectations of its teaching and learning through clearly stated objectives and performance indicators and the top priority required actions (which relate to the values within the strategic plan). These two plans provide the dynamic and framework for the staff development and other work undertaken by the TLG. Through these, the TLG is enabled to influence actions upwards as well as across the system.

To give one example of how the TLG encourages and supports moves into more open and flexible learning by representing the interests of the staff it seeks to serve, one of the first initiatives of the newly merged TLG was to commission a survey into staff perceptions of teaching and learning and how they perceived these to be valued by their schools and senior management (Baker 1993). The findings of this survey indicated that staff were strongly committed to teaching and learning and interested in alternative modes of delivery but that there was scope and need for greater recognition and reward for teaching. These findings led the TLG to negotiate 'recognition and reward for good teaching' as one of the five objectives in the university's teaching and learning plan. The TLG has subsequently been pro-active in developing guidelines for enhanced position classification standards for staff at all academic levels. These position classification standards include mention of flexible modes of programme delivery and reflective practice in line with the expectations of the teaching and learning plan and the reality of staffs' changing roles. The academic union has accepted these guidelines and human resources is now developing core selection and promotion criteria which focus on sensitivity to students' learning needs through flexible delivery and internationalisation of the curriculum. Consideration is also being given to enterprise agreements, salary supplementation and performance bonus schemes in line with these changing work patterns (Mueller 1996). The TLG has also reviewed and improved a student appraisal of teaching system which is an integral part of a quality cycle and which embraces all forms of educational delivery. These two initiatives help the institution to obtain and keep good staff, and demonstrate that senior management do more than pay lip-service to the importance of teaching and staff development.

Conclusions

Staff selection, training and support form the engine that will drive profound and comprehensive transformations in the nature and practice of teaching and learning. The writers therefore argue that staff developers should help to shape the institutional missions and policies that provide the contexts for change as well as directly address the needs of the staff. However, within such an extended model, staff developers run the risk of becoming too diversified and over-stretched. Staff development priorities therefore need to be carefully planned and related to institutional strategic directions rather than being serendipitous and shaped by localised or individual concerns. For staff developers' advice to university policy-makers on teaching and learning to be credible and sustainable, their work needs to have a strong theoretical and epistemological basis and be in accord with institutional plans, procedures and values. A further challenge for staff developers in a climate of accountability and competitiveness is to balance the autonomy of the teacher against the institutional need for consistent quality assurance. Perceptions of a 'managerialist', top-down approach will result in tensions across the institution, with some staff supporting management in recognising the need for change and others setting their faces against management and those they regard as the 'instruments' of management.

The youthful state of this new model of staff development, coupled with an extended history of precariousness in such units, makes it difficult to recruit middle- to senior-level staff developers with the necessary practical and theoretical expertise. Strategic alliances, staff exchanges, secondments, using academic affiliates within teaching areas and joint appointments to both schools and service areas are ways of overcoming this difficulty. But staff developers need to identify, nurture and develop knowledge and skills within teaching staff in such ways that these can be passed on by staff to their colleagues. The real answer therefore lies in staff developers creating the climate, conditions and academic work patterns that will inculcate a new form of staff self-management based upon continuous improvement and the notion of a learning organisation.

References

Andresen, L. (1991) 'Educational developers: what do they know?' in HERDSA News, 13(1): 5–7.

Australian Vice-Chancellor's Committee (1995) Development Bulletin 2/95, AV-CC Staff Development and Training Programme, University of Queensland, Brisbane.

Baker, R. (1993) Valuing University Teaching and Learning: Academic Staff Perceptions, Teaching Learning Group, Curtin University of Technology, Perth, WA.

Campus Review (1996) 'Rewards will flow from focusing on staff development', Campus Review (7–13 March), p. 8.

DEET (1994) Resource Allocation in Higher Education: Report of the Joint DEET/HEC Working Party, Canberra, Australian Government Publishing Service, pp. 1–48.

De la Harpe, M. (1996) 'Virtual universities better than new campuses, says Murdoch VC', Campus Review (11–17 April), p. 5.

Duning, B. (1990) 'The literature of management', in M.G. Moore (ed.), Contemporary Issues in American Distance Education, Potts Point, NSW: Pergamon Press, pp. 30–43.

Elton, L. (1995) 'An institutional framework', in A. Brew (ed.), Directions in Staff Development, Bristol, PA, and Buckingham, UK: The Society for Research into Higher Education, and Open University Press, pp. 177–88.

Jevons, F. and Northcott, P. (1994) Costs and Quality in Resource-based Learning On- and Off-Campus, Commissioned Report No. 33, National Board of Employment, Education and Training, Canberra: Australian Government Publishing Service.

Latchem, C. (1996) 'Flexible and cost effective delivery around the world', paper presented at Technologies for the New Millennium: The 10th Australian International Education Conference, IDP Education Australia/Australian International Education Foundation (1–3 October), Adelaide, SA.

Latchem, C. and Parker, L. H. (1995) 'Developing a teaching and learning strategic plan: a case study', in A.C.L. Zelmer (ed.), Higher Education: Blending Tradition and Technology, proceedings of the 1995 Annual Conference of the Higher Education Research and Development Society of Australasia, University of Central Queensland, Rockhampton, pp. 458–63.

Latchem, C., Parker, L. and Radloff, A. (1996) 'A strategic role for an academic staff development unit: the Teaching Learning Group at Curtin University of Technology' in the proceedings of the conference, Higher Education in the 21st Century: Missions *and Challenges of Developing Countries*, vol. 1, Vietnam National University and Royal Melbourne Institute of Technology, Vietnam (14–17 May), pp. 109–17.

Moran, L. (1995) *National Policy Frameworks to Support the Integration of Information Technologies into University Teaching/Learning*, report of a search conference commissioned by DEET, Centre for Academic Development, Deakin University, Vic.

—— (1996) *Flexible Learning: Convergence at Work*, paper presented at the 1996 Conference of the Canadian Association of Distance Education (May), Université de Moncton, New Brunswick.

Mueller, W. (1996) *Transformation of Teaching and Learning in Higher Education*, report on Management Frontier's study tour of selected US universities, institutes of technology and community colleges (6–18 October), by the Director, Human Resources, Curtin University of Technology, Perth, WA.

Schön, D. (1983) *The Reflective Practitioner: How Professionals Think in Action*, London: Temple Smith.

Senate Employment, Education and Training References (EETR) Committee (1995) *Inquiry into the Development of Open Learning in Australia, Parts 1 and 2*, Canberra: Australian Government Publishing Service.

Taylor, P.G., Lopez, L. and Quadrelli, C. (1996) *Flexibility, Technology and Academics' Practices: Tantalising Tales and Muddy Maps*, Higher Education Division, Department of Employment, Education, Training and Youth Affairs Evaluations and Investigations Programme, Canberra: Australian Government Publishing Service.

Tinkler, D., Smith, T., Ellyard, P. and Cohen, D. (1994) *Effectiveness and Potential State-of-the-Art Technologies in the Delivery of Higher Education*, Occasional Paper Series, Higher Education Division, Department of Employment, Education and Training, Canberra, ACT.

8

PRO-ACTIVE STAFF DEVELOPMENT

The Indira Gandhi National Open University experience

Badri N. Koul

Tertiary-level correspondence courses were formally introduced into dual-mode settings in India in 1962, but in-service workshops in study material development for academics only began in the late 1960s and, for support staff, not until the early 1980s. Such early staff development was limited and episodic. It operated in a context of ideological differences and institutional inertia. Even when the first Indian open universities were established, staff development was not conceived of as an integral part of such educational enterprise. There were no models to guide the planners and there were many detractors among the academics and senior managers. This was the environment in which the Indira Gandhi National Open University (IGNOU) opened in 1985, and its Division of Distance Education (DDE) was created in 1986 to provide staff development.

Staff development at IGNOU

Early introspection and consultations at IGNOU suggested that a staff development plan was required to accord with the needs of three types of clientele:

- *policy-makers, planners and educational administrators*, who needed to be acquainted with the philosophy and operational intricacies of integrating the academic, organisational and administrative aspects of distance and open learning;
- *academics*, who needed to be orientated towards communicating with the learners who were studying *in absentia* or with only short spells of tutorial contact; and
- *non-academic and technical staff*, who needed to be guided in dove-tailing

75

their expertise with the specific requirements of distance and open education.

There appeared to be need for three levels of staff development provision:

- *short-term orientation programmes*, focused upon single activities or concepts and designed to meet the immediate needs of part-time staff and policy-makers and planners from institutions all over the country;
- *medium-term training programmes* for the full-time staff of IGNOU and other institutions involved in distance and open learning, organised as a series of workshops ranging from basic principles and operations through to advanced levels and special themes; and
- *long-term human resource development* based upon perceptions of future needs.

The DDE's first long-term development programme was a Postgraduate Diploma in Distance Education, developed in 1986, piloted in 1987, revised in the light of the evaluative feedback from the first cohort of students, and offered from 1988 onwards. By the time that the DDE had developed its second long-term programme, the MA in Distance Education, about 900 non-academic and technical staff had received training through fifty-two short-term orientation programmes and about 500 academic staff had engaged in twenty-two medium-term training programmes through the Division.

At this stage, the selection of content for these staff development programmes derived entirely from perceived needs and it was recognised that the programmes needed a more empirical basis to ensure academic credibility and to inform the trainers better. Accordingly, a survey was conducted to see what tasks each category of staff was expected to perform and what training inputs they required in the cognitive, psychomotor and affective domains (Koul and Mirugan 1989). The findings largely confirmed the perceived needs but this feedback certainly helped to focus, improve and deepen the content. This work also provided the basis for a later survey, sponsored by the Commonwealth of Learning (COL) and conducted in 1994, which aimed to identify the training needs of open and distance educators in South Asia and ensure that the IGNOU training programmes were relevant to the needs of the region, as well as to those of the institution.

By 1989–90, the IGNOU expertise and Diploma materials had gained a sufficiently high reputation to be used in a COL-IGNOU training programme for South Asia, and in 1990, IGNOU was also invited to participate in a COL-sponsored, four-nation collaborative exercise on postgraduate training programmes in distance education. This exposure to international concerns made it possible to provide a global context to IGNOU's Diploma courses and the five additional courses being prepared for the launch of a Master's programme in 1993. A subsequent review of these materials by COL experts confirmed their utility and relevance beyond the Indian context.

The government of India's Ministry of Human Resource Development also came to recognise the quality and potential of these IGNOU courses. At a 1989 regional conference held in Islamabad, Pakistan, and designed to explore various national initiatives for the region, the Ministry proposed that IGNOU's work had regional application. This led to the recommendation that a specialist institute for staff development in distance and open education should be established at IGNOU under the stewardship of a Pro Vice-Chancellor. The government approved but would not fund this proposal, suggesting that since it was visualised as serving regional needs, the initiative should at least in part be internationally funded. COL was approached for funding and committed C\$150,000 as a development grant and IGNOU matched this by providing the accommodation, infrastructure and recurrent budget for routine expenditures. In 1993, the DDE was upgraded to become the Staff Training and Research Institute of Distance Education (STRIDE), with a new mandate not only to organise staff development activities including those leading to degrees but also to conduct and promote systemic research in distance and open learning. Such was IGNOU's contribution to staff development that in 1994 COL declared IGNOU to be a COL centre of excellence for staff development.

In 1994, IGNOU also agreed to offer its Postgraduate Diploma and Master of Arts (Distance Education) programmes to about twenty developing Commonwealth countries under the Rajiv Gandhi Fellowship Scheme which had been instituted by COL in 1993. These courses were reviewed by COL experts and then restructured and updated in-house to ensure that their content, design, distribution, depth and treatment met the necessary international standards. The revised postgraduate programmes were offered nationally in 1994. In 1995, they were offered to an international clientele comprising 103 students. These students were supported by STRIDE staff from a distance and by local tutors/counsellors prepared specifically for this role by STRIDE through special orientation programmes conducted in India, Solomon Islands, Trinidad and Tanzania. STRIDE also initiated various administrative procedures to ensure flexibility in scheduling examinations and other activities to suit local conditions within the different countries.

The Postgraduate Diploma in Distance Education entails 900 study hours and comprises five courses:

- Growth and Philosophy of Distance Education;
- Instructional Design;
- Support Services;
- Management of Distance Education;
- Communication Technology for Distance Education.

The MA (Distance Education) can only be taken by those who have successfully completed the Postgraduate Diploma. It comprises five courses which again require 900 study hours:

- Curriculum Development in Distance Education;
- Research for Distance Education;
- Distance Education: Economic Perspectives;
- Staff Development in Distance Education;
- Project Work (on a selected topic).

Each programme package comprises study materials including audiovisual programmes, assignments and tutorial/counselling sessions, and each six-credit course and the project requires 180 study hours. To date, about 1,000 academics (including 53 from outside India) have obtained the Diploma and about 150 have gained the Master's degree.

The second major concern of STRIDE, systemic research, has so far remained a lower-key activity, partly because of the absence of a research policy and a shortage of staff, and partly for want of a critical base for the growth of indigenous research. However, there have been a few undertakings – programme evaluation conducted by STRIDE, a major COL-sponsored international study into the language needs of Commonwealth students studying at a distance through the medium of English (Creed and Koul 1990), and various research exercises, some pertaining to MPhil and PhD studies. To encourage indigenous research in diverse forms and disseminate research findings, in January 1992 STRIDE launched a biannual refereed research journal, *The Indian Journal of Open Learning*. IGNOU established a firmer institutional research policy in 1995, and this, together with the coordinating role of a Distance Education Council and other initiatives, including the development of training materials in the regional languages of India and the introduction of satellite technology for support services, augurs well for STRIDE as it approaches the next century.

Lessons learned through hard experience

Overcoming ideological barriers and constraints

In the early days at IGNOU, many questions were raised about the relevance of a training unit and its functions, activities, personnel and place within the organisation. Typical questions were: 'Was staff development to be a continuous process?' 'Why not run a few workshops rather than establish a training unit which would burden institutional resources?' 'Where would we find the local experts to run such a unit?' 'How could such a training unit have the academic pretensions of offering long-term programmes which were the preserves of the teaching schools?' 'What would be the purpose of a Postgraduate Diploma or Masters in distance and open learning?' 'Was distance education a *discipline*, sound enough to sustain such courses?' And 'Would the money spent on a dedicated centre bring any real returns?' These concerns were expressed by (among others) Lord Perry, then an ODA adviser to the first Vice-Chancellor of IGNOU. He felt that IGNOU, in following the course-team approach, might well manage without a dedicated training unit.

The advocates for the unit and continuous staff development adopted a pro-active stance, addressed these questions emphatically at every possible opportunity, progressively built up the training resources, and introduced programmes in conjunction with supporting policies and incentives. They argued that given the rapid development and change in theory, pedagogy and communication technologies, one-off workshops could not serve the academics' needs or help the institution or its programmes to discard weaker approaches in favour of better practices. It was also advanced that distance and open learning was like other corporate enterprises in which every change in product design or service delivery entailed corresponding staff development programmes and a continuous cycle of review and development.

From the outset, the training unit was perceived as needing to function, and be seen to function, as an academic unit and as an innovator. The challenge was to find the personnel with the appropriate track record, values, communications skills and commitment. However, the DDE succeeded in building a team of nine staff in its very first year of operation. These staff had very limited, if any, acquaintance with distance and open education, its philosophy and/or operations, but committing their existing knowledge and skills to the work, they emerged as the pioneering core who were subsequently responsible for staff development at, and through, IGNOU.

From the outset, DDE staff development and postgraduate programmes were also seen as needing not only to meet the professional needs of IGNOU and other universities' staff, but to empower and extend individual and institutional horizons. Whether or not it is a 'discipline', distance and open learning has shown itself to be penetrative, purposeful and dynamic. So central to the teaching and learning enterprise has it become that in just two decades it has really outgrown its current appellation.

In regard to the question of cost and returns, about 75 per cent of the DDE course materials were developed in-house, and to date these have been the least costly of any in the university. However, the benefits should not be measured simply in these terms or by the number of students attracted to the programmes. Ultimately, staff development at IGNOU must be judged by what it yields and saves in the years to come as a consequence of well-trained human resources.

The IGNOU experience has been that the assumption that the course-team approach can serve the purpose of staff development everywhere is flawed, and that strategies which work well in one culture may not necessarily do so in another. The course-team approach, although a desirable gaol, is expensive and time-consuming, and remains problematic in a culture such as India's, where academics have yet to learn to work in teams.

Developing the staff roles and expertise

The IGNOU experience taught us that any group of course coordinators, writers and content editors undergoing the orientation programmes would invariably break into three sub-groups, usually of comparable size. The first sub-group would honour deadlines, adhere to the house-style and complete their units satisfactorily. The second sub-group would genuinely try to fulfil their commitments, but would require additional support to make their units usable. This sub-group evidenced the need for flexible training approaches as each trainee came onto the programme with different levels of competency and efficiency. The third sub-group would not respond to reminders or would keep on asking for extensions of time for family and other reasons. They would fail to fulfil their commitments or would delegate their work to inexperienced junior colleagues or even senior students, and they would write only essays or textbook chapters and ignore the pedagogical dimensions of the work. We finally established that this third sub-group was simply not suited to the work, but only after expending valuable funds, time and energy on these staff. The staff who received training in tutoring and counselling followed much the same pattern and a sharp decline in attendance at the tutorial/counselling sessions was not unusual. It was a costly realisation to the DDE that single, short orientation programmes were not enough to transform every conventional classroom teacher into an effective tutor/counsellor, and that not every academic was suited to work in distance and open learning.

We experimented with the involvement of deans and other senior academics in our activities, partly to acquaint these conventionally minded stalwarts with the processes of distance and open learning, and partly to lend academic and political credibility to the study materials and tutorial services being planned. The exercise served the former purpose to some extent, but the latter aim was not realised. We learned that devoting resources and time to the pursuit of academic and political credibility through such involvement is generally a bad bargain, some notable exceptions notwithstanding.

Through our work at DDE, we found that more open staff selection criteria and procedures coupled with continual training can yield up some really dependable part-time staff. For example, in enlisting course writers or tutors/counsellors, we found that we did not need to restrict our choice to the academic fraternity. Good academic or instructional communication is not the sole prerogative of the 'academic' instructor. Persons who are not necessarily from educational institutions, but who are appropriately qualified, know the content, can communicate effectively, are willing to benefit from orientation programmes and are prepared to put their minds and hearts into the tasks at hand, can be much more effective course writers, tutors or counsellors than unwilling academics who are involved unwittingly or driven by ulterior motives. We also established that the hiring schemes for part-time staff needed to provide for a mix of rewards and penalties; in our experience, strict observance of contractual procedures works far better than attempts at 'management by goodwill'.

In extreme cases, the DDE or STRIDE simply could not find suitably trained or experienced part-time staff. For example, the DDE faced such a situation when its Postgraduate Diploma in Distance Education was launched in 1987. For the first two years of this programme, twice-a-year, short, intensive contact programmes were organised at selected study centres by the full-time staff of the DDE. For the third cohort admitted in January 1989, regular tutoring/counselling sessions were arranged by hiring in the services of those in the first two cohorts who had performed well on the Diploma programme and organising intensive orientation programmes to train them for this purpose. The deserving new diplomates found their Diplomas providing immediate returns, the students found the continuity of tutors and contacts more satisfying, and the DDE staff found they had more time to work on the more advanced materials and activities required for the Master's degree.

Overcoming 'fallacious inhibitions'

Change and staff development at IGNOU was inhibited by certain fallacious arguments. One 'fallacious inhibition' encountered by the DDE was that of *academic elitism*. The earliest workshops did not attract the professors, for they believed that their status provided them with immunity from the ignominy of their colleagues – and in many cases their juniors – telling them how to go about their work. Their typical defences were: 'I have five books to my credit. Why do I require orientation to write for distance students?' or, 'I have seven years' teaching experience. Am I not experienced enough to write or talk on themes which I have taught several times over?' It was not unusual to hear of conflicts between the junior academics, working in accordance with what they had learned in the workshops, and the more senior staff who had not attended them and wanted the study units to be anything but self-instructional. The latter staff were only concerned with scholastic excellence in the specific linguistic register of their discipline and the frustrated junior staff often had to be cajoled to keep on with the task. It took five years of the workshops' operations before newly appointed professors attended them voluntarily and with any real commitment. It took all of this time for it to become evident to these more senior appointees that the workshops could help them to reduce tensions within their schools and interact with their colleagues purposefully and effectively, thus saving resources, time and energy. In the DDE we learned that patience and time, as well as knowledge and skill, are needed to find solutions in staff development.

Uniqueness of the discipline was another belief upheld by many academics. Quite often, in the orientation programmes, science teachers would say that the 'mechanical approaches' of instructional design might well apply in the humanities or the social sciences, areas in which most of the distance education programmes were offered, but would not work for their particular disciplines. On the other hand, humanities faculty would often claim that their focus was on pluralism and creativity and that such structured instruction would not work in these contexts, being best-suited to the science subjects. These misconceptions were overcome by involving diverse faculties in various joint tasks wherein they came to realise that whatever the discipline or learning milieu, they were all essentially engaged in pedagogy, they were all first and foremost teachers, and the principles of instruction were the same, whatever the discipline.

The third major belief that had to be addressed was that *only live teaching transactions provide for creativity*. The teachers on our staff development programmes had to be persuaded to consider how particular teaching transactions in the classroom led to creative activities and how instructional design could replicate such transactions in distance education courseware or strategies. By involving the staff in all of the stages of course and coursework development, it could also be demonstrated that preparing study units with effective explanations, telling examples, explicit illustrations and apt access devices can be as creative an experience as any live teaching transaction.

Conclusion

Staff development, in any field of activity, is accorded true professional status only after its human resource and economic relevance are fully acknowledged. Until that time, staff development goes through an uncertain period of problems and conflicts, which, however, provide ample scope for pioneering work and valuable interventions. The work at IGNOU has thrown up some interesting problems.

The first problem occurs when politicians and policy-makers become carried away by success stories of distance and open learning without any idea of the levels of professionalism required for the actual operations. The failure of the Nalanda Open University, established in 1987 in Bihar, provides a case in point – this was a glaring example of a failure to recognise the importance of expertise and human resource development needs.

Second, being at different levels of technological and economic development, different countries provide, use and maintain different communication technologies at differing levels of sophistication. This in turn gives rise to differing perceptions of the what, why and how of staff development in various distance and open education systems. What is modern in one context is already dated, or outdated, in another, and only a dream for the future in yet another. It is difficult to achieve acceptance of the fact that such differing situations actually coexist and form a spectrum of need-strands; the advocates of one kind of delivery system either try to haul all the others onto their bandwagon – the current hype about 'Information Superhighways' is an example – or seek to denigrate what others may advocate. Indifference to, and ignorance of, these multiple need-strands creates a situation which is worsened by the immense variation in management styles and managers' perceptions of the value of technology and staff development. Within one and the same context, no two power-centres think about these issues in similar ways. To conceive, put into shape and implement well-planned training programmes in such a situation is fraught with inaptitude, scepticism, and disbelief by management, academics and funding agencies. This composite handicap can only be overcome by positive and imaginative interventionism by staff developers.

Third, honouring professionalism in distance and open learning is rare in developing countries. For instance, although IGNOU has established policies, procedures and substantial monetary incentives for its staff to obtain professional training and postgraduate qualifications in distance education, the overall potential and range of purposes such training can serve is not generally or unequivocally accepted. In selecting tutors/counsellors, the university's regulations continue to ask for academics with teaching experience in conventional, face-to-face institutions. A qualified and trained person without such experience will *not* be considered for the position. Faith in teaching experience in conventional classroom settings may have a sound basis, but to ignore the potential of trained persons from other backgrounds only indicates the strength of the biases working against the positive measures taken to promote professionalism in this field. To give another example, as reported earlier, although the Indian government gave approval to the establishment of STRIDE, they would not fund it; even IGNOU has yet to fulfil its commitment of providing space and facilities for this purpose. In the interests of distance and open learning and the vast numbers of students it seeks to serve, the quicker such anomalies are addressed, the better.

Fourth, the size of the overall operation, the nature of the infrastructure, the clientele and the financial and temporal limits within which targets have to be achieved have significant implications for the selection of appropriate training models. The larger the clientele, the more diverse their characteristics, levels of concern and commitment. This diversity requires the content of training to be stratified, the course packages to be modularised and the training process to be flexible, both in terms of policy and delivery. With a relatively small clientele and pragmatic projections for human-resource requirements, *participatory* models emphasising more *reflective* approaches may be employed. In developing countries, planning typically takes a back seat and 'instant policies' prevail, driven by top management's desire to engrave their names on the plate of national progress. Pressures of time, funds and size force the institutions to develop staff development models which tend to be *prescriptive*, and can degenerate into being *restrictive*. Such prescription promotes absolutist tendencies among the recipients. Consequently, the trained personnel are less innovative and more dependent. Only a minority can provide the necessary creative energy and this does not create a culture of true professionalism. One of the solutions lies in those practitioners who structure and prescribe these programmes changing, modifying and improving them and thus making their own training a continual activity. Such staff, however, do not find it easy to keep pace with the changes in content, methodology and technology. The solution may therefore lie in *collaboration*. Multilateral collaboration may be problematic but long-term bilateral relations serve well.

Experience at IGNOU has shown that the dynamism inherent in an uncertain and uneasy situation, if matched with appropriate pro-active interventions, is bound to improve it. If staff development is to benefit distance and open learning systems universally, it needs pioneers to display vision, perseverance and operational sagacity, for we have miles to go and far-reaching goals to attain.

References

Creed, C. and Koul, B.N. (1990) *Study of the Language Needs of Commonwealth Students Studying at a Distance through the Medium of English*, Vancouver: Commonwealth of Learning.

Koul, B.N. and Mirugan, K. (1989) *Training Trainers: Needs, Content, Strategies*, New Delhi: Indira Gandhi National Open University.

9

HELPING FACULTY TO MAKE THE PARADIGM SHIFT FROM ON-CAMPUS TEACHING TO DISTANCE EDUCATION AT THE INSTITUT TEKNOLOGI MARA, MALAYSIA

Szarina Abdullah

In the late 1980s and early 1990s, when there was so much talk about a 'paradigm shift' in higher education, I thought that this was just another passing fad. I was wrong on at least two counts. First, in recent years, leaders in Malaysian government, industry, commerce and education have acknowledged that the continuing economic development of the country can only be maintained by major investment in the education and training of its people. Within higher education, there has been a parallel acknowledgement that a major paradigm shift is required among the staff if the institutions are to help the nation achieve its developmental goals.

Second, I was charged with the new responsibility of developing and managing distance learning at the Institut Teknologi Mara (ITM), the largest institute of higher learning in Malaysia and an institution that has enjoyed forty years of successful practice and outcomes by teaching conventionally. Within such an environment, I have become convinced of the need for a paradigm shift by the institution and by its staff. This chapter describes the strategies and processes that have been employed at ITM to help faculty envisage and accommodate the change from on-campus (face-to-face) teaching to distance learning.

Why a paradigm shift in staff development?

During national seminars organised by ITM in 1993 and 1994 to create more awareness of distance education among the Malaysian public and academic community, typical comments and questions put forward by my teaching colleagues were: 'There is no way I can teach law at a distance'; 'How are we going to achieve good behaviour and mould character when the students are not on campus and interacting with us daily?' 'How can such a degree be recognised? There's no classroom teaching, no laboratory work, no library work. How are the students to learn? They never meet their professors', and 'When you accept students without any entry requirements into the programme, this makes it appear that the programme is not of good quality.'

These remarks typify the perceptions, or rather misperceptions, traditionally held by many Malaysian academics. Another group of academics, the members of the Technical Committee on Qualification Recognition for the Public Service Department, share the concerns of the latter speaker. Most of the distance education programmes offered by ITM and the other public universities are based upon a full-time, on-campus curriculum. The degrees awarded do not indicate whether they were obtained via on-campus study or distance learning and these have long been recognised by the Public Service Department. However, we have yet to see a single mode education programme gain recognition on its own merits.

Given these attitudes and traditions, it is no surprise that the then Vice-Chancellor of University Malaya (UM), the country's oldest university, failed to persuade his staff to agree to his idea of UM offering distance learning programmes when he first suggested this in 1970. Only the far-sighted and assertive Vice-Chancellor of University of Science Malaysia (USM) managed to establish the Unit for Off-Campus Study in 1971 to administer bachelor degree programmes in arts, humanities and social sciences by distance learning. Between 1973 and 1975, USM added bachelor programmes in science, physics, mathematics, biology, chemistry and foundation science. However, it was not until 1990 that a second institution of higher learning, ITM, came to offer programmes in the distance mode. The reaction and resistance evident at UM were also experienced at ITM. The fact that only three out of 120 programmes taught on campus were offered at a distance reflected the attitude of staff towards this mode. Furthermore, the general public did not initially view distance education positively, and few graduates or students who studied through off-campus programmes spoke openly about their status or experiences as distance learners.

The wind of change swept through Malaysia in 1995. Propelled by rapid economic growth which necessitated an increasingly skilled workforce, the Malaysian government made human resource development one of its top priorities. In his 1995 Budget speech, the Finance Minister declared that all universities in Malaysia should introduce distance education courses as a means of upgrading the knowledge and skills of the workforce. The Minister of Education (Mohd Najib 1996) re-emphasised this initiative by stating that the government's vision was for 40 per cent of the population to have tertiary qualifications by the year 2020 and that distance education was to be one of the prime mechanisms by which the number of graduates would be raised from the current 13.9 per cent to achieve this target. By 1996, in pursuit of this policy, there were seven public institutions of higher learning offering dual-mode programmes and a number of private institutions offering distance education programmes in collaboration with local and overseas universities. The latest data on students, programmes, learning materials and staff in Malaysian distance education may be found in Abdullah (1997), while the development of distance programmes in Malaysian dual-mode institutions are described by Saleh (1995); Silong (1995); Hapsah (1995); Abdullah (1994); and Ahmad (1993).

The implementation of such major policy and educational changes requires leadership, new priorities in policies and actions, and staff to be helped in managing their feelings, thinking positively about new approaches and adapting to the paradigm shift.

Strategies for change that worked well for ITM

The following strategies were used to bring about change at ITM.

Recognising the fact that resistance to change is normal

Everyone involved in leading and managing change needs to recognise that resistance to change is normal and something to be planned for. Unless this is acknowledged, those charged with managing change will inevitably find themselves involved in a major and continuous tug-of-war between what the organisation expects and demands of its staff and the staff members' personal aspirations. The consequences are likely to be a high degree of frustration, despair and staff turnover.

Most academics at ITM teach their students in the ways they were taught and believe that they have sound reasons to say that this method has worked well for the Institute. Over the years, such approaches have produced many graduates who are now successful leaders, managers, political figures, entrepreneurs, business people, academics and professionals in a wide range of fields. The teaching staff's resistance to being told that they now have to change the ways in which they teach, use new delivery methods and enable more students to learn flexibly is therefore both normal and understandable.

Having acknowledged the existence of such resistance, we needed to address the issue. We found two books which provided insights into the process of change to be particularly useful. These were by Scott and Jaffe (1990) and Tan (1994).

Scott and Jaffe's portrayal of the four stages of transition that individuals and groups go through when confronted with change is given in Figure 9.1. Confronted with the need to change, the initial reactions of the individual or the group are to look to the past and indulge in 'Denial' (denying the external imperatives that suggest a need for change) and 'Resistance' (protecting self). In time, and with the necessary encouragement and support, these give way to the 'Exploration' stage and ultimately, the 'Commitment' stage where the orientation is now to the future rather than the past.

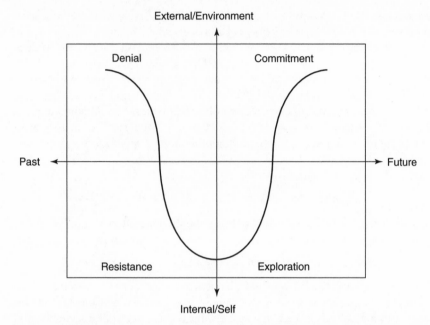

Figure 9.1 The four stages of transition when confronted with change (Scott and Jaffe
1990: 35)

Our experiences in trying to involve staff in distance education at ITM
conformed with this model. Several deans initially rejected or denied the need
for change and our attempts to get the earliest distance education programmes
off the ground met with some resistance. However, this model showed us that
we were experiencing a normal and predictable pattern of human behaviour
and once these stages were recognised, we set about devising ways of addressing
them.

Providing vision-orientated leadership from the start

We were fortunate in that the Rector of ITM had previously managed change in
another large organisation and was well aware of the tensions created by such a
profound change process as moving into dual-mode delivery. He was in a strong
position, and saw the need to transform the second-level managers and enlist
their help in effecting the desired changes down and across the institution. In
1995, he announced the Institute's vision, namely, to achieve an enrolment of
50,000 on-campus and 50,000 off-campus students by the year 2000. He urged
every member of staff to think seriously about using distance learning as a
mechanism to achieve this target (Laidin 1996). At that time, ITM's student
enrolment was about 37,000 full-time on-campus, and about 8,000 off-campus.
Over 125 programmes were on offer, but only four of these were delivered in the

distance mode. The challenge lay in increasing the number of distance students from 8,000 to 50,000 within a time-frame of four years.

Communicating, educating and informing

Change of this magnitude seldom occurs automatically or easily – it needs to be managed. We managed the resistance to change at ITM by adopting the steps in Figure 9.2. Having acknowledged that many key staff were, in Scott and Jaffe's terms, at the 'Resistance' and 'Exploration' stages, we made a concerted effort to create more awareness of the needs for change and inform the staff about the nature and purpose of distance education.

The Rector never failed to 'advertise' the vision and the strategies that were planned to achieve this vision in his formal and informal discussions with staff and students. This is clearly a critical role for senior managers in organisations facing change. He also alerted staff to the nature of the impending changes and, acknowledging the staff's self-concern, talked of the unease which many would inevitably experience during the transition stage. He explained that he expected all staff to learn new skills in developing and delivering a modular curriculum and flexible learning, engage in Total Quality Education (TQE), and undertake many other new tasks. As a consequence of this critically important awareness-building and counselling, the Scholarship and Training Division of ITM found itself busier than ever before, providing numerous demonstrations and staff

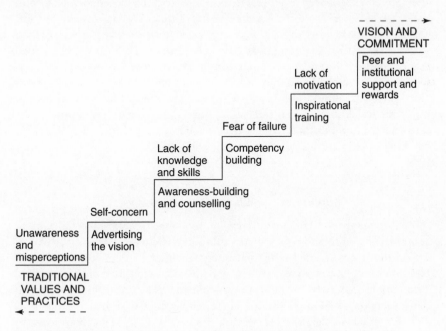

Figure 9.2 Helping faculty make the paradigm shift at the Institut Teknologi Mara

development programmes for the 2,750 academics and 3,800 general staff. The Minister's 1995 address acted as a further spur to change and, by 1996, to the three programmes established in 1990 in Business, Banking and Public Administration, we had added a fourth diploma programme in Accounting. And in 1997, two more programmes at Bachelor level were being planned.

Introducing Total Quality Education (TQE)

Total Quality Education (TQE) was found to provide an effective induction into the culture of continuous improvement that is so essential in an increasingly competitive world and every ITM staff member has been trained in this approach. TQE identifies the students as prime customers, and shows that flexible programmes, methods and materials that are geared to their needs are more likely to be viewed and received favourably by the students. Moreover, we show that TQE is a fundamental part of distance education planning and implementation. Once our teaching colleagues are aware of the principles of TQE, we find that they readily apply these to all distance education operations.

Learning from external sources

It was very important for us to acknowledge that we could not depend solely upon our own experiences and knowledge and that there was a considerable reservoir of experience in other organisations that had been involved with distance education over a considerable period of time. We saw a need to enable staff to visit these other institutions to gain new insights and to open up their 'world view'. We found that this helps to achieve the required attitudinal changes and commitment. As funds permit, deans, coordinators and lecturers involved in distance education travel abroad for academic visits, conferences and short courses. External and overseas experts are also brought in to run workshops and seminars for staff. As an interesting side note, the author's papers on the paradigm shift and distance education received scant attention from the ITM staff until speakers from other universities made reference to these (Abdullah 1994).

Enhancing qualifications and knowledge

ITM also recognised the importance of providing scholarships for staff to further their formal studies in distance education. Between 1994 and 1996, ten scholarships were awarded – three at postgraduate and seven at doctoral level. The courses followed were in open and distance education administration; instructional materials design and development; educational technology; and learner support in adult education. These scholarships have had a symbolic as well as a practical significance, because they evidence ITM's commitment to increasing the number of staff well-qualified in distance learning. They also signal the institutional view that distance education is a status activity requiring specialists with relevant research experience.

Creating public awareness

As mentioned earlier, there were some public and institutional misperceptions about distance education and, in 1993 and 1994, in an attempt to address this, ITM organised two national seminars for academics, administrators and the general public. These gave further exposure to the government's and ITM's visions, the principles, practices and technology of distance and open learning, and the work already under way. The participants heard distance education success stories from people who had been managing such programmes in Hong Kong, Indonesia, Malaysia and the USA. At the 1994 seminar, the Minister of Education and the audience witnessed a videoconferenced lecture from the president of the US Distance Learning Association and this helped to demonstrate the potentials of the new technology. From these events we learned much about the public and academic views and concerns about distance education. We found that ITM's staff became more interested in distance learning as they observed that this was being actively embraced by their peers, respected scholars and other institutions, as well as by the general public. This also contributed to the new sense of purpose and direction in the work.

Publicising the positive values

Helping staff to internalise the positive values of their learning is recommended by Cartey (1996) through what he calls 'inspirational training'. He argues that when individuals and groups are more aware that they are contributing in a positive way, they are more likely to be committed.

We found that there were many positive features in distance and flexible learning that could be communicated and reinforced through words and actions; for example, the opportunities for staff to be more innovative, to be more learner-centred, to experiment with new educational technology, to research and publish in the area, to collaborate in achieving wider access to education, and to make a significant contribution to societal well-being. Interestingly, after identifying and discussing these points during staff development sessions, some staff began to come forward to tell us that they themselves had graduated through off-campus programmes.

Providing counselling and support

Change is seldom comfortable or easy. However, those who have experienced change and know 'the pain' and 'the gain' can often provide invaluable insights, advice and support to those who are experiencing the uncertainties of the transition period. In setting up and expanding distance and open education at ITM, we were well aware that merely to establish writing teams, provide them with technical training, and then leave them to get on with the work was to court disappointment and disillusionment all round. When staff embark on such a new, challenging journey, they are unsure of the right path or where the end point is, and there are many distractions along the way. We found that we needed continually to show that the senior and middle managers shared their commitment, to reaffirm peer and institutional support, to provide suggestions and administrative assistance, and to ensure that there was a positive working atmosphere. Good interpersonal relations were as critical to this work as any of the more formal elements in the staff development process.

Being prepared for things not to work out

Change involves risk. One can never be sure whether one will be better off or worse off as a consequence of doing different things or doing things differently. We found that senior and middle managers as well as the staff developers had an important role in reassuring the staff that even if they put in their best efforts, they could not always be assured of instant success and that nobody would be blamed for failure. Failure is only an outcome of venturing into new things, and at ITM we have found that we need to encourage risk and openness so that after each new venture we can collect feedback to evaluate and improve our products and services.

Changing students' attitudes towards distance learning

Malaysian students in general have poor reading habits (Abdullah 1996) and this is also evident in adult learners. Also, the idea of taking responsibility for one's own learning is foreign to many Malaysian students, and the earlier distance education students tended to come to the monthly seminars offered in the ITM distance education programmes in the expectation of being lectured to, rather than discussing what they had been studying. Questionnaire results have shown that most of the students would like these sessions to be more frequent and such teacher-dependent approaches to the work make it difficult for lecturers to stimulate or sustain discussion. Invariably, in such a situation, conventional classroom teaching becomes the easy way out, both for the teacher and the taught.

Clearly, these perspectives and practices have to be changed. Attendance at an orientation day is now a requirement for all learners registering in a distance education programme. Here they are introduced to the new ways of learning through specially prepared packages and self-directed learning, supported by the monthly face-to-face meetings and on-demand telephone or face-to-face counselling. This orientation programme also helps them with their study skills, motivation and lifestyle management.

We have found it essential for both learners and teachers to have common understandings of what distance education entails. The information given to the students in these orientation programmes is therefore also communicated to all of the lecturers involved in developing, delivering and supporting distance learning.

Students are also encouraged to establish formal and informal networks through which they can share experiences and assist one another towards common goals, academically and personally. It has been found that branch campuses with active student associations record higher pass rates and shorter periods to graduation than campuses without such peer support.

Conclusion

Change is ongoing at ITM and the other Malaysian universities. Referring again to the Scott and Jaffe model in Figure 9.1, to date most of the ITM staff are still essentially at the stages of 'Resistance' and 'Exploration'. But some are already at the 'Commitment' stage. To encourage more staff to the 'Commitment' stage will take even more effort in providing information and training and demonstrating the new ways of teaching and learning.

In this chapter, I have focused on staff development for attitudinal change. At ITM, we have also come to recognise the many external factors that affect change – for example, restructuring the organisation, changing working hours, reorganising accommodation and facilities, and not least, providing incentives and rewards. However, in the ITM experience, no amount of external motivation can match internal motivation and the change that comes from within the individual is most likely to be long-lasting and reliable.

References

Abdullah, S. (1994) 'Pendidkan Jarak Jauh di Malaysia dan Peralihan Paradigma', *Seminar Kebangsaan Era Baru Pembangunan Sumber Manusia di Malaysia: Pendidkan Jarak Jauh*, 'Distance education in Malaysia needs a paradigm shift', paper presented at the National Seminar on a New Era for Human Resource Development in Malaysia: The Role of Distance Education (27–28 September), ITM, Shah Alam, Malaysia.

—— (1996) *Kajiselidik Mengenai Tabiat dan Minat Membaca Di Kalangan Siswa-Siswi di Institutusi Pengajian Tinggi di Malaysia, (Survey of the reading habits and reading interests among students of the institutions of higher learning in Malaysia* (Report no. IRPA 4–07–01–006), Selangor, Institut Teknologi Mara.

—— (1997) 'Managing technology through cooperation', paper presented at The International Conference on Distance and Open Learning, 27 February–1 March, Universiti Sains Malaysia, Pinang, Malaysia.

Ahmad, Q. (1993) 'The administration of distance learning programs: the USM experience', 'Seminar Kebangsaan Ke Arah Peningkatan Program Pendidkan Jarak Jauh', paper presented at the national seminar *Towards Improving Distance Education* (20 July), Selangor, Institut Teknologi Mara, Malaysia.

Cartey, R. (1996) *Inspirational Training: How to Inspire Action*, London: Ascgate/Gower, Advanced Training Group.

Hapsah, S. (1995) *Pewujudan Pembelajaran Berjarak di Fakulti Perubatan UKM: Cabaran Perkembangan*, Syarahan Perdana (11 November), Fakulti Perubatan, Universiti Kebangsaan Malaysia, *The Establishment of Distance Learning at the Faculty of Medicine*, Kuala Lumpur: UKM.

Laidin, A.Z. (1996) 'Making reform work: a case study', Institut Teknologi Mara, Malaysia, paper presented at the *Seminar on Public Administration Reform for Economic Transformation* (14–18 October), Hanoi.

Mohd Najib, Dato' Sri (1996) *Reducing the Outflow of Funds from Overseas Education: Towards Making Malaysia a Regional Education Centre*, Speech by the Minister of Education at the National Economic Forum (11 January), Kuala Lumpur.

Saleh, M.N. (1995) 'Managing the distance learning programme of the Universiti Sains Malaysia', paper presented at the *Workshop on Distance Learning: Issues and Implementation Strategies* (26 June–1 July), Serdang, Universiti Pertanian Malaysia.

Scott, C.D. and Jaffe, D.T. (1990) *Managing Organisational Change: A Guide for Managers*, London: Kogan Page.

Silong, A.D. (1995) 'Challenges in implementing distance education in Malaysia', paper presented at the *Workshop on Distance Learning: Issues and Implementation Strategies* (26 June–1 July), Serdang, Universiti Pertanian Malaysia.

10

STAFF DEVELOPMENT IN OPEN LEARNING AT THE HONG KONG POLYTECHNIC UNIVERSITY

Hilary Mar and Diana Mak

During the past decade, the Department of Applied Social Studies (APSS) at the Hong Kong Polytechnic University (HK PolyU) has been adopting a more open and flexible approach in the delivery of some of its programmes, namely, a Certificate in Pre-Primary Education, a Diploma in Social Work, and a module for a Bachelor of Education in Guidance and Counselling. This has involved twenty-three subjects and has engaged about 50 per cent of the departmental staff in authoring, programme delivery and continuous teaching and learning improvement.

This chapter describes how staff development helped these staff transform the Diploma in Social Work (DipSW) – a foundation course for social workers – into the open mode, employing delivery methods that enable learners to learn at their own pace, time and space (Rowntree 1992). The writers were advocates for this approach and foresaw its potential to not only improve teaching and learning but also to develop staff attitudes competencies (Meacham 1982; Race 1989). The chapter derives from semi-structured interviews with six of the lecturers engaged in the DipSW who were invited to give their views on the development process and how it contributed to their personal development. Five of these staff had been involved in writing and delivering the open learning packages; one had used a package developed by a colleague. Two of the staff had recently joined the department from the profession, two had been teaching the programme for a few years, and two were teachers of long standing. A comparison of original intentions and the participants' perspectives highlight some important issues of staff development.

Introducing open learning at HK POLYU

There are no geographical barriers to access in Hong Kong and the APSS programmes have always been delivered in the on-campus, face-to-face mode.

However, in the late 1980s, the APSS faced a number of external and internal challenges in regard to the DipSW. There were staff shortages in the social work profession and the government responded by commissioning the APSS to expand the numbers of DipSW graduates quickly. Such a sudden and large increase in student numbers would inevitably result in greater variability in entry ability and require a proportionate increase in staff, a development complicated by staff mobility as Hong Kong moved into a transitional phase before returning to Chinese sovereignty in 1997. The DipSW was due for revalidation and the staff were reformulating the programme's philosophy. They perceived that there was too much content and too little space for reflection and that the better way forward was to develop students as reflective practitioners (Schön 1983) and self-directed learners, and that the theory should build upon local practice. The main questions were these: how could the curriculum and teaching and learning methods be designed to prepare the graduates for change in the community and the profession? And how could consistency of standards be maintained across student groups with a fluctuating staff profile?

Open learning was seen as providing the answers to these questions. Open learning ideology and methods had been used elsewhere in HK PolyU to increase access and ensure standards for continuing education programmes. It had been established that such an approach could help to reorientate the Hong Kong student, accustomed to passive learning in their former schooling (Biggs and Watkins 1993), to more active and self-directed learning. Learning packages could be designed to accord with the course requirements and needs of the students. Interaction, feedback and study guidance could be built into the learning materials in the form of cognitive and reflective exercises, activities, questions, discussion and so on. Such materials could provide continuity of professional expertise, have multiple applications, and maintain a baseline standard of teaching across student groups. They could also be a vehicle for generating local material.

After much discussion, the DipSW course team, comprising all teachers on the course, agreed in 1991 to transform the DipSW into an open learning programme in accordance with the desired philosophy and the external expectations. Print-based learning packages were to provide explicit, comprehensive content coverage, study guides to readings, learning activities and local examples. These packages were not conceived as totally replacing classroom teaching – the students were to work independently through them before they came into class. The classroom sessions were to be for interaction with lecturers and peers, integration of concepts into practice, clarification of issues and promotion of independent and critical thinking. In order to give the students more time for such study and reflection, contact time was to be reduced by 20 per cent.

Staff development issues

Introducing open learning into a conventional on-campus teaching institution raises important staff development issues. Such a shift of control, with students learning through a combination of self-study and face-to-face interaction, creates uncertainties in the staff. New skills are needed – skills which may not be covered by job descriptions, accorded status, or rewards. Staff consent has to be obtained and staff development and support have to be provided to help staff develop the materials and learning system, redefine their role from that of teacher to that of facilitator, respond to the ways students learn and help the students assume responsibility for their own learning.

In discussing planned change, Chin and Benne (1976) analysed three possible strategies: power-coercive, empirical-rational and normative-re-educative. Power-coercive strategies make use of political and economic sanctions; empirical-rational strategies persuade through reasoning, information or research data; and normative-re-educative strategies involve change agents in reorientating values and practices. McNay (1987) discusses these in educational contexts and suggests that a mix of the three strategies is generally the best practice. Higher education institutions reporting on successful educational innovations have also described an integrated strategy of management support, retraining and peer interaction – for example, the Miami Dade Community College Project, in Badley (1990); and the McMaster problem-based learning approach, in McMaster University (1987). In transforming the DipSW into open learning, APSS adopted a supportive approach to staff development, using strategies that may be understood from the perspectives above. At the time of writing, APSS has gone through three stages in the development process: involving the staff; designing the learning system and materials; and implementing the open learning programme. There are structures to support each stage and a continuous process of review and improvement.

Involving the staff

The head of the Department of Social Work's 'power-coercive' role was crucial in initiating change. Recognising the potential of open learning to resolve the problems of the DipSW, the head consulted senior staff in charge of the programme and obtained their support. To initiate the development, an incremental approach was adopted to staff decision-making (Lindblom 1980). The head allocated funding and arranged for an instructional design and editorial team from the Educational Development Unit (then the Educational Technology Unit) of HK PolyU (then the Hong Kong Polytechnic) to provide training and development services. Staff who took part in the development were given time release and the work was recognised as scholarly activity.

To start off the normative-re-educative process, a series of seminars on open learning were offered to all of the subject teachers in 1990. The intended outcome was the production of subject outlines and objectives in preparation for the full development of courseware. The seminars were conducted by the EDU instructional designers who encouraged staff discussion on open learning concepts and their transferability into the training of social workers.

A Course Committee, responsible for curriculum development and programme management and operation, became the forum for empirical-rational exchange, wherein staff for and against the development were allowed to advance their arguments. Staff scepticism about the self-learning packages derived from both intrinsic and extrinsic concerns: could the materials be used to move students away from rote learning and provide opportunity for quality interaction? Would these replace the teacher as role model which had always been the preferred basis of social work training? Would the reduced contact hours lead to staff cuts?

After considerable debate, the Course Committee agreed in 1991 to transform the DipSW by stages and by subjects into open learning by 1996. An Open Learning Packages Committee was established comprising project leaders and subject authors. This Committee reported on progress to the Course Committee; the subject authors reported to their subject panels.

This committee structure provided good opportunities for peer interaction and reflection and sustained the necessary empirical-rational discussion. Initially, discussions were at the theoretical or hypothetical level, but as the packages were developed and used, and as students' reactions and teachers' experiences fed into the debate, the discourse moved from generalisations and matters of content to educational principles and methods.

Designing the learning system and materials

Development was a collaborative process involving the authors and the instructional designers who acted as facilitators in the normative-re-educative process. The instructional designers organised workshops for the first group of authors who agreed to participate, and these were phased in to link with the actual tasks undertaken by the authors – for example, identifying target student abilities, specifying learning objectives, concepts and skills, selecting and sequencing content, and designing learning activities. The instructional designers' role was to advise on the methodology, the ways in which the content and learning activities could be presented and the learning package combined with face-to-face interaction to form an integrated learning system, rather than the content itself. Teaching colleagues were responsible for the content review. The authors produced sample units for comment and, when the approach was agreed on, presented further drafts for review by the instructional designers who assumed the roles of student advocate and critical friend.

The final drafts were then developed into packages for trialling. Student and teacher feedback were used to make improvements. New staff joining the teams reviewed materials already developed. This provided useful role modelling and examples of the levels of teaching and learning aimed for.

The role of the instructional designer initially generated tension. A typical staff comment was: 'As academics, we are used to commenting on student assignments, and teaching is an individual activity. It is difficult to accept critical comments from the instructional designer.' But it became increasingly clear to staff that the instructional designer could provide useful comments from the learner's perspective. One staff member later said of this approach: 'It was positive because it gave us a chance to rethink and to see things from the student's viewpoint. The instructional designer came from outside our discipline and identified gaps in the written communication which would not have been evident to us as subject experts.'

Staff comments revealed that the discipline of research and writing expanded and consolidated their knowledge base and teaching skills:

> In writing up [the material], I had to do additional reading, and integrate the new knowledge with existing knowledge. After this process of internalisation and writing, you felt that the knowledge had truly become yours. There was greater clarity.

> In the design of learning activities, I had considered so many different possibilities. This was like a rehearsal, thoroughly preparing me for my classroom teaching.

> I could bring in my experience from the field and this makes my teaching unique.

> I could integrate theory with practice.

> I could now look around me and pick everyday examples to illustrate my teaching with ease.

These remarks show how, as Race (1989) suggests, open learning can be a catalyst for staff development. DipSW development process had various personal meanings for the staff involved, according to their developmental or career stage. These ranged from viewing the educational product as a useful 'scholarly publication' to more personal concepts of, and commitment to, student-centred teaching and learning. This was said by an experienced teacher:

> I started off with cognitive understanding of openness in tertiary education, but through the experience of writing the package, through mastering the subject matter and through reflection, I have learned how to become a social work teacher. . . . It has become a personal enquiry process of what teaching and learning is. I have gained confidence and my teaching methods are more flexible. Teaching method can be so diversified, it does not stop at one-way transmission and role-modelling.

I can easily pick an event from yesterday and use it for discussing values with students, rather than give a lecture on theory. Indeed, I can do without the package, and conduct discussions with other methods.

The systematic design of an open learning programme helped new staff entering higher education from the social work field to move from the role of practitioner to educator, learn to pitch the content to the level of the students and make use of practical experience in the learning activities. This came from a new teacher:

I write from a student-centred, student learning perspective. . . . [I] start from where students are and build on what they know. . . . In the development process, I have to read up, digest, understand, and then write it all out in my own words. I have to decide how to present this content to fit in with the student's level, have to think about which examples to use. There is a long period of in-depth study reflection and orientation to students.

Implementing the open learning programme

As each package was completed and used, personal experience and student feedback brought fresh and useful insights into the application of open learning in an on-campus setting and reinforced empirical-rational exchange among staff. Some of the authors used student evaluation questionnaires with closed- and open-ended questions, and others employed focus group discussions (Chun and Cheng 1996). The feedback provided invaluable material for the subject panels, the Open Learning Packages Committee and the Course Committee.

Implementation of the DipSW open learning programme is still at an early stage, but student feedback has been positive, as evidenced by the following remarks from student focus group discussion on the packages:

The content is well-structured and inter-relationships are clear.

The localised examples help understanding of theory.

The packages are written in simple English and easy to understand, thus increasing efficiency in learning.

They free teachers of time which could be spent more productively with students to further understanding.

Students can take a more active part in class, think and ask questions more as opposed to passively taking notes in a lecture.

Where learning activities are well designed, they help students to stop and think, and thus help synthesis and application of knowledge.

However, in the event, neither the students nor the teachers used the packages or the classroom sessions in the idealised mode. The original assumption was that the students would take responsibility for their learning, study the materials and work through the activities on their own, and prepare themselves for addressing the more open-ended issues in class. In reality, not all of the students completed the learning activities in the packages, some skipped classes when they needed time for other assignments, and some became over-dependent on the package, using it as the ultimate source of knowledge and reproducing it at examination time.

It is at the earliest phase of implementing an open learning innovation that it is put to the severest test, when the teacher's perceptions of self, the learning package and the approaches are confronted by the variety of student responses. Although challenging, this can also provide the basis for staff development of most lasting value. One staff member indicated some broadening conceptions of teaching and learning:

> We cannot assume that at Diploma level, students are self-directed learners. I have to guide and persuade. Open learning packages have to be used in the context of the total learning experience. If we can promote student responsibility for learning, the open learning packages are useful. If not, they may lead to rote learning. . . . I have to learn how to use the learning package, not just students. I have to see how students react, then make adjustments. . . . Students are supposed to read at home but they do not necessarily read nor understand, so we need to discuss how to apply these. [The] open learning package is first-level learning, it handles more objective knowledge and concepts, it is theoretical. Face-to-face interaction is second-level learning, students discuss, defend, argue . . . through discussion, knowledge becomes internalised and students learn how much of that knowledge is truly his or hers. We have made space for discussion . . . Both teachers and students have to participate in the implementation process to get best results. . . . I ask students to express their views through an individual learning journal and I give feedback. Students indicate that they value the feedback and feel excitement about the learning activities.

Some staff commented about the packages and flexible use of learning time, for example:

> Skipping classes is a way to gain space. When students have several assignments at one time, they can flexibly use their time and pick up the learning later if a package is available. . . . The package has to be part of a total learning experience. The face-to-face interaction has to extend the package. The assessment scheme has to cover both the material in

the package and the face-to-face interaction. If the assignments are just reproduced from the package, of course students will rote learn.

The approach had clearly extended some staff's teaching skills. One staff member commented:

> In the writing process, I have done a lot of reading. I use this as the basis for reflection and debate in class. For class discussion I use some activities from the package and add others, I use up-to-date examples. I spend more time on controversial topics and use a lot of group work. ... We have to show students how to use the package as a medium for learning, to explore the value base in social work, what lies behind the knowledge presented in the package.

Another said: 'I have been more at ease in varying my teaching strategies to meet student needs. It has become a spontaneous strategy for me to pick local, everyday examples to illustrate theory; so many perspectives can be generated from one case.'

A few staff viewed the package as an end in itself. For example, one staff member reported: 'The learning packages are the instructional materials, so I follow them closely in my teaching.' Used thus, the package provides no solutions and, not surprisingly, the students continue to rote learn. Successful implementation clearly depends on continuing staff development to address such staff variability. But the change agents can come from within, and social work staff recognised the value of collegial exchange:

> We could use formal and informal meetings for information sharing. Perhaps we could have a focus group discussion for teachers before beginning of term, to share our experience of using the package, to discuss different methods for face-to-face interaction.
>
> The packages provide a common ground and point of departure for peer learning among teachers. We could discuss how to use the packages to make the implementation successful. We could use the packages to train fieldwork supervisors.

Through the committee structure and other meetings, changing practice and building upon conceptions such as those above took the work beyond individual competence to influence group practice and move staff development into a continuous improvement process.

Extending the programme

Social Work studies have only recently been introduced into the People's Republic of China (PRC). One university and several post-secondary colleges in

Beijing have been mandated to develop programmes but there is a scarcity of resources and expertise. In late 1995, as part of an academic exchange process, six staff from one of Beijing's colleges visited HK PolyU, and paired off with the APSS authors to begin the task of translating the DipSW packages into Chinese. This on-going work is an important process of cross-cultural exchange for both parties. The differences go beyond semantics, for underlying the terminology and sentence constructions in the Chinese translations there are different conceptions, social and cultural practices, and values. Such exchange is helpful, given Hong Kong's gradual convergence with China. For the Hong Kong staff, the gains relate most to social work practice:

> We agree on basic principles, but there are differences in service delivery. These derive from the two different social systems. . . . Social work cannot be seen in isolation from social, cultural background, development stage, and concept of society. It's influenced by how resources are allocated. . . . We may not be able to communicate each other's message clearly through discussion, for example, in discussing disability, a paradigm shift is required; but we are closer in our work values when discussing rehabilitation services. They have their strengths. There is mutual learning.

For the Chinese counterparts, the gains in understanding go beyond social work practice to openness in learning:

> The learning approach is very different from the conventional method used in PRC. This new approach gives students more thinking space, enables students to be more active learners. . . . The process centres on student needs and is extremely demanding on teachers. . . . The exercises in the learning packages are most rigorous, students need to search and examine their values and world views in life . . . they also enhance student competence as change agents.

At the time of writing, the first drafts of fourteen subjects have been completed, but the process of exchange has only just begun.

Conclusion

As Rowntree (1992: 18) has argued, and the DipSW experience has shown, open learning can be introduced into conventional, on-campus teaching institutions. How this is interpreted, planned, developed and put into operation depends on the teachers' conceptions of what teaching and learning means within specific disciplines. Staff development can use a combination of power-coercive, empirical-rational and normative-re-educative strategies. The instructional design, implementation and evaluation process develops staff as educators, adding to their knowledge base and teaching skills. Most importantly, it advances their conceptions of teaching and learning. Where structures are established for continuing collegial exchange, educational development may move beyond the individual to stimulate cultural change in the wider academic community and even beyond institutional and national bounds.

References

Badley, G. (1990) *Improving College Teaching and Learning: An American Case Study* (SCED Paper 59), Birmingham, Standing Conference on Educational Development (July).

Bell, R. and Malcolm, J. (1993) *Open Universities: A British Tradition?* Bristol, PA, and Buckingham, UK: The Society for Research in Higher Education and Open University Press.

Biggs, J.B. and Watkins, D.A. (eds) (1993) *Learning and Teaching in Hong Kong: What Is and What Might Be*, Education Paper 17, Faculty of Education, University of Hong Kong.

Chin, R. and Benne, K.D. (1976) 'General strategies for effecting changes in human systems', in W.G. Bennis, K.D. Benne and R. Chin (eds), *The Planning of Change*, 4th edn (1985), New York: Holt, Rinehart & Winston.

Chun, P.K. and Cheng, C.H. (1996) 'Innovation in teaching and learning: development of open learning packages for the Diploma in Social Work Course of the Hong Kong Polytechnic University', paper presented at the Joint World Congress of International Federation of Social Workers (IFSW) and International Association of Schools of Social Work (IASSW), Hong Kong.

Lindblom, C.E. (1980) *The Policy-Making Process*, 2nd edn, Englewood Cliffs, NJ: Prentice-Hall.

McMaster University (1987) *The Health Sciences Briefs*, vol. II, *Education*, Hamilton, Ont.: McMaster University.

McNay, I. (1987) 'Organisation and staff development', in M. Thorpe and D. Grugeon (eds), *Open Learning for Adults*, Harlow: Longman.

Meacham, E.D. (1982) 'Distance teaching: innovation, individual concerns and staff development', *Distance Education* 3(2): 244–54.

Race, P. (1989) *The Open Learning Handbook: Selecting, Designing and Supporting Open Learning Materials*, New York: Nicholas Publishing.

Rowntree, D. (1992) *Exploring Open and Distance Learning*, London: Kogan Page.

Schön, D.A. (1983) *The Reflective Practitioner: How Professionals Think in Action*, New York: Basic Books.

11

FACULTY DEVELOPMENT PROGRAMMES IN DISTANCE EDUCATION IN AMERICAN HIGHER EDUCATION

Charlotte N. Gunawardena and Rebecca H. Zittle

The first part of this chapter reviews recent North American literature on teaching and learning in two-way interactive distance education systems and discusses the implications for faculty development programmes. The second part provides examples of distance education faculty development programmes in operation across the United States, what is common to these programmes and some of their unique features. Some of these programmes were developed by institutions which have been engaged in distance education for decades – for example, the Penn State University and the University of Wisconsin. Others represent institutions new to distance education, such as El Paso Community College. All reflect a move towards a learner-centred, active learning philosophy and away from a teacher-centred approach.

A review of the literature and the implications for faculty development

The literature review discussed in this chapter was published initially in Gunawardena and Zittle (1996), and focuses predominantly on papers published since Dillon and Walsh's (1992) comprehensive survey of distance teaching in *The American Journal of Distance Education*. Most of the papers examined provided descriptions or anecdotal evidence of teaching via two-way interactive systems. Very few of these papers provided empirical evidence of the effectiveness of specific teaching and learning strategies. The interactive distance learning systems covered in these papers included audioconferencing, audiographics, videoconferencing or instructional television (ITV) using transmission technologies such as satellite, Instructional Television Fixed Service (ITFS), microwave, fibre optics and compressed digital video or synchronous and asynchronous computer conferencing using a combination of E-mail, groupware, bulletin boards and resources on the Internet and World Wide Web (WWW).

Most US higher education distance teaching institutions are dual mode, primarily serving traditional on-campus students but also offering selected programmes to distance learners, extending the on-campus classroom by employing a combination of interactive technologies. In this model, faculty have to be capable of teaching to two types of audience: the on-campus students and the distance learners, and researchers point out that teaching in such a distance education environment may require skills not commonly found among higher education faculty (Beaudoin 1990; Thach and Murphy 1995). It is shown that instruction is most effective where faculty who engage in distance education can change their roles as well as their practices (Catchpole 1992; Gunawardena 1992). It is argued that the changes in teaching and newly assumed roles of faculty in distance education reflect a shift from a behaviourist approach to learning to one which is cognitive-constructivist (Garrison 1993).

This review of the literature identified four major teaching and learning issues that needed to be addressed in faculty development for teaching via interactive systems: learner-centred instruction; interaction; social presence; and collaborative learning. These issues are discussed below.

Learner-centred instruction

It is difficult to determine whether the shift to more learner-centred instruction has been driven by the technology or by instructors bringing such an orientation into the distance education context. There is evidence that, in some instances, technology has stimulated change in instructional practice (for example, Moore 1993), but there are also indications that the instructors have conceived, designed and delivered their courses from a learner-centred orientation (Worley 1993; Schmidt et al. 1994). To give but one example of the latter, a pilot programme designed to teach algebra to migrant students was conceived using a constructivist approach, and the evaluation indicated that a learner-centred course can effectively deliver difficult concepts such as algebra at a distance, even using such low-end technology as audioconferencing (Schmidt et al. 1994).

Gunawardena (1992) observes that instructional design must address the complex inter-relationships between the intended learning tasks, the media attributes and the learner's cognitive processes. Two-way interactive telecommunication systems provide opportunities to develop learner-controlled instructional systems that make frequent interaction mandatory for effective learning experiences. Describing her teaching experiences using an audiographics system, Gunawardena (ibid.) discusses the design of a learner-centred graduate course wherein the focus was on learner-initiated enquiry and exploration. The course assignments were designed to strike a balance between independent, interactive and interdependent activities. In such an approach (Figure 11.1), the learner was central to the learning process and in control of the learning experience.

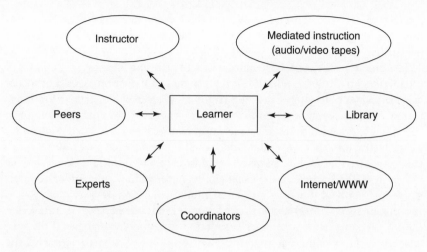

Figure 11.1 Learner-centred instruction

The learners were connected to a variety of instructional resources, including other on- and off-campus learners, the library and databases available through the Internet, and the teacher. Each learner was constantly interacting with these various resources and receiving feedback. Gunawardena (1992) observed that in adapting to this mode of delivery, she had to learn to change her role from that of the teacher in front of the class to that of the facilitator at one with the participants. Her primary role was to guide and support the learning process by helping to link the learners to the other resources and providing sufficient support to empower the learner to exercise control over his or her learning experiences. In developing faculty for work with such a learner-centred instructional system, it is important to focus on the need to ensure that the human and non-human support systems are such as to provide such empowerment and obviate undue failure and attrition.

Interaction

In regard to 'interaction', two questions are of particular interest: what types and levels of interaction are essential for effective learning? And what does real-time and time-delayed interaction contribute to the learning process and outcomes? Moore (1989) makes distinction between three types of interaction: learner–content interaction; learner–instructor interaction; and learner–learner interaction. Kearsley (1996: 84) observes that 'interaction in distance learning needs to be differentiated according to content versus teacher versus student, immediate versus delayed, and types of learners'. Fulford and Zhang (1993) found that the critical predictor of student satisfaction in the course that they studied was not the extent of personal interaction but the perception of overall interaction. If the students perceived that there was a high level of interaction in the course, they were satisfied – even if they did not or could not interact personally.

The literature stresses too the importance of planning for appropriate forms of interaction in distance education programmes. Interaction does not occur automatically or simply because the technology is capable of supporting inter-action but, as Kearsley (1996: 88) notes, 'the idea that interaction must be explicitly designed in distance education courses seems a difficult concept for many instructors to accept and understand'. The University of Wisconsin's faculty guide, *Bridging the Distance: An Instructional Guide to Teleconferencing* (Monson 1978), provides some excellent examples of how to incorporate inter-active instructional strategies into such distance education delivery.

Hillman *et al.* (1994) argue that Moore's (1989) three types of interaction do not account for all aspects of interaction in technology-mediated distance education. They point out that the new technology systems necessitate the conceptualisation of another form of interaction – learner–interface interaction. Instructors and learners have to learn to interact with the new high-technology devices and manipulate interfaces in order to be able to communicate with one another, and have to be at ease with the technology, but this dimension is often overlooked in faculty and student induction.

Social presence

Dede (1989) observes that successful distance instruction depends on more than competence in classroom management strategies, knowledge of subject matter, pedagogical expertise, and the ability to use technology. The capacity to create an intellectually and emotionally sustaining 'telepresence' and the capacity to build 'virtual communities' are also vital attributes in the distance instructor. Telepresence or 'social presence' is defined by Short *et al.* (1976: 65) as the 'degree of salience of the other person in the interaction and the consequent salience of the interpersonal relationships'. Social presence means that the remote instructor, whether 'on-screen' in the instructional television context or the computer conferencing context, is perceived to be a real person with a genuine interest in the distance learner's needs, interest and progress. This characteristic is variously described in terms of the on-screen instructor's 'immediacy', 'closeness in space/time' and 'emotional closeness'. It also describes the degree to which a distance learner is able to feel that he or she can establish an on-going student–teacher relationship with the on-screen instructor.

Hackman and Walker's (1990) study provides evidence that 'teacher immediacy' contributes to student satisfaction and learning in an interactive television class. They argue that there are differences between telecommunications-delivered instruction and traditional face-to face instruction, specifically in terms of the climate of 'social presence' created. Social presence techniques can be taught and faculty who teach using interactive systems need to be trained in these techniques.

Collaborative learning

Research indicates that collaborative group work can increase motivation, completion rates, student satisfaction and, depending on the number of students in the group, even performance (Wells 1990). However, until the advent of the newer communications technologies capable of facilitating interaction among groups for extended periods of time, it was difficult to arrange for collaborative learning by distance learners. Asynchronous computer-mediated communication (CMC) is an excellent medium for introducing various forms of group work into distance learning and many distance educators are now adopting this medium, using the resources available through the Internet and the Web, to design collaborative learning experiences based upon constructivist principles. McIsaac and Ralston (1996) describe the design of such a course using the Internet, the Web, First Class computer conferencing software, and audio-conferencing facilities.

Jonassen (1994) discusses the implications of constructivism for instructional design, and observes that purposeful knowledge construction may be facilitated by learning environments which provide multiple representations of reality, focusing on knowledge construction and not knowledge reproduction, real-world case-based learning, fostering reflective practice, facilitating context- and content-dependent knowledge construction, and supporting the collaborative construction of knowledge through social negotiation. Employing constructivist principles, CMC environments can be designed to provide multiple perspectives and real-world examples, encourage reflection, and support person-to-person and large- and small-group discussion at a distance. Gunawardena *et al.* (1996) developed a constructivist interaction analysis model to analyse learning from an on-line debate which included five phases: sharing/comparing; dissonance; negotiation; testing tentative constructions; and statement/application of newly constructed knowledge.

Garrison notes that constructive learning environments do not reduce the instructor to a mere optional resource:

> While the focus is on learning and the learner taking responsibility to construct meaning, this does not diminish the role of the teacher . . . the teacher carries a heavy responsibility to structure content that provides a framework to connect and make sense of ideas and facts. The goal is not simply the assimilation of facts.
>
> (Garrison 1993: 203)

This is only possible where the instructor has the innate capacity for, and/or has been trained to the point where he or she is comfortable with assuming many roles, among them those of moderator, mediator, modeller and motivator.

Common and unique elements of faculty development programmes across the United States

The four issues discussed above serve to show how fundamental and critical is the need to change instructors' roles and practices in the development and delivery of distance and open learning. The following section outlines the elements of faculty development which are common to many US dual-mode institutions and should form the foundation of any distance education faculty development programme, and then provides some specific examples of programme provision.

Our survey of faculty development programmes across the United States covered the University of New Mexico, New Mexico State University, University of Utah, University of Maryland, Penn State University, University of Alaska, Indiana University, Oklahoma State University, Rochester Institute of Technology, El Paso Community College and the University of Idaho. It revealed the following common provisions:

- Orientation to the use of technologies. Even though some technologies such as television or the telephone are familiar household items, institutions hold that their utilisation in educational contexts requires faculty to be encouraged to revise their conceptions of each medium, consider its qualities, capabilities and limitations, have opportunities for hands-on practice, and reconceptualise it as a tool to assist teaching and learning.
- A presentation on how instructional design must be revised and adapted for distance courses/programmes. This typically covers: the types of material that need to be developed to support instruction and learning; the graphics and other visual elements that need to be created with the capabilities of the delivery medium in mind; the instructional strategies and methods that are needed to maintain students' interest and promote interaction; and the need for increased planning, organisation and time to design and develop an effective distance course/programme.
- Discussion of the presentation methods and 'social presence techniques' which can be employed to decrease interpersonal distance between the instructor and distance students. In the context of instructional television or videoconferencing, these 'social presence techniques' include addressing the distant students by name, making 'eye contact' with the camera, maintaining a relaxed posture, and speaking with an informal tone of voice while varying pitch and pace in discussions, questioning and answering.
- A presentation on the importance of formative evaluation early in a course/programme to identify and remedy any problems which may prevent students from fully participating in, and benefiting from, their studies, and summative evaluations to gain end-of-course input to revise and refine content and methodologies in accord with students' needs.
- Recommendations to staff to visit each distant site at least once to meet the

110

students and, if possible, deliver sessions from these sites in order to decrease any sense of distance or isolation.

- A session on providing on-going support for students. Many support functions, such as library access, advisement, admissions and registration, financial aid and so on are taken for granted by faculty and students accustomed to on-campus classes. Distance education programme developers and faculty need to ensure that their students not only have access to those support elements listed, but also to the all-important technical and logistical support, psycho-social or affective support and tutorial/ counselling/ mentoring support. The capacity to provide, or arrange access to, these services and support systems is critical if faculty are to make the role transition from sole disseminator of knowledge in the classroom to team member and facilitator of learning to the distributed group.

The examples below illustrate how certain institutions approach faculty development – and encourage recalcitrant faculty to participate in their programmes. The University of New Mexico's Distance Education Center, in addition to faculty development workshops for resident distance teaching faculty, offers workshops for institutions new to the distance education enterprise. The Center stresses that the development of successful programmes requires the efforts of a *development team*. It therefore strongly recommends that whole development teams, comprising administrators, programme developers/managers and faculty, should attend these workshops which address both general and role-specific needs. Hands-on training is utilised and faculty experienced in distance teaching offer advice on those techniques that work and those that do not.

At New Mexico State University, faculty are trained in the development of Interactive Study Guides (ISGs) which are used with ITV courses and pre-packaged, self-paced videotaped courses. In their book *Teleclass Teaching: A Resource Guide*, Cyrs and Smith (1990) explain how an ISG is designed to minimise the verbatim note-copying behaviours of students and maximise their attention on instruction and interaction with content. An ISG utilises the format of a lecture outline, complete with reproductions of graphics and other visuals used during a presentation, and incorporates elements such as word pictures, small-group activities and directions on how to complete activities and assignments.

The Penn State University programme includes a Faculty Development Forum, at which invited speakers make presentations on topics or issues of interest to faculty engaged in distance teaching. These presentations are face-to-face, or audioconferenced. The latter provides access to a far wider range of resources than at Penn State itself and the experience of being on the 'receiving end' of a distance presentation. Such an approach also allows for comparison and sharing of instructional practices and media between Penn State faculty and various distance education centres across the country.

The University of Maryland has adopted a particularly creative approach in its faculty orientation programme. One component of this is a humorous videotape designed to illustrate good and bad ITV teaching techniques. This video, *ITV Nationals*, features two sportscasters who give a running commentary on the performance of a distance instructor 'competing' in a national event. A second video, *Confessions of an ITV Student*, and the accompanying manual, serve as a self-contained training package for students new to ITV. To encourage faculty to attend the training programme, a lunch or dinner is organised and the videos are shown in an informal atmosphere with time for discussion.

At El Paso Community College in Texas, the emphasis is on authentic experience and practice, and faculty receive much of their training at a distance. The El Paso dictum, which guides both faculty training and instructional design for teaching at a distance, is 'Active monitor or active students'. 'Active monitor' refers to a frequent change in presentation mode, and 'active students' are those who are solving problems, writing, making decisions or answering questions together. Faculty are required to demonstrate facility with the technology as well as with a variety of presentation techniques and tools. They are trained in multimedia (including video) development, Internet tools, testing and evaluation, and the facilitation of cooperative learning. Participation in the programme is mandatory but faculty do receive time-release to attend.

The University of Alaska's faculty development programme addresses the cultural diversity of its distance students. Faculty are instructed on how cultural attributes may affect communication styles and interaction, reminded that English may not be the first language of all of their students, advised on how values and humour may differ, and encouraged to localise content so as to make it as meaningful and relevant as possible to the students. Faculty new to distance education are given the option of participating in a mentoring network wherein 'veterans' are paired with 'novices' to share their experience and offer advice and support as needed. This staff development network uses E-mail extensively to help conquer the enormous distances within the University of Alaska's distance education system.

The University of Idaho has developed a series of guides, *Distance Education at a Glance*, which deal with a range of distance education issues of interest to administrators, facilitators, teachers and students. These guides may be downloaded from their Web site, and printed for non-profit educational purposes.

Conclusion

The underlining theme in this chapter is that faculty who are accustomed to, and secure in, conventional teaching methods will have to assume new roles and learn new skills if they are to be facilitators in a learner-centred distance education system. They need to be able to exploit the potential of new tele-communication technologies, encourage deep learning and generally extend and enhance their roles as teachers. Thach and Murphy (1995) surveyed 103 distance educators working in academic institutions in the USA and Canada. Using the combined responses of two surveys, they came up with a competency model which they suggested would serve as a foundation for the design of faculty development programmes in distance education. They identified eleven roles for faculty teaching at a distance. These roles, which might be assumed by one or by several people, include: instructor, instructional designer, technology expert, technician, administrator, site facilitator, support staff, editor, librarian, evaluation specialist and graphic designer.

Faculty development programmes alone will not change roles. Distance teaching requires faculty to devote much more time to preparation than they would for a face-to-face classroom. In order to encourage faculty to teach at a distance, they must be provided with financial and other incentives such as adjustments in course load, adequate time-release, peer recognition and credit toward tenure and promotion (Beaudoin 1990; Dillon and Walsh 1992; Gunawardena 1992).

References

Beaudoin, M. (1990) 'The instructor's changing role in distance education', *American Journal of Distance Education* 4(2): 21–9.

Catchpole, M.J. (1992) 'Classroom, open, and distance teaching: a faculty view', *American Journal of Distance Education* 6(3): 34–44.

Cyrs, Thomas E. and Smith, Frank A. (1990) *Teleclass Teaching: A Resource Guide*, 2nd edn, Center for Educational Development, College of Human and Community Services, New Mexico State University, Las Cruces.

Dede, C. (1989) *The Evolution of Distance Learning: Technology-mediated Interactive Learning*, Washington, DC, Office of Technology Assessment, Congress of the United States.

Dillon, C.L. and Walsh, S.M. (1992) 'Faculty: the neglected resource in distance education', *American Journal of Distance Education* 6(3): 5–21.

Fulford, C.P. and Zhang, S. (1993) 'Perceptions of interaction: the critical predictor in distance education', *American Journal of Distance Education* 7(3): 8–21.

Garrison, D.R. (1993) 'A cognitive-constructivist view of distance education: an analysis of teaching–learning assumptions', *Distance Education* 14(2): 199–211.

Gunawardena, C.N. (1992) 'Changing faculty roles for audiographics and online teaching', *American Journal of Distance Education* 6(3): 58–71.

Gunawardena, C.N., Anderson, T. and Lowe, C.A. (1996) 'Interaction analysis of a global on-line debate and the development of a constructivist interaction analysis model for computer conferencing', paper presented at the Annual Convention of the American Educational Research Association, New York (April).

Gunawardena, C.N. and Zittle, R. (1996) 'An examination of teaching and learning processes in distance education and implications for designing instruction', in M.F. Beaudoin (ed.), *Distance Education Symposium 3: Instruction*, ACSDE Research Monograph, No. 12, University Park, PA, Pennsylvania State University, pp. 51–63.

Hackman, M.Z. and Walker, K.B. (1990) 'Instructional communication in the televised classroom: the effects of system design and teacher immediacy on student learning and satisfaction', *Communication Education* 39(3): 196–209.

Hillman, D.C.A., Willis, D.J. and Gunawardena, C.N. (1994) 'Learner–interface interaction in distance education: an extension of contemporary models and strategies for practitioners', *American Journal of Distance Education* 8(2): 30–42.

Jonassen, D.H. (1994) 'Thinking technology: toward a constructivist design model', *Educational Technology*, pp. 34–7 (April).

Kearsley, G. (1996) 'The nature and value of interaction in distance learning', in M.F. Beaudoin (ed.), *Distance Education Symposium 3: Instruction*, ACSDE Research Monograph, No. 12, University Park, PA, Pennsylvania State University, pp. 83–92.

McIsaac, M.S. and Ralston, K.D. (1996) 'Teaching at a distance using computer conferencing', *Techtrends* 41(6): 48–53.

Monson, M. (1978) *Bridging the Distance: An Instructional Guide to Teleconferencing*, Madison, WI, University of Wisconsin-Extension, Instructional Communications Systems.

Moore, M.G. (1989) 'Editorial: three types of interaction', *American Journal of Distance Education* 3(2): 1–6.

—— (1993) 'Is teaching like flying? A total systems view of distance education', *American Journal of Distance Education* 7(1): 1–11.

Schmidt, K.J., Sullivan, M.J. and Hardy, D.W. (1994) 'Teaching migrant students algebra by audioconference', *American Journal of Distance Education* 8(3): 51–63.

Short, J., Williams, E. and Christie, B. (1976) *The Social Psychology of Telecommunications*, London: John Wiley & Sons.

Thach, E.C. and Murphy, K.L. (1995) 'Competencies for distance education professionals', *Educational Technology Research and Development* 43(1): 57–79.

Wells, R.A. (1990) *Computer-mediated Communication for Distance Education and Training: Literature Review and International Resources*, Boise, ID: US Army Research Institute.

Worley, L. (1993) 'Educational television and professional development: the Kentucky model', *Technological Horizons in Education* 20(11): 70–3.

12

DESIGNING THE *REBBELIB*

Staff development in a Pacific multicultural environment

Claire Matthewson and Konai Helu Thaman

Concern within the open and distance learning profession about cross-cultural transfer, globalised curricula and 'appropriateness' issues has increased commensurate with the expanding potential for international practice that disregards them. This expansion of potential substantially derives from technological advance, tightened fiscal policies and the new demands of a knowledge-based society.

Within the University of the South Pacific (USP), however, concern about cross-cultural transfer, globalised curricula and appropriate models is as old as the institution itself. Such issues – although now of heightened interest for developed/developing world debate – have confronted USP internally since the time of its inception.

Multi-ethnic and regionally governed, the university within itself is a cross-cultural artefact. Moreover, being an institution of higher learning, it also confronts the challenge of being this cross-cultural artefact within yet another culture – that of academia itself. The new debates are, therefore, old debates for USP.

In such a unique environment, staff development is a complex issue. This chapter discusses the particular, rather than general theory and paradigms. It focuses, therefore, on practice and some context-related policies. It considers the issue of a dominant educational model and the submergence (or commodified adding) of others' cultures within that. It includes in its findings that the magnitude of possible achievement within multicultural staff development policies is inseparable – as with virtue – from the grandeur of challenges to them.

'Designing the *rebbelib*' refers to a Micronesian stick chart, an ancient aid for navigation in a sea of islands. It is chosen both for its figuring of vastness and for its implication of understandings without which the chart's directional framework serves little effective purpose.

The University of the South Pacific

The University of the South Pacific (USP) is a regional institution and, as such, rare in the international community. It has within the Commonwealth only one sister institution, the University of the West Indies (UWI). USP has twelve proprietors exercising its collective governance: Cook Islands, Fiji, Kiribati, Marshall Islands, Nauru, Niue, Solomon Islands, Tokelau, Tonga, Tuvalu, Vanuatu and Western Samoa.

USP was formally established by Royal Charter in 1970. The university was dual-mode in its founding vision and documentation. Distance education provision began almost as soon as the university started in 1971, with an up-grading programme for teachers. These initial six courses had become 30 by 1979, 75 by 1984, and 148 by 1989. In the 1990s, the number of courses stabilised at around 165. Distance enrolments (by head-count) now number over 15,000, excluding Summer Schools and distance non-credit courses, and credit enrolments have become about 65 per cent of the total FTES roll (Solofa 1996: 4). Being base-funded relative to FTES load, many academic departments derive their major income from distance education. In practice as well as philosophy, therefore, distance education is central to the university's mission.

In 1991, Vice-Chancellor Geoffrey Caston re-affirmed institutional policy thus:

> Each extension student, on any course, has a claim to the attention of the Department which is *equal* to that of each on-campus student on the same course [and] every academic staff member has an obligation to participate in distance education to the extent . . . that the Head of Department . . . specifies.
>
> (Caston 1991: 1)

Context

The university's distance students live in a sea of islands and atolls spanning 33 million square kilometres. Their countries' resource bases are generally aid-dependent or aid-augmented, with population majorities in rural, subsistence economies that have long been sustainable in their own context.

Students variously inhabit four time zones and at least sixty distinct cultures. The ethnic heritage of the majority of students is Polynesian, Micronesian, Melanesian or Indian. All are bilingual and many are multilingual. More than 265 languages are spoken in the USP region. In consequence, students' communities do not inhabit a common non-English world but, rather, myriad linguistic worlds of differing conceptual frameworks. These can vary from province to province, even between neighbouring villages or atolls. Their higher education must, therefore, bridge 'distances' uncommon in measure and implication, for the relationship between cultural patterns and the educative process is tripartitely symbiotic and synergetic with the world of language. These considerations were perceived by a Commonwealth of Learning review to have massive implications for USP (Renwick *et al.* 1991: 41).

Educationally, students are variously prepared by national educational systems and basic curricula that have evolved from British, Australian, New Zealand, French or North American models – reflecting former political ties and/or colonial history. All derive from formal education systems as yet non-comprehensive in sector coverage, in some cases even at primary level. All belong to the region's elite cohort of 4 per cent with opportunity to access further education between the ages of 18 and 25 (Fairbairn 1992: 6). These students are seeking qualifications that have currency, dignity and relevance simultaneously within both their own and wider cultures.

The university's faculty and professional staff can be even more diversely multi-ethnic than the student body. The academic, professional and technical staff substantially comprise Pacific Island nationals (65 per cent), but women are under-represented (31 per cent) in the staff and student groups, and representation is not balanced among Pacific cultural groups. All world continents have some representation so that, in the non-Pacific cohort, linguistic and cultural profiles are also diverse.

Staff, all contractually committed to distance education provision, derive from multiple education jurisdictions with nil-to-conceptually different distance mode experience. Personnel – and thus the necessary focus of staff development policies – are, like the student body, physically dispersed across 33 million square kilometres. Their bases are variously one of the three campuses (Laucala in Fiji, Alafua in Western Samoa and Emalus in Vanuatu), eleven national Extension Centres or a growing number of outer island sub-centres.

Multicultural issues

Thaman (1995: 3) describes culture as 'that complex all-embracing phenomenon which manifests itself in the way of life that is shared by a group of people, perceived by them to be unique. It includes language, a body of accumulated knowledge and understandings, skills, values and beliefs.' Thaman (1995: 8) further cites Goldsmith's definitive view that 'there is no better way of destroying a society than by undermining its educational system' and that this is effected commonly by the destruction of cultural patterns through the educative process (Goldsmith 1993: 285).

There are many ways in which the cultures of Pacific communities and the classical culture of a university cannot avoid being in essential tension. USP could be said to inhabit a cultural dichotomy comprising broadly, on the one hand, its indigenous multicultures (including learning systems and knowledge bases) and, on the other, the formal culture of academia. Students in both delivery modes are seeking access to these 'worlds in integration'.

That both symbiosis and synergy exist between educational structures, culture and language raises vital issues for all education planners, teachers and staff developers. In ironically diverse practice, the richer the diversity of culture and language, the more reductive the educational process seems to have to become. Thus, English as the sole language of instruction from the USP represents an outfall as much from the wealth of students' linguistic diversity as it does from their countries' colonial histories. Matthewson (199: 37), subscribing to the view of education as the most functionally powerful conduit of culture and the teacher as a key transmitter of cultural values, considers the increased destructive possibilities in inter- and trans-cultural distance education.

If culture is what we always teach, overtly or implicitly, then the physical separation of teacher and learner becomes only one of several, more serious 'distances' to consider. The separation between the distance teacher and the learners in their ethno-linguistic, religious, economic and historical traditions increases the potential of dominant 'globalisation', the risk of submerging other cultures, learning systems and knowledge bases. Staff development policies for distance education need to be informed by basic concern for such potential.

Globalising the curriculum

'Globalisation' is a euphemism. In essence and in practice, it means 'Westernisation'. Moreover, 'curriculum' extends to assumptions of an absolute (Anglo-American) pedagogy and includes – almost without question – the instructional systems themselves. 'Globalising the curriculum' could be regarded, therefore, as 'Westernising education'. Within the educational providers' culture, there are some opponents of this process, just as in the culturally dominated there are those who would gladly embrace it.

> the expert says
> that my country is sick
> I'm glad his isn't
> . . .
> our director of education
> supports vernacular studies
> for other people's children
>
> a champion of multiculturalism
> he preaches equality of opportunity
> only for himself
> . . .
> look at the mango tree
> full of fragrant flowers
> promises promises
> . . .
>
>   (Thaman 1993: 54–60)

The view that a culture-free or culture-neutral curriculum is possible is both Eurocentric and invalid. This view would regard subjects such as mathematics, engineering and many vocational trades as inherently 'free' or 'neutral' and would concede that other subjects (such as the fine arts and philosophy) are not. Proponents of this view believe also that localisation can be effected at a curricular content level.

Cosmetic changes to vocabulary and examples cannot and do not, of themselves, transform context, for context is both informed by and expressive of culture; and culture, in turn, transcends its contextual or linguistic expression. Within the view that localisation is possible through 'item-substitution', culture is commodified, perceived as a separable commodity that can be added or subtracted as a component. The view is culturally exclusive, moreover, in that it not only assumes the existence of fields of absolute knowledge within a commonly apprehended world; it also denies the existence of complex, non-Western fields of knowledge – such as physics in Micronesia, mathematics in Polynesia, sustainable development theory or the biological sciences in innumerable other cultures.

The separation of concern for 'what' is taught from concern for 'how' it is taught is equally artificial. The separation assumes the existence of absolutes in good teaching practice – that, apparently sharing a common humanity, learners will also share a common responsiveness to particular pedagogical procedures. Staff development workshops at the USP, however, cannot proceed on such a blithe assumption. A student's silence in response to direct questions might denote neither rudeness nor ignorance nor lack of attention; it might equally relate to teacher respect or the peer group's social composition. A student's faithful reconstruction of prescribed texts might denote neither dishonesty nor incapacity for critical thinking; it might equally relate to culturally valued skills. A student's negative response to a negatively phrased question might semantically mean the same as a positive response from another.

In such a context, staff orientation and development need to focus not merely on ways of transferring knowledge and skills but on the cultural dimensions to assessment systems, teacher–learner relations and status, selection and emphases within the curriculum, interdisciplinary connections, classroom organisation and, for distant study, the design of the support systems.

The writers subscribe neither to the paradigm of increased 'flexibility' or 'openness' in education delivery as having an absolute, culture-free value nor to the view of mode-convergent staff development as entirely desirable. In regard to flexible or open delivery, value judgements are implied in regard to education that is designed otherwise. Self-paced, independent learning is presumed to be, or even reified into, an educational virtue regardless of context. The primary issue here is that community or cultural traditions do not uniformly (and only erroneously are presumed to) value learner independence and autonomy. An absence of valuing these relates to value differently placed both within the learning process and the realm of knowledge-based skills. Staff development for distance education needs to be sensitive to the fact that learner autonomy may be valued differently by the teacher's and learners' respective cultures.

In regard to the second paradigm – that of mode-convergence – the concern relates to higher education in the international arena. There are two types of convergence: that of distance and face-to-face modes of education, and that between communication technologies and these modes of teaching and learning. In regard to the first convergence, distance education has long woven many, various and positive interfaces between totally independent learning and the provision of local tuition. The new danger lies in the realm of pedagogical politics – that what has been regarded as support for distance learners loses its structural role as augmentation, and that all delivery components fall consequently into a basket of miscellaneous valency. In the world now seeming to be under some threat, the distance learner is central and recognised as needing to be served. In the brave new world of mix-and-match convergence (often accompanied by restructuring and decentralisation), she or he loses position as a particular focus of care.

The second convergence – that of communication technologies themselves and forms of education delivery – intersects with this transfer, particularly in dual-mode universities, shifting pedagogical and political power away from distance education. Distance educators have been at the forefront of technology's teaching and learning applications which have proved to be useful to education at large. However, there are dangers of uncritical acceptance and application, of technological determinism and purely politico-economic concerns driving the agenda.

Blanket acceptance by distance educators of both the teaching mode-convergence and technology's capacity to eradicate distinctions between distance and internal teaching, ultimately risks a commandeering of their professional skills to service enhancements of on-campus education and a loss of specific resources and structures that have championed the genuine learner-at-a-distance.

Staff development at USP

USP assumes responsibility for the academic development of its (Pacific) staff. Although 'losses' are inevitable from this investment – higher qualifica-tions being transportable to Rim countries – the university's ethos of service to its region is ultimately unconditional. Advanced education and further qualifications for the nationals of the region are seen as an important invest-ment in personnel who are integral and essential to a Pacific institutional culture within the simultaneously imperative framework of international academic culture.

Staff development policies, therefore, must balance a consideration of the university's appointment and promotion systems (based, under the terms of the institutional charter, solely on performance excellence) with that of providing opportunity for regional staff to be appointed and promoted under this same criterion. 'Localisation' has never been practised at USP. However, in the appointment process, expatriates need superior qualifications or previous Pacific experience in order to offset their relative lack of desirable cultural understandings.

At USP, tenure does not exist. All academic staff, including the Vice-Chancellor and personal Chairs, and regardless of nationality, hold three-year contracts that have been internationally advertised. Contracts are only renewed on the basis of satisfactory performance – and, in this, both worlds of the cross-cultural artefact are regarded as context. Within this system of triennial review, many staff retain their positions on a continuing basis.

Staff development policy is the overall responsibility of the Staff Development Committee (SDC), which has functional relations with the Staff Review and Staff Policy Committees. The SDC's budget in the main comprises Overseas Development Assistance from the governments of Australia, New Zealand and Britain. Development funding is allocated on a competitive basis for two main categories of award: for overseas study towards higher academic qualifications, and for short-term overseas attachments or study leave to enhance professional development. These awards tend to be tied to the origin of donor funding. Awards for short-term attachments, study and conference leave are open to all staff regardless of citizenship, but training leave for the acquisition of higher qualifications is available only to Pacific nationals.

Only academic staff located in University Extension and at the regional Centres have any interest in formal studies in distance education. Even among these staff, higher degrees have traditionally been sought in the prior subject specialisation. This pattern shows recent signs of change, however, with an increasing number of staff completing or currently pursuing doctoral and postgraduate programmes in (and in some cases by) distance education.

The pattern of teaching staff's lack of interest in formal study in distance education shows less sign of change. As elsewhere, this is unsurprising since academic reputations in the international community are rarely enhanced by research and studies in a mode of delivery. The university's policies, however, have overtly moved to address this circumstance. Staff involvement and performance in distance education have become politically very strong criteria for academic promotion and contract renewal, and the review procedures for academic staff have, for many years, provided for specific judgement from the Director of University Extension. Service to the regional community is also a formal criterion for promotion and contract renewal.

Short-term attachments, study leave and international conference attendance that directly focus on distance education concerns have a high priority in the allocation of the limited staff development funds. Indeed, their funding priority increases with the growth of distance-accrued FTES. Grants are available to all levels of staff regardless of citizenship and infrastructural status – academic, administrative, technical and clerical. Notable also is the larger number of teaching staff now applying for professional opportunities for distance education development.

In USP's unique environment, staff development is a complex issue. Indeed, planning activities and strategies to address region-specific issues is not unlike designing a *rebbelib*. This Micronesian stick chart for navigating vast seas provides true direction only in a context of cultural understandings. Like sticks of a *rebbelib* – effective only with contextual insight – the basic framework for USP staff development includes the following:

- General orientation workshops organised by the Centre for the Enhancement of Learning and Teaching (CELT) but also involving staff input from University Extension. These focus mainly on increasing understanding of the students' particular learning cultures and the related behaviours that staff should expect and respect, and to some extent on acceptable general behaviour by staff in relation to students.

- More specific workshops organised by University Extension – for example, on USP's particular model for development of distance education courses; instructional design for Pacific materials; the conduct of science practicals in a Pacific environment, relying often on local specimens and services; the multiplier-role of Centre Directors in their respective national locations; multi-currency accounting procedures for distance students from various jurisdictions; basic librarianship skills enhancement for outpost para-professionals serving distance students. Where these require participants to travel from their home countries to the training location, funding has to be acquired through outside agencies such as COL, and the Commonwealth Fund for Technical Cooperation or a range of ODA programmes.

- Staff travel between and among the twelve member countries' Centres. The University expends substantial resources on staff movement intra-regionally. Airfares within the Pacific Basin are, by international standards, very high and staff travel schedules can also be expensive in terms of time, so this is a choice based on principle rather than practicality. Whether the in-country experience relates mainly to mandatory tutorials, the training of Centre staff, or general liaison and consultation, it is always found to bring benefits in terms of improved multicultural understandings. Indeed, those USP staff who do not travel among member countries, whether these be Pacific nationals or non-regional staff, can be noticeably lacking in 'regional perspective' relative to those who do.

- Involvement of teaching staff in course writing and the revision of their own or others' material. Special considerations in this include:

  - text readability levels for students who generally are not first-language speakers of English but need to encounter internationally acceptable levels of content difficulty;
  - foreign and/or culturally meaningless concepts and examples that have no local referent;

- cognisance of the locally possible or impossible in course delivery and design, academic support and media components;
- assessment procedures and schedules that social patterns, geography and transport infrastructures can accommodate.

Within the same basic *rebbelib*, the above aspects are addressed in a less formally inductive way through the course-team model of materials development. The consultation, advice and guidance and team coordination provided by University Extension staff are crucial in this regard. The course-team model provides deliberately for a collegial sharing of academic expertise, distance education theory and practice and regional circumstances, cultures and experience among writers, instructional designers, editors and media specialists. Each team is overseen by the Head of Distance Education, through the Coordinator of Instructional Design and Development, and ultimately by the university's Instructional Strategies Committee especially established for distance mode courses.

USP in-house staff development activities have also recently related to the wider Pacific region that includes Papua New Guinea. Constrained by the politics of aid programmes, which typically specify where professional development may be located, the region's distance educators have sought funding schemes which are not thus tied, and specifically for Pacific-located attachments and consultancies. Since 1994, the Australian government has resourced an intra-Pacific Islands consultancy scheme for the region's twelve autonomous providers of formal distance education. This accommodates exchange and consultancy for all levels of staff. The New Zealand government is likely soon to introduce a similar scheme.

Conclusion

Staff developers engaged in distance education within a multicultural environment may, broadly speaking, fall into two main categories: those who are already resident and working within such a complex environment, and those who are engaged, or planning to be engaged, in delivery projects from outside it. Both groups undoubtedly share a concern to 'get things right', but some differences can be apparent in their approaches to development issues. These differences could be said to reside in the culturally based concepts of the *rebbelib* and the *recipe*.

The *rebbelib*'s apparently simple framework embraces the challenge of vastness and the undefinable within that; it also requires interpretative understandings to be brought to bear. The *recipe* is a prescription that has expectations inseparable from a Western, scientific, positivist culture. Both the *rebbelib* and the *recipe* are valid in their own terms: however, neither can be wholly transplanted into the other's environments. Staff developers – particularly when working in jurisdictions outside those Western cultures – are advised to accept that definitive or comprehensive multicultural recipes are simply not possible. However, a concern for the ingredients of the recipe, however partial and incomplete, might well be the beginning of a *rebbelib*–prescription compromise. The USP, both at the interfaces of its multicultures and in its essential bicultural dichotomy, continues also to face this challenge.

An holistic staff development programme in an essentially multicultural university needs to reflect and encompass in its strategies the following understandings:

- education has a crucial role in the conservation or undermining of culture;
- teaching and learning methodologies are cultural matters (as much as of content);
- no subject discipline is culture-free or culture-neutral;
- regardless of context, the international academic culture of universities is valid for universities since they are essentially defined by it;
- it is incumbent upon their common protagonists and subscribers to achieve the optimum interface between academic culture and community culture;
- to understand any culture, one needs, at least to some extent, to have lived it.

Since its inception, USP has never truly *not* held these understandings. In its various departments and areas there have always been key staff who were 'awareness carriers' of these ideas. Indeed, being educationally central, these issues are difficult to avoid. However, after almost three decades – or perhaps because their proponents are now more sure of their right and duty to inform such educational practice – USP is now an academically and cross-culturally mature institution. In some specific fields, it has become an international centre of excellence. The Pacific region, which academically the university both serves and leads, has itself become politically independent. Received models in many spheres are increasingly being scrutinised and many things long quietly known are now finding a stronger advocacy.

The on-going challenges confronting a regional, multicultural institution are formidable. The partnership between the Pacific and academic worlds of cultural dichotomy cannot avoid some compromise of and by each. If this is done appropriately, the reward will be a third, unique and enriched creation, yielding the culturally dysfunctional in each and honouring the essential best of all. USP has, in ways that deserve international recognition, charted its own voyage between this Scylla and Charybdis.

> Whose chart is this
> behind our eyes
> Who has placed
> its sticks
> to guide our journey

Speak to us, sailor
of rebbelib
and wind song

of shark's tooth
and frigate bird

of the singing sea

See
our strong fingers
and hands
filled with kapkap
See how the magimagi
has striped our skin
with blood
Look
how the wind
can lash
our bones
for masts
These are what
we bring
you
Gift for gift
. . .
   (Matthewson 1996)

References

Caston, G. (1991) 'Memorandum to Heads of Departments and Schools', in *Annual Report 1993*, Suva, University Extension, USP, p. 19 (27 September).

Fairbairn, T. (1992) *Report of Seminar of South Pacific Post Secondary Education*, Suva, Institute of Social and Administrative Studies, University of the South Pacific.

Goldsmith, E. (1993) *The Way: An Ecological World View*, Boston: Shambhala (also in Thaman 1995).

Matthewson, C. (1994) 'Whose development, whose needs? Distance education practice and politics in the South Pacific', paper presented at the 16th ICDE World Conference, Bangkok, 1992. In *Journal of Distance Education* 9(2) (Fall): 35–47.

—— (1996) 'Navigating Song', in *Practices and Resources in Distance Education: Pacific Islands (With Particular Reference to Pre-Tertiary Education)*, a study commissioned by the Commonwealth of Learning and USP, Vancouver and Suva.

Morris, C. (1966) *Report of the Higher Education Mission to the South Pacific*, London: HMSO.

Renwick, W., Shale, D. and King, St C. (1991) *Distance Education at the University of the South Pacific*, report of a review commissioned by the Commonwealth of Learning, Vancouver.

Solofa, E. (1996) 'More students enrol at USP', in *Fiji Times*, Suva (press release), (31 May).

Thaman, K. (1993) 'Reflection', in *Kakala*, Suva: Mana Publications, South Pacific Creative Arts Society, pp. 53–65.

—— (1995) 'Culture and distance education: a view from the Pacific Islands', plenary address given at *Distance Education: Crossing Frontiers*, the 12th Biennial Forum of the Open and Distance Learning Association of Australia (21–25 September), Port Vila.

13

SEEING THE WORLD THROUGH TWO PAIRS OF EYES

Staff development issues in distance/open
learning programmes for First Nations peoples
in Canada

Barbara Spronk

Tertiary-level educational programmes are an important part of the struggle by members of Canada's First Nations peoples to realise, within Canada's political and economic structures, their rights as enshrined first in the various treaties they signed with the Crown and, more recently, in the Canadian Constitution. Out of these struggles, many aspects of Aboriginal life are coming under Aboriginal people's own control. As a consequence, appropriately trained and educated Aboriginal people are needed to manage the resources and educational and health-care programmes that are coming under their jurisdiction.

Currently, the majority of these programmes are provided by educational institutions working at the request of, and in partnership with, First Nations communities and councils. Given the predominantly rural, and often remote, location of Aboriginal communities, and the unevenness of educational pre-paredness that is a legacy of colonial educational practice, these institutions are by necessity employing open and distance methods and approaches, and in a variety of creative ways. In this provision, institutions face a number of challenges, all of which require awareness-raising among staff and at all levels across these institutions.

It will be argued that the primary challenge facing all those involved in Aboriginal education in predominantly non-Aboriginal contexts, whether learners or providers, is to come to see the world 'through two pairs of eyes' (McAlpine *et al.* 1990).

Historical context

Until very recently, First Nations peoples have been expected to enter mainstream Canadian society. This expectation has generated countless disputes

127

between governments pursuing the assimilation of Aboriginal populations and the elimination of their rights, and Aboriginal populations intent upon preserving their identities and rights. During the fur trade era, Aboriginal peoples were commercially useful to Europeans and politically useful as fighting allies of one power or another. With the coming of agriculture and settlement in the Canadian territories, the Europeans responded

> by developing an 'Indian policy' that for the first time in Canadian history had a civil rather than a military purpose. As this policy took shape ... it increasingly acquired an assimilationist and coercive quality. Since Indians were an obstacle, they would be removed, not by extermination but by assimilation. They would be settled in compact communities, or reserves, where they could be proselytised by missionaries and taught Euro-Canadian ways by government and church alike. Above all else, they would be taught European occupations ... so that they could support themselves in ways that would not interfere with the economic activities of the now-dominant white population.
>
> (Miller 1987: 3)

Despite these concerted efforts, however, Indians did not disappear. On the contrary, by the 1930s the population of status Indians had begun increasing. Subsequently, with economic development in post-war Canada orientated more than ever to frontier, resource-rich areas that were occupied by Indians and Inuit, prospectors, entrepreneurs and governments came into direct conflict with Indian peoples, who were organising themselves to press their claims to be allowed to control their destinies (Miller 1987: 3).

The educational context

Education is a major arena in which this continuing battle has been fought, and in which assimilationist policies, made flesh in the form of residential schools, have been most evident. The horrors of these schools have been comprehensively documented (for example, Bull 1991; Haig-Brown 1988). Children were torn from their homes for ten months out of every year and confined to institutions where they were punished for speaking their own languages, and subjected to treatment at times so abusive that reading and hearing accounts of it chill the soul. Despite even this assault on their physical and spiritual existence, however, First Nations peoples survived to fight. Horrendous as they were, the lessons meted out in the residential schools served ironically to motivate and equip the leaders of the movement for 'Indian control of Indian education'. Their National Indian Brotherhood policy document of 1972, produced in response to a federal government White Paper that clothed continued assimilationist positions in contemporary political jargon, remains an eloquent and powerful statement of the rights of First Nations peoples to control their own destinies within the framework of the Canadian state.

The educational system has continued to be a core focus of this struggle for control, and over the past two decades, primary and secondary education for Aboriginal children on reserves has been shifted largely to federally funded but Aboriginally controlled schools. In urban areas, off-reserve Aboriginal children attend municipally funded schools, but even here efforts are made by public school boards, in cooperation with local Aboriginal groups, to establish schools that provide an Aboriginal approach to the teaching of provincially mandated curricula. There are also a growing number of Aboriginally controlled tertiary institutions with provincial mandates to grant diplomas and degrees; these include the Saskatchewan Indian Federated College, Mohawk Community College in Ontario, and Kwantlen Community College in British Columbia.

In addition to these credentialling institutions, there are many more Aboriginal agencies that deliver tertiary-level programming, not as independent entities, but in cooperation with non-Aboriginal institutions. Typically, the Aboriginal learners in question enrol as students of the non-Aboriginal institution but attend classes in learning centres that are leased or owned and staffed by employees of the Aboriginal agency, and located either on or near to reserves, or in cities with significant Aboriginal populations. Funding for such undertakings comes primarily from the federal government and is channelled through the Aboriginal agency. This means that the collaborating institution typically enters into a contract with the Aboriginally controlled agency to recover the costs of providing teaching staff for the programmes, and only has access to these funds on the basis of its collaboration with this agency.

One example of this is the Yellowhead Tribal Council (YTC), which comprises five Aboriginal bands located in central-western Alberta. The YTC contracts with a number of universities and colleges to deliver courses and programmes out of a building they own on the western edge of Edmonton. Primary among these collaborating institutions is Athabasca University (AU), an open university that offers YTC students a range of on-site courses that are taught by AU tutors but use material from the course packages from AU's largely distance delivery system. One significant outcome of this AU/YTC collaboration has been the development and delivery, with federal funding, of a two-year University Certificate Programme in Health Development Administration, aimed at equipping Aboriginal people with the knowledge and skills to administer their own community-based health-care facilities and programmes.

An example of a different type is the Contact North network of northern Ontario, which is funded by the Ontario government to meet the secondary and post-secondary educational needs of small, remote and dispersed communities. More than three dozen such communities, several of them Aboriginal, have Contact North-provided learning centres with satellite dishes, audio-conferencing and, increasingly, videoconferencing facilities. These technologies are used to deliver courses provided by a variety of universities and colleges which recoup their delivery costs from Contact North. Institutions have also had access to a provincially provided fund for the development of courses for delivery via this network, and a number of courses and programmes offered on the network have been developed for a primarily Aboriginal audience. One such programme is the Native Community Care, Counselling and Development programme, developed in collaboration with Aboriginal community representatives, community health workers, the Union of Ontario Indians, and the Association of Iroquois and Allied Indians, delivered by Mohawk and Cambrian Colleges, and administered by the Anigawncigig Institute. Another example is the Native Resource Technician programme, developed in collaboration with a number of Aboriginal agencies and offered by the Sault College of Applied Arts and Technology, which is aimed at equipping Aboriginal people to work in modern renewable-resource management organisations.

These kinds of collaborative arrangements between Aboriginal agencies and non-Aboriginal educational institutions provide the context for the discussion of staff development issues, needs and strategies which follows.

Staff development issues

Organisational needs

Inter-institutional and inter-sectoral collaboration is increasingly a fact of life for Canadian universities and colleges, and particularly those involved in open and distance learning. Sharing the costs of courseware development via co-development, sales and leasing arrangements, and the costs of delivery via consortia and other types of inter-institutional enterprise, make scarce dollars go further at a time when public funding for education is declining, and provide more learning opportunities for more people. And increasingly Canadian provincial governments are forcing institutions to see the sense of such collaborative arrangements by making these a condition of funding for the development and delivery of new programmes.

However, such inter-institutional collaboration is by no means easy to establish or maintain. Each organisation has its own structures and norms, and in any collaboration, those who manage, develop and deliver distance and open learning are brought face-to-face with the hard realities and peculiarities of their institutional politics and intransigence – see Moran and Mugridge (1993) for a comprehensive discussion of these issues. I would argue, however, on the basis of over twenty years' experience in making collaborative arrangements happen, that collaborations with Aboriginal agencies push such reality-facing to its limits, for three reasons. First, Aboriginal groups insist, rightly and with the force of centuries of colonial oppression behind them, on equal partnerships with institutions, and will not tolerate junior partner status. Second, when Aboriginal groups encounter institutions which insist on treating them as junior partners, they are quite capable of taking their federal and other dollars elsewhere, and will do so. And third, the realities which the Aboriginal groups bring before institutional managers and faculty are not just those of institutional rules and structures, but descend much deeper into the foundations of the educational enterprise – the origins and ownership of knowledge and what constitutes wisdom.

The implications of this difference are far-reaching. For example, university senior managers are accustomed to deal-making with other senior managers. When the 'deal' in question is with an Aboriginal agency, however, the discussion may initially involve agency bureaucrats who are knowledgeable and skilled in manipulating the rules of deal-making in the white man's world, because these are critical to the continued funding and hence survival of their agencies. At later stages, university bureaucrats will inevitably find themselves at meetings that involve the ultimate reference group for Aboriginal bureaucrats, the elders.

Meetings will open with a prayer of thanks to the Creator, who will be acknowledged as the true source of knowledge and wisdom. The elders will be deferred to as the embodiment of the values, skills and knowledge which have enabled their people to survive. These elders regard words as things of value to be used with care and respect, and hence will remain silent for long periods at such meetings. When the elders determine that it is time for them to speak, they will do so in stories which convey their message in image and metaphor that come from the ancestors and the spirit rather than from any management texts or educational theory. Institutional representatives who treat such events as necessary but essentially meaningless ceremony, and demonstrate impatience to get on with the 'real' meeting, do so at their peril. In such encounters, experience is clearly on the side of the elders, who embody generations of dealings with white men that have taught them hard lessons about which white men can be trusted, and which cannot. It has become a cliché in the literature that partnerships will only endure on the basis of trust and respect. Partnerships with Aboriginal groups give these terms new, and profound, meaning.

Curriculum and course content needs

Assuming that these 'deals' actually get made, in determining what gets taught and why, the issues of the origins and ownership of knowledge will come to the fore. This is a continuing and emergent process, however. At the most superficial level, initial discussions concerning curriculum and course content will tend to involve the kinds of give and take that characterise any attempt to tailor content to the needs of a specific group. But for those working in Aboriginal contexts, there will be even more specific needs to take into account – for example, in regard to health education, the exigencies of Aboriginal politics within which managers have to negotiate, the particular spectrum of diseases that characterise

Aboriginal communities, and the recognition of indigenous knowledge about the provenance of illnesses and their treatment.

Acknowledging and including such issues in a curriculum, especially those involving kinship-based politics or spiritually based medicine, will be a major accomplishment for academics accustomed to courses that adhere to some academically defined canon. Such agreement is, however, still only the beginning. Once the courses are being delivered to the students, more issues will emerge, or, more accurately, the same issues will emerge in a somewhat different form.

Students will complain that their workloads are far too heavy. They will not be accustomed to doing a lot of reading, especially of academic prose. They may be faced with courses that are overstuffed with content as course authors attempt to deal with the two kinds of knowledge, that defined by the academic canon and that defined by cultural practice and wisdom. In addition, students will likely be unprepared by either the formal education they have received to date or the largely oral culture in which they live, to write analytical essays of the kind required in tertiary-level courses. They will rebel at having to learn things they do not believe they will ever need or use. As a consequence, course authors will be called upon to assess the validity of these claims as best they can, to rethink, rejustify, rewrite and re-do, all of which require a great deal of good will and hard work (and pay or workload relief), to say nothing of open-mindedness to content requirements that go beyond those of the academic discipline.

Delivery needs

Other issues will surface in regard to delivery. First, face-to-face contact, preferably prior to or at the beginning of delivery, is an essential component of any successful course for Aboriginal learners. Any technologies, assuming they function technically, will also function pedagogically in First Nations contexts, as long as students have actually met the instructor face-to-face at least once, or preferably on several occasions. This point has been made by the designers of virtually every programme intended for an Aboriginal audience; see Spronk (1995) for a representative sample.

Second, in regard to the tutor or instructor, experience with and knowledge of Aboriginal communities and cultures will clearly be an asset. However, such experience and knowledge is not the critical feature of effective teaching in Aboriginal contexts. Those who make the most effective facilitators in these contexts are the same as those who are the most effective in any teaching context. They require a firm, clear but not arrogant grasp of the subject they are teaching, a keenness to learn as much from their students as they impart to them, a sizeable toolkit of techniques and communication skills, and above all, a sense of humour. In much the same way as the elders are quick to recognise and write off the rigid or insincere bureaucrat, Aboriginal students are quick to distinguish the genuine teacher from the grim-faced proclaimer of truth.

Third, there are issues which arise beyond classroom walls but which materially affect what happens within them. Those responsible for delivering programming for Aboriginal learners must be prepared to accommodate the fact that the adults who come to their programmes lead exceedingly burdened and complex lives. They are enmeshed in networks of kin and community that are the foundation of their lives and the source of most of their joys and sorrows. So, for example, when there is a death in the community, classrooms will be close to empty, since nearly all of the students will be kin to the deceased. Women bear most of the burden of family life, and, since most students in any Aboriginal setting are women, attendance at class will be subject to students' ability to find adequate care for their children or for ageing or ill kinfolk (Spronk and Radtke 1987). Class attendance will take second place to the need to accompany a relative to the doctor or a court appearance. Money, housing and transportation will be chronic and continuing problems for many students. Under these circumstances, programmes that are as flexible as possible in allowing students to work with others, catch up on late assignments, or receive extra help from the instructor are going to be the most successful in helping the students to achieve their goals.

Strategies for staff development

In the case of Aboriginal education, there is at least one specific, and highly recommended, training programme available in Canada, from the Secwepemec Centre in Salmon Arm, British Columbia. It would be valuable for any institution seriously involved in providing education to Aboriginal populations to send one or two faculty members to this programme and then use them as a resource and as mentors for other faculty in the institution.

These notions of 'resource' and 'mentor' merit more attention than the idea of 'training' in this context. Because the issues involved in learning to see with two pairs of eyes are emergent and continuing, once-off training is going to be of limited value. Building various forms and levels of mentoring into an institution has the virtues both of providing long-term and continuing support to staff who are struggling to improve their 'dual vision', and of modelling the type of teaching and learning that characterises informal education in Aboriginal communities. According to Dr Clare Brant, a Mohawk psychiatrist, children in Aboriginal communities are not 'taught' correct or appropriate ways of behaviour; such 'teaching' would constitute an interference in the rights, privileges and activities of these children. They are expected to learn on their own, by watching and emulating those around them. This process neither involves explicit cajolery, praise or punishment, nor the withholding of privilege or promising of reward. It is up to the child to observe constantly, carefully and autonomously. It is also incumbent on children to respect their elders as repositories of experience and wisdom, and as models for their own behaviour (Ross 1992).

How can institutions build opportunities for this kind of learning into their structures and organisations? I would suggest that this already happens in a number of institutions, even though it may not bear the explicit label of mentoring. For example, at the executive level of a number of colleges and universities, there exist Native Advisory Committees, whose membership is drawn from prominent members of the Aboriginal community and whose role is to advise the institution on policies and programmes for Aboriginal communities and students. The province of Ontario has taken the lead in this practice, making it a requirement for institutions who receive Aboriginal development funding to have in place such Advisory Committees. Furthermore, these committees must have more than token existence; they are to be sub-committees of the institutions' Boards of Governors, and hence able to operate at the highest level of institutional policy-making, safe from interference or obstruction by middle-level academic managers (indicating that whoever designed this set of conditions had a profound understanding of academic politics!). Of course, simply having a committee in place does not mean that those whom it advises actually listen. None the less, putting such committees in place, and ensuring that Aboriginal communities are represented on governing boards, opens the possibility of mentoring at the highest levels of institutional decision-making.

At the more operational level, specific programmes can have advisory committees whose members are responsible for vetting and approving the content of curricula and courses and their attendant delivery modes. Such committees are an appropriate way of formally acknowledging Aboriginal/institutional partnerships. However, they can all too easily become *pro forma* bodies which are seen as just one more hoop in a long series of hoops through which faculty members must jump in getting approval for courses and programmes. There are more informal means of providing faculty involved in Aboriginal programming with support and guidance in developing their second pair of eyes.

First, less experienced faculty can be teamed with more experienced faculty (preferably Aboriginal) to whom they can go for advice and assistance in developing and delivering appropriate and workable courses. This strategy will be most effective, of course, if the experienced faculty actually have this mentoring role recognised as part of their official workloads. This both acknowledges the importance of their knowledge and experience, and gives them adequate time for their mentoring tasks.

Second, peer meetings can provide a great deal of support to faculty who are struggling to develop and deliver Aboriginal programmes. Sharing one's problems and successes with others who are dealing with the same issues, and perhaps the same students, can enhance a feeling of community, reduce feelings of isolation and inadequacy, and help solve any number of very practical problems, such as how to deal with students wandering in and out of class, or whether to dock marks for late submission of assignments.

Third, faculty members and other support staff should be encouraged to spend time in the communities from which their students come. All too often, the site visit is actually a flying trip, in for the morning and out in the afternoon. A few overnight stays, meals and other activities with the students and other community members can work wonders in building rapport between faculty and community and thereby the mutual knowledge and understanding that is the basis of seeing with two pairs of eyes. Again, this requires investment by the institution, but it is a modest investment, and one which pays considerable dividends in terms of community good will and faculty acceptability.

Finally, faculty members should be encouraged to invite the elders to their class sessions from time to time, to share in the teaching and mentor both the teachers and the students. Many Aboriginal programmes already make this a practice. Others pair the tutor or the subject-matter specialist with an Aboriginal teaching partner whose task it is to bring the other pair of eyes to the subject matter and help both teacher and students make the appropriate transitions from one way of seeing to the other (see Spronk 1995 for examples).

Conclusion

Mentoring systems, advisory committees, peer support, faculty/community visits, and elders' involvement in class sessions are low-cost, culturally appropriate and institutionally effective means of fostering the kind of staff development that is essential to genuine partnerships between educational institutions and Aboriginal agencies and communities. Educators who work collaboratively with Aboriginal learners and communities are in fact privileged, since they are given the opportunity to learn as much as they impart, not only about the nature of teaching and learning, but about the way the world looks through two pairs of eyes. By accepting this gift and working with it, and by sharing what they learn with their non-Aboriginal students, they can participate in challenging the forces and dismantling the barriers that keep First Nations peoples from taking their rightful place in Canadian society.

References

Barman, J., Hebert, Y. and McCaskill, D. (eds) (1986) *Indian Education in Canada*, vol. 1: *The Legacy*, Vancouver: University of British Columbia Press.

—— (eds) (1987) *Indian Education in Canada*, vol. 2: *The Challenge*, Vancouver: University of British Columbia Press.

Bull, L. (1991) 'Indian residential schooling: the native perspective', *Canadian Journal of Native Education* 18 (Supplemental Issues): 1–64.

Haig-Brown, C. (1988) *Resistance and Renewal: Surviving the Indian Residential School*, Vancouver: Tillacum Library.

McAlpine, L., Cross, E., Whiteduck, G. and Wolforth, J. (1990) 'Using two pairs of eyes to define an Aboriginal teacher education programme', *Canadian Journal of Native Education* 17(2): 82–8.

Miller, J. (1987) 'The irony of residential schooling', *Canadian Journal of Native Education* 14(2): 3–13.

Moran, L. and Mugridge, I. (eds) (1993) *Collaboration in Distance Education: International Case Studies*, London and New York: Routledge.

National Indian Brotherhood (1972) *Indian Control of Indian Education: Policy Paper Presented to the Minister of Indian Affairs*, Ottawa, Ministry of Indian Affairs.

Ross, R. (1992) *Dancing with a Ghost: Exploring Indian Reality*, Markham, Ont.: Octopus Publishing Group.

Spronk, B. (1995) 'Appropriate learning technologies: Aboriginal learners, needs, and practices', in J. Roberts and E. Keough (eds), *Why the Information Highway? Lessons from Open and Distance Learning*, Toronto: Trifolium Books, pp. 77–101.

Spronk, B. and Radtke, D. (1987) 'Distance education for native women', in K. Storrie (ed.), *Women, Isolation and Bonding: The Ecology of Gender*, Toronto: Methuen.

14

STAFF DEVELOPMENT IN SUPPORT OF EFFECTIVE STUDENT LEARNING IN SOUTH AFRICAN DISTANCE EDUCATION

Christine Randell and Eli Bitzer

Since the historical election of April 1994 , everyone involved in South African education has to cope with the huge backlogs, discrepancies and inequalities inherited from the past, the challenges of global change and technology, and the need to be relevant to the demands of an emergent democratic society. There are enormous resource constraints and in the words of one of South Africa's Vice-Chancellors: 'The plane has to be serviced in flight.'

South Africa's national education policy states that

> the overarching goal . . . must be to enable all individuals to value, have access to and succeed in lifelong education and training of good quality. Education and management processes must therefore put the learners first, recognising and building on their knowledge and experience, and responding to their needs.
>
> (Department of Education 1995: 21)

Translating these ideals into reality presents a major challenge to open learning and distance education, which are seen as having the potential '[to] give practical effect to policies for affirmative action aimed at addressing past injustices' (International Commission into Distance Education in South Africa 1995).

The quality of distance education in South Africa is under close scrutiny. The 1995 International Commission into Distance Education concluded that distance education's contribution to the priorities for education and training has been marginal, inefficient and, in respect of the values sought for democratic South Africa, dysfunctional (SAIDE 1994). Research into the quality of teacher education offered at a distance supports this conclusion (SAIDE 1995), and the

Draft White Paper on Higher Education also reflects serious concerns 'about the efficiency, appropriateness and effectiveness of much current distance education provision' (Ministry of Education 1997: 20).

The discussion document, 'A Distance Education Quality Standards Framework for South Africa', highlights several developments which might provide the basis for improvement. These include: the establishment of the South African Qualifications Authority and the National Qualifications Framework; the proposed establishment of a Higher Education Quality Committee; the development of a Human Resources Development Strategy and a National HRD Council; the development of new legislation, and revision of existing legislation, to create an environment conducive to meeting the policy objectives set out in the White Paper on Education and Training; the development of new curriculum at national and provincial levels which will focus on lifelong learning; and the formation of a National Association of Distance Education Organisations of South Africa (Department of Education 1996a: v–vi).

Such policy and infrastructural developments are essential in creating a more open educational environment more responsive to the socio-economic and cultural needs of our new democracy. There are encouraging signs that the concept of open and flexible education is starting to take root, and some exciting projects are being piloted by both existing distance education and traditional contact institutions in such provinces as Gauteng, Free State, Kwa-zulu Natal and Western Cape. However, many factors frustrate these transformation efforts.

Impediments to effective learning

Geidt (1996) observes that the model of distance education which initially inspired South African distance educators was developed within the context of the United Kingdom where the constituency of students could be assumed to be monolinguistic and within a class-structured but essentially homogenous state. By contrast, South African outreach education has to operate in regions and districts differentiated from one another by language, custom, political affiliation, economic factors, access to resources and practically everything else that counts in life.

There are also major barriers within the institutions themselves. Rigid bureaucratic structures severely constrain flexible learning initiatives. Institutions often use lack of funding as a compelling argument for not providing comprehensive course development and delivery, well-integrated and decentralised support systems and sustainable and coherent staff development programmes. However, institutions which claim to be committed to change cannot escape their responsibility for creating systems which promote and support quality and ease students' progress rather than hampering it. New priorities and funding allocations are needed, based upon student need and national policy directives.

Many teachers are struggling to adopt a more interactive style of teaching. Glennie (1995: 8) attributes the current all-pervasive authoritarian pedagogy to the paternalistic influences of Afrikaner Christian National Education. The dependent behaviour of students only strengthens teachers' convictions that the students are at the heart of the problem, are unprepared for independent study and are incapable of logically structured discourse. Overcoming years of reinforcement of a teacher-focused model of teaching and learning and changing underlying conceptions of learning and teaching will be a lengthy process requiring a great deal of skilful professional development.

For many students, distance education was – and indeed still is – perceived as a second-rate version of the preferred traditional face-to-face education model. The students also lack confidence and ability in independent study because of their experiences with an authoritarian methodology which promoted rote learning and rewarded dependent behaviour. Distance education is also constrained by a relative lack of well-designed courses appropriate to a diverse cultural community and in languages spoken by the majority of students. As a consequence, distance education students often flounder in their studies, the providers perceive the students' difficulties as requiring remedial or palliative interventions, and the outcome is a reintroduction of teacher-dependent approaches.

Some new ventures

Although many staff quite understandably feel overwhelmed and even paralysed by the enormity of the tasks confronting them, some individuals have seized opportunities for pioneering new models of teaching and learning. Two innovative flexible learning approaches that appear to have the potential to be transferable to other South African programmes are the Resource-Based Career Preparation Programme (RBL Career Prep) offered by the University of the Free State (UFS) and the Adult Basic Education and Training (ABET) course offered by the ABET Institute at the University of South Africa (UNISA). Both of these ventures provide effective learning support and demonstrate commitment and responsiveness to the learners' needs.

RBL Career Prep

The UFS is a traditional contact institution which is now actively exploring the feasibility of becoming a mixed-mode institution (Bitzer and Pretorius 1996). Since 1992, the UFS, Technikon Free State, two technical colleges, two nursing colleges and Glen Agricultural College have participated in providing the on-campus inter-institutional bridging Career Preparation Programme for Free State students who would not normally qualify for admission to university or further education. Demand has totally outstripped supply with up to 2,000 students having to be turned away annually and so an alternative was piloted in 1996; namely, the open distance mode RBL Career Prep.

From the outset, this project has been conceived as an exemplar for the UFS and its future on- and off-campus provision. To research the implications of adopting such a resource-based learning approach, the RBL Career Prep is being closely monitored in terms of the learners, course materials, student engagement with materials, learning support provision, staff factors and costs, and capacity to serve rural communities and sub-regions.

ABET

The ABET Course, piloted in 1995, is aimed at ABET educators. In 1997, student registrations in ABET were in excess of 6,000 and included students from other Southern Africa countries. ABET illustrates how a well-designed distance education course using materials specifically designed for the South African context and supplemented by an innovative learning support model can lead to effective learning (McKay *et al.* 1996).

ABET provides a model of learning support well-suited to the South African context. Students participate in the delivery process and are encouraged to take ownership of their own tutorial sessions. They form self-help groups, organise their own venues and negotiate tutorial times and dates with their tutors to suit their particular circumstances. They meet in different venues within reasonable reach of their homes and they negotiate to use these free of charge. Some groups use their employers' facilities, and this has enabled many employers to become more knowledgeable about, and supportive of, this course. Each study group decides exactly how it wishes to use the four hours per month contact time offered by the ABET tutors. Learners opt to meet weekly, fortnightly or monthly and are not restricted to one group but can attend any group of their choice. The learners, particularly in rural areas, value the tutorial sessions highly and about 80 per cent of the students are regular attenders. Some learners form self-help learning groups between tutorials and organise field trips and visits to various workplaces and communities. Some even continue to meet after completing the course. Such learning support arrangements respect the ability of adults to organise themselves, encourage greater self-confidence and stimulate greater self-reliance in learning.

The ABET course materials actively discourage rote learning and encourage deep learning. They are designed to provide students with insights into their own experiences and the ability to link these with the academic discourse and relevant social issues. The materials incorporate study skills and are supplemented by a study guide. The National Education Secretary of the Congress of South African Trade Unions (COSATU) says that:

> The study materials are user-friendly and help build our confidence . . .
> through a coherent and systematised course. What the course has done

so far, has been positive aspects like: recognition of our experiences; opening the doors of a learning culture amongst adults; recognisable certificate; lifelong learning process.

(McKay *et al.* 1996: 53)

The ABET assignments are designed to encourage learners to give expression to their own ideas and build on their own experiences. They are marked by tutor markers who are trained to be responsive to the self-expressive mode of the assignments and capable of providing learners with detailed feedback. Continuous course assessment encourages theory–practice integration. The final course mark is for assignments, an examination and a practical research project. Many projects are based upon work the learners are engaged in and their findings may be subsequently applied within the workplace or community.

Part-time tutors are assigned to groups of between twenty-five and thirty-five students and work face-to-face at the chosen venues or by telephone. Most of the tutors are graduates and some have experience in adult education and training. Like the students, these tutors require orientation and support. They attend an introductory workshop focused on promoting and facilitating group activities and the 'discourse model' of teaching and learning, are given a manual containing relevant information and guidelines and may call upon more experienced regional tutor coordinators for further support.

ABET demonstrates the wisdom of building up a learning support system, encouraging 'student managed' tutorial groups and developing the capacity of learning support staff. This decentralised learning support system represents a major innovation in a predominantly correspondence institution. It also shows the importance of ensuring that funds are used to provide meaningful learning experiences for the students, employ part-time tutors at the locations where students live and at times that suit the learners, and ensure on-going staff training and development.

Staff development issues

There is a growing awareness of the need to provide 'a continuum of educational provision in which contact, distance, mixed-mode and dual-mode educational opportunities should be available to all learners' (Ministry of Education 1997: 20). This requires a massive re-orientation to more learner-centred provision. Course and materials developers need to be enabled to develop programmes which encourage deep and autonomic learning and which are culturally and linguistically appropriate. Tutors and counsellors need to acquire new student-centred approaches to teaching and learning and develop their diagnostic, problem-solving and inter-personal skills in assisting culturally diverse students. Managers and administrators need to be given the knowledge and ability to provide and evaluate relevant support systems for staff and 'two-way communication with students through the use of various forms of technology . . .

counselling (both remote and face-to-face), and the stimulation of peer group structures' (Department of Education 1996a: 63).

Managing a culture of change

Staff within South African institutions are confronted with a myriad of new policies, legislation and qualifications frameworks. There are governmental, institutional, community and student demands for new political awareness and commitment, the 'Africanisation' of curricula and the addressing of language issues. Many young, inexperienced and largely African teaching staff are being appointed and there are severe financial constraints. Thus, although change may be embedded in the legislation, there is often little evidence of real transformation at institutional or faculty level. Audits and research into distance education (SAIDE 1994), teacher education (SAIDE 1995) and educational management (Department of Education 1996b) reveal dysfunctions between visions and realities due to the interplay of a complex web of factors. These include the enduring influence of structures and systems of a fragmented and discriminatory past, passive or even hostile resistance to change, and inadequate resources to achieve significant and sustainable change.

It is clear that academic managers need to develop the capacity to respond to rapidly changing situations and, no less than the teaching staff, engage in structured reflection on experiences, problems, ideas and models (Middlehurst 1995). Our experiences with some innovatory projects at SAIDE and UFS have confirmed that staff are better able to cope with the stresses of adopting new approaches where there is a clear vision and a plan driven by inspired managers, where information and communication among all levels flows freely and effectively, and where staff are enabled to reflect frequently and openly on their experiences and participate in in-work training tailored to their immediate tasks.

Dealing with culture bias and discrimination

Nowhere in the world have discriminatory practices been more comprehensively and meticulously organised and entrenched than in South Africa. At the national level we are finding ways of healing our broken and fragmented nation. The removal of all statutory discrimination is complete, the implementation of legislation based on democratic principles is continuing, and the Truth and Reconciliation Commission aims to heal the wounds caused by the perpetrators of racial and political violence.

Within institutions discriminatory structures and staffing policy and practices are being vigorously challenged and transformation forums assist in the implementation of equitable practices. Various evasive or stalling tactics sometimes bedevil the work of the pressure groups for change. However, every inch of progress is a victory for democracy. Two urgent issues are the implementation of affirmative action appointments and the education of staff in multicultural matters.

Affirmative action appointments have the potential to restore balance in a distorted staffing provision. However, working relationships between staff of different cultures are usually left to chance and tensions stemming from cultural bias may be allowed to simmer until they cause deep-seated conflicts which are time-consuming to resolve and which hamper transformation efforts. Differences in cultures need to be handled sensitively and institutions need to work out ways in which newly appointed and existing staff can receive adequate staff development and support in order to avoid friction and disenchantment. Fortunately, there are useful South African-developed training resources which can be used in staff group sessions to build bridges and develop common understandings.

Awareness of the languages, customs, experiences, beliefs and social contexts of the various learners from different cultures is essential for course designers and tutors. The capacity to provide course materials and tutorial sessions which reflect these will improve the quality of the learning and likelihood of success for the students.

Designing appropriate support systems

Although senior management may subscribe to the notion of learning support, they often fail to provide adequate funding for this. Learning support may therefore be restricted to a few programmes or not integrated into the institution as a whole; rigid systems may endure which are unresponsive to the needs of students; plans for decentralised learning may proceed at a snail's pace; and support staff may be inexperienced, untrained and/or under-resourced.

Recognising similarities of context and need, SAIDE is facilitating a process whereby learning support staff can come together to share and reflect on their experiences and problems. Inter-institutional support groups have been found to be very useful in raising staff motivation and collaboratively resolving solutions. Another useful strategy is guided seminars facilitated by experts in learning support systems in which staff outline their specific context and current stage of development and receive focused guidance in planning the next steps.

Changing staff perceptions

Information collection and analysis can provide a basis for staff development discussions, interventions and cultural change (Lewis 1991; Elton 1994), and another staff development strategy which has proved to be effective in the South African context is the involvement of students in staff development sessions with a view to changing staff perceptions and practices (Du Plooy and Steinberg 1996).

This approach was used in the RBL Career Prep where the student feedback through questionnaires was initially and superficially interpreted by staff as indicating that the students were coping with the course materials and satisfied with the learning support. However, on interacting with the students in a staff workshop, the providers discovered that their personal mind-sets had influenced their interpretations of the students' responses. They became more sensitised to students' problems in regard to assignment turnaround times, poor course design, lack of confidence in their own responses, applying their learning, and breaking the rote-learning habit. They came to realise that questionnaires have only limited application and that greater care was needed in formulating questions to elicit the students' underlying assumptions, concerns and difficulties and in establishing strong contact with the students.

The students at this workshop also revealed that initially they were not very interested in using the audiotapes in the learning packages because they did not have access to cassette players and felt that listening to these would be a waste of time anyway. Once shown how these tapes had been designed to assist their learning, they completely changed their views about the usefulness of this resource. This experience alerted the staff to the need always to check upon equipment availability and the orientation of the students to particular materials and media. Such first-hand understanding of students' attitudes, experiences and concerns is more likely to lead to improved provision and support for the students.

In the RBL Career Prep the information recorded and monitored by staff enables them to reflect upon student attendance at tutorials, face-to-face and telephone counselling, assignment results and comments, student feedback on learning experiences, and facilitators' reactions to the students' performance in tutorials and assignments. Such information forms the basis for discussions at regular staff support meetings and enables staff to identify common problems and determine appropriate follow-up. Such a structured reflective process is encouraging a gradual shift from teacher-driven to student-focused approaches.

Enabling staff to help students become independent learners

Students' lack of confidence in taking responsibility for their own learning is a major problem for South African distance educators. It has been found that staff development programmes need to include activities focused on motivating and enabling students to become independent learners. The RBL Career Prep suggests one approach to building students' confidence. One of the four RBL Career Prep courses is the Foundation Course in Lifelong Learning which focuses on acquiring study skills for university study. The development of the self-directed learner is a key element in this programme, and learners and tutors alike are made aware from the outset that contact time will gradually be reduced as the learners progress and develop confidence in their ability to learn independently. The use of contact time and the on-going needs of the learners is carefully monitored and this provides a useful feedback loop for staff development purposes.

It can also be demonstrated to staff that where programmes involve large numbers of adult learners, student-managed tutorial groups may provide a viable learning support model. Evaluators from the University of Hull conducting an in-depth investigation of the ABET project reported that the course and the use of this model have contributed significantly to the students' self-reliance. Past students are also involved in a number of community projects as a direct consequence of their ABET training.

A *professional development consortium*

Staff developers in South African institutions are in general agreement that a more coherent and integrated staff development policy and strategy needs to be implemented in distance and mixed-mode institutions. An important step in this direction is the formation of a professional development consortium comprising the major distance education institutions and two non-governmental organisations – the South African Committee for Higher Education (SACHED) and SAIDE. The consortium recognises that collaboration between institutions facilitates more rational use of resources. It aims to improve the quality and professionalism of distance education by obtaining and/or developing and evaluating courses and modules for distance education practitioners appropriate to the South African context and by undertaking work on other staff-related issues such as quality assurance and research into professional development.

Conclusion

South Africa urgently needs quality distance education which is efficient and cost-effective. Integral to this is the availability to students of effective learning support within the course materials and through a range of services provided by tutors/facilitators and administrative staff. Staff engaged in innovative programmes are evolving diverse models of learning support well-suited to the South African context. Their contribution to viable and sustainable open and flexible learning needs to be more widely acknowledged, and ways must be found to integrate these models into the provision of mainstream distance education.

Many of the existing management systems, processes and structures employed in distance and contact institutions are inappropriate for the provision of distance education programmes for students from disadvantaged backgrounds. Recent recommendations to the Minister of Education for a comprehensive capacity-building approach to effect fundamental transformation in learning and teaching also apply to distance education institutions. The proposed framework comprises the five major elements that are needed to achieve the desired transformation: strategic direction; organisational structures and systems; human resources; infrastructural and other resources; and networking partnerships and communication (Department of Education 1996b: 36).

Development of staff and management is crucial at this time of transformation. Now is the time for '*Masakhane*', a Xhosa and Zulu word meaning 'let us build together'. Until adequate resources are invested by institutions and people have the will and capacity to dig at the very foundations and rebuild a distance education system based upon open learning principles and guided by the new policies, we shall be failing the thousands of students who depend on us to gain access to quality education and training.

References

Bitzer, E.M. and Pretorius, E. v. E. (1996) *Resource-Based Learning at the UOFS: Background, Meaning, Implications and Possible Solutions*, Academic Development Bureau, UFS, Bloemfontein.

Department of Education (1995) *Government Gazette*, White Paper on Education and Training, 357 (1632), Notice No. 196 of 1995, Pretoria: Government Printer.

—— (1996a) 'A Distance Education Quality Standards Framework', a discussion document prepared by the Directorate, Distance Education, Media and Technological Services (September–December), Pretoria.

—— (1996b) *Changing Management to Manage Change in Education*, a report prepared by the Task Team on Education Management Development (December), Pretoria.

Du Plooy, G.M. and Steinberg, S. (1996) 'Transition in distance education: a pilot study', *Open Learning in South Africa (Olisa) Review*, OLASA.

Elton, L. (ed.) (1994) *Management of Teaching and Learning: Towards Change in Universities*, report of a seminar, London: Committee of Vice-Chancellors and Principals of the Universities of the United Kingdom (CVCP) (March).

Geidt, J. (1996) 'Distance education into group areas won't go?' *Open Learning* 11 (1): 12–21.

Glennie, J. (1995) 'Putting the Student First: Learner-centred Approaches in Open and Distance Learning', in the Proceedings of the Cambridge International Conference on Open and Distance Learning, Churchill College, Cambridge.

International Commission into Distance Education in South Africa (1995) *Open Learning and Distance Education*, Manzini: Macmillan Bolwesa.

Lewis, K.G. (1991) 'Gathering data for the improvement of teaching: what do I need and how do I get it?' *New Directions for Teaching and Learning: Effective Practices for Improving Teaching* 48, San Francisco: Jossey-Bass, pp. 7–20.

McKay, V., Sarakinsky, M. and Sekgobela, E. (1996) 'Distance education into group areas won't go? A response', *Open Learning* (June) 52–6.

Middlehurst, R. (1995) 'Top training: development for institutional managers', in A. Brew (ed.), *Directions in Staff Development*, London: Society for Research in Higher Education and Open University Press.

Ministry of Education (1997) *Draft White Paper on Higher Education, Government Gazette*, vol. 382: Notice No. 712 of 1997, Pretoria.

SAIDE (South African Institute for Distance Education) (1994) *Open Learning and Distance Education in South Africa: Report of an International Commission, January to April 1994*, Johannesburg: Macmillan.

—— (1995) *Teacher Education Offered at a Distance in South Africa: Report for the National Audit*, JUTA in association with SAIDE, Johannesburg.

Webb, G. (1996) *Understanding Staff Development*, Bristol, PA, and Buckingham, UK: Society for Research in Higher Education and Open University Press.

15

TUITION AND COUNSELLING

Supporting the teachers for competitive advantage

David Sewart

The tasks which the United Kingdom Open University (OU) requires of those engaged in the tuition and counselling of its students are unique in UK higher education. As the OU's support services to students have evolved, it has had to create and continuously amend a staff development programme which not only defines the necessary competencies but also develops these competencies at a distance. Over the years, this has led to major changes in the roles of approximately 9,000 part-time tutorial and counselling staff, and these role changes have resulted in a body of staff who originally operated on an annual contract basis now being integrated into the institution's overall human resource strategy.

The early years

Although there exists within the UK an accepted tradition of certification for those teaching at primary and secondary level, the reverse is true at tertiary level. Here, the academic staff are hired to engage in both teaching and research, and whereas it might be said that there exists an apprenticeship for the latter in terms of research degrees and a lifelong updating and cross-fertilisation through subject related conferences, seminars, journals and, on a day-to-day basis, interaction with departmental colleagues, there is no comparable range of support activities in regard to teaching. Teaching competence is something which is assumed, a private matter in which the individual academic relates to a large or a small group of students, without any peer judgement of the efficacy or otherwise of the interaction.

It was against such a background that the OU began to teach its students in 1971. But the OU was not part of the long tradition of higher education; it was attempting something new – namely, distance education – and on an unprecedented scale. I have argued elsewhere (Sewart 1993) that UK higher

148

education had been moving throughout the last sixty years of the twentieth century towards a more industrialised model. But this had been a gradual movement, hardly noticeable in such a time-scale. The OU, by contrast, was posited from the start on structures and concepts associated with mass production and industrialisation, not least in a rigid division of labour which allowed a rationalisation of the elements of the teaching process, and introduced technology to ensure a product of constant quality in volumes which were theoretically unlimited (Peters 1973).

This was a significant step forward and, in more than twenty-five years, the pattern established at the launch of the OU has hardly changed. Course teams, working under the umbrella of particular faculties or schools, and supported by specialists in various elements of production (designers, editors, TV and radio producers and so on), produce courses which are suited to distance learning, lead to recognised qualifications, and are set within a properly designed and modular curriculum. This element is commonly and loosely referred to as 'course production'. Course presentation takes place through the agency of thirteen Regional Centres distributed throughout the UK. The role of these Centres is to ensure support for the students, by selecting, training and monitoring locally hired, part-time tutors and tutor counsellors and by these staff providing advice and guidance to help students pursue their studies successfully. These two functions are not discrete. Underpinning both course production and course presentation is another set of functions which might be classified as administrative.

It was in the area of course presentation that the OU faced the greatest change. New teaching media had been entering teaching for some time and the OU's course production was but a further step, albeit a significant one, along a developmental continuum with precedents in Australia and South Africa. But what was planned in course presentation was very different. The courses were to be tutored and assessed by people who had not been involved in any aspect of their production. Further, this was not to be done by full-time staff but by a large number of part-time staff organised through the Regional Centres throughout the UK. The students' main source of teaching reinforcement might be these tutors but they would only meet them from time to time – the core relationship was through correspondence tuition, marking and commenting on written assignments. The part-time tutorial staff would be largely recruited from traditional higher and further education, but their role was to be entirely different from that of tutors in the more conventional institutions. The basic academic content would be transmitted to the students via print, radio and television and the tutors were to focus on support for students and interpretation of the curriculum. Alongside this narrow academic support would be developed the broader academic support which the university called counselling. This was not envisaged as subject-based but more concerned with the student as an independent learner. This function too would be carried out by part-time staff. Launching all of these changes into a tradition of higher and further education wholly lacking any elements of training for teaching, the OU introduced in 1971 the rudiments of what was then known as a 'briefing and training' programme. The fact that it was allowed to do so at all is probably a testament to, and acknowledgement of, the very special and unprecedented roles which the OU had conceived for those engaged in its course presentation.

A reassessment of roles

The early years witnessed considerable reassessment of these part-time staff roles. In its first year, the OU established three functions, often, indeed normally, carried out by separate individuals. The 'correspondence tutor' commented on and evaluated the students' written work and, since this function could be carried out at a distance, might be anywhere in the country; the 'course tutor' offered face-to-face tutorials specific to the course being studied at local Study Centres; and 'the counsellor' offered broad educational guidance on how to study, again at a local Study Centre. It was soon found that there were problems with this model. It was difficult to differentiate between the roles in terms of the briefing and training programme and, more importantly, the students did not understand the division of labour and were confused over who to ask for advice.

By the start of the second year, the OU had amalgamated the correspondence and course-tutor roles. The students now had access to two forms of support, one strictly academic, relating to the particular course being studied, the other more broadly supportive. This was more easily focused in the briefing and training programme but the roles had still not been properly thought through. In the first year or so, approximately 25,000 students had taken one of four foundation courses. This had translated on the ground into support through most of the university's 250 Study Centres, effectively providing a local service of face-to-face contact right across the UK for any students willing to travel a relatively small distance. However, as the university's range of courses expanded, this 'course population' rapidly diminished. Tuition had to change from local week-day evening provision to sub-regional 'Saturday school' provision as students moved from the high-population foundation courses and dispersed among a far greater number of post-foundation courses. For these, the average populations were about 500.

In addition to amalgamating the correspondence tutors and face-to-face tutors, the OU now gave the counsellors a defined role. Instead of being responsible for a range of students across a range of courses at a local Study Centre, the counsellors were now linked to various foundation courses and involved in study skills related to particular subject areas as well as the broader aspects of distance learning. But these new roles proved equally confusing for the part-time staff and students. While the briefing documentation might have been able to draw distinction between the various roles, in reality, student needs caused the tutors and counsellors to encroach on each other's preserves, and job descriptions supported by briefing and training programmes were set aside in everyday practice. It was from this experience and observation of failures that the university moved in 1976 to establish the support service which carried it through the next two decades.

The roles of foundation course tutor and local counsellor were now combined. When students began their studies on one of the foundation courses, they were assigned to a local tutor counsellor in their local Study Centre. This tutor counsellor was responsible for all first-year tuition and counselling and was available on a regular basis at the local Study Centre to help with the academic aspects of the course as well as the broader educational needs of the student. As a supplement, or a substitution where the students chose not to attend that Study Centre, student–tutor counsellor contact was achieved by other means, principally by correspondence and telephone. The tutor counsellors were also responsible for assessing and commenting on the assignments on the particular first-year course. Even more significant in the new tutor counsellor role was the development of a philosophy of 'continuity of concern'. When students progressed from their first-year foundation courses, correspondence and face-to-face tutorial support became the province of the specialist tutor. However, the tutor counsellor continued to provide an element of stability and continuity in the life of the students since the broad role of student adviser was retained for the whole of their time with the OU.

It was this dimension to the role of the tutor counsellor that began to expand. The tutor counsellors became 'the face of the university', a resource the OU could depend on, the person(s) to whom the students addressed all manner of questions about their studies and progress. Where the tutor counsellors could not provide immediate answers to the student, they could find the answers through the specialist advice at the Regional Centres. As far as the student was concerned, the tutor counsellor was the omniscient support service provider. And it was through this tutor-counsellor role, which had emerged over the university's faltering initial five years of experience, that the OU finally settled on the basis for its student support services and course presentation for new students. The notion of counsellor had its origins in the concept of moral tutor and student adviser in the traditional university. But the concept of tutor counsellor was unique. Such staff were not merely advisers, not simply supportive teachers and evaluators, but from the student point of view, the academic and administrative face of the university.

Staff development and the human resource
strategy

As the tutor-counsellor role evolved, it became clear that the original briefing and training programme, which had seemed so far ahead of its time in 1971, was insufficient. A comprehensive staff development programme was seen to be needed to help the university's 2,000 tutor counsellors in their complex academic role. A draft training document, 'The roles of the part-time staff in the Open University', introduced in 1976 and revised for 1977, provided the university's educational rationale, policies and guidelines for its part-time staff. Far more radical, however, was the *Handbook for Tutorial and Counselling Staff*, which set out to provide a comprehensive analysis of student progress, identify an extensive list of student questions based upon the university's study requirements and provide guidance and answers to these questions as well as to the possible inter-relationship of these various queries. Not surprisingly, a perfect and comprehensive handbook to support all tutor counsellors in all eventualities proved to be a goal to be continuously pursued rather than instantly attained, but this initiative was central to the new briefing and training programme which, within a few years, was renamed 'staff development'. This handbook came to be copied by distance providers throughout the world, even though its contents were largely unique to the OU and the conditions which had necessitated its creation.

The popular concept of distance education is of a system dominated by a highly structured package. If this were the sole or major success factor in educating distance students, we would be witnessing a global victory for distance education over traditional provision. But this is not the case, largely because the rush into open and distance education and technological determinism all too often ignores the individual needs of the student, learning alone and at a distance. When the OU began its operations in 1971, it did so in an environment almost wholly lacking in competition. Not only was the OU unique in offering distance education, it was unique in concentrating on part-time adults. Its success identified a market, and within a decade competitors emerged, not so much from among the traditional universities but from the (then) polytechnics.

During the 1980s, none of these competitors came anywhere near the OU in size, but together they began to offer meaningful competition in many con-urbations. Social, economic and political factors gave rise to enormous increases in demand for part-time higher education, and the government was favourably inclined to expanding higher education. However, the OU still maintained its dominance in the new market through its unique funding arrangements. All of this changed in the early 1990s when the government abandoned the binary system of universities and polytechnics and created what amounted to a competitive bidding situation among all higher education institutions for full- and part-time students. Now the competition was local. Almost every university was offering a range of part-time courses in its catchment area. Developments in new technology – and particularly desktop publishing – had removed the competitive advantage which the OU had initially held through its course materials. Now the OU's competitive edge – indeed its only sustainable competitive advantage – was the local support service which it offered to its students through what it now calls Associate Lecturers. As a consequence, the OU is now more than ever before reliant upon this support service and this body of staff.

Staff development is therefore critical in ensuring quality of performance and outcomes and it is vital that this body of staff is well integrated into the institution's overall operations. This represents a change from traditional 'personnel management' to a more comprehensive 'human resource strategy'. In employment terms, it is apparent in the move away from short-term and annual contracts which began in response to legislation in the late 1970s. But the OU has gone far in advance of the purely legislative requirements. It has now completed an agreement with the relevant union which offers continuity of employment for all tutorial and counselling staff for as long as their course is being offered, provides maternity, annual and sick leave, and integrates them into the institution's overall human resource strategy.

Another major element in this strategy is the institution of a process of 'organisational entry' which embraces recruitment, selection and induction. Recruitment is geared to attracting candidates with the required experience and attributes and is carried out through press advertisements and booklets describing the job and competency requirements. Selection is a comprehensive process which in all cases involves interviews conducted by at least two full-time staff and the taking up of references. A manual details the rationale and conduct of this process, which accords with the university's equal opportunities and fair selection policies. Induction is provided through mandatory staff development sessions over the first two years of service, supported by mentoring relevant to the particular role. Appointees are also given a booklet offering a welcome and an introduction to the work and a Reader containing a collection of articles about key concepts and skills relevant to teaching, supporting and counselling open learners. All of these articles derive from the team of Associate Lecturers and full-time regional staff and the accent is on the experience of open learning practitioners. Hence they cover intensely practical aspects: for example, the correspondence tuition element includes the creation of a dialogue, commenting and assessment, with examples of good and bad practice.

This package of materials leads directly into locally provided, face-to-face briefing sessions which concentrate on both the role and the actual course being taught. The former is generic while the latter is specific and may involve explanations and guidance from those involved in the writing of the course materials. Participation in these sessions is a mandatory part of the contract and covered by payments for attendance and travel. Further documentary support is provided through a Reference File (the development of the original *Handbook*) and a variety of Toolkits which cover broad areas such as 'Effective Tutorials' and 'Revision and Examinations' as well as specialist areas such as 'Students with Disabilities'.

All new staff are assigned to a mentor. The mentor is an experienced member of the Associate Lecturer staff who is paid to provide informal peer support during the first year of service and maintains a supportive contact, both pro-active and re-active, throughout that period. Mentors will have long experience of a specific role and within the same or a cognate subject area. They will also be 'local' to the new member of staff and may meet on a face-to-face basis if this is felt to be appropriate.

Performance management is another part of this human resource development strategy. The staff development materials and mandatory sessions set the standards for good practice in each role. The evaluative role of tutors is monitored through such elements as Kosmat analysis, which reviews their written comments on students' assignments and provides staff with feedback on their performance compared with their peers. Broader performance management is achieved through these tutors' contacts with full-time staff in the Regional Centres who are responsible for appointing and managing these part-timers. The staff development materials are also a resource to which part-time staff can be referred if there is any need for realignment of individual standards. One element which is not in place at the moment but exists in the institution's human resource strategy for its full-time staff is an appraisal scheme. Discussions have begun as to how this might also be applied in the context of these particular part-time roles.

Another major element of the human resource strategy concerns redundancy and retirement. The employment of these tutorial staff is dependent firstly on the courses which the university offers at any given time and the numbers of students enrolled throughout the UK. Continuity of employment cannot therefore be guaranteed, but the university has moved from annual contracts as an earnest indication of its intentions. Having made considerable investments in human capital, it will always seek to redeploy staff wherever possible and, because of its range of operations, will normally expect to do so. However, the possibility of redundancy always remains and, where necessary, this is actioned through a policy which is public and seen to operate fairly and without discrimination or bias.

Future directions

It is in the context of such a staff development programme, now fully integrated into the overall human resource strategy for the institution, that the university looks to its position in UK higher education. This position will be determined by changes in the university's internal environment – its culture, personnel and structure – and in the external environment in which the major drivers will be competition and social, employment, financial and legislative factors. These external factors will have an impact on the institution as a whole, and it may be useful to highlight those of particular significance:

- efficiency gains will remain a factor throughout the next five years;
- competition will continue to increase;
- the market will increase as part-time employment becomes more common

and changes in skill and competency requirements make the theoretical concept of lifelong learning a practical reality;

- the so-called 'Social Contract' will effectively abolish the traditional distinction between full- and part-time employment;
- there will be a major impact from developments in new technology which are robust enough to be part of standard services and operations.

We may surmise that by the end of the millennium the university will have a staff of about 12,000 and that more than 70 per cent of these staff will be employed in and from Regional Centres as Associate Lecturers. The traditional divisions between the terms and conditions of full- and part-time staff which were enshrined in the legislation of the 1950s and 1960s will have disappeared. The legislative reform which began in the UK in the late 1970s with the so-called 'Employment Protection' legislation and is now, in the mid-1990s, popularly referred to as the 'Social Contract', will establish a continuum of employment which includes all aspects of what we now know as full- and part-time work within a single set of employer/employee rights and obligations. The OU will have similar obligations to all of its staff and, perhaps more importantly for the university, this new and sizeable body of staff will owe a basic allegiance, both morally and legally, to the university as its employer. On current trends, the university will be the sole or major employer for some 75 per cent of these staff.

In a few years' time, the university will possess an information system which embraces its students, staff, curriculum and regulatory framework and which will be unparalleled in UK further and higher education. This information will, as now, not be circumscribed by the confines of the university's offices. There will be robust 'home-based' links, and the expanded staff will have immediate access from wherever they live, through a PC and modem, to a range of databases. Expert systems will mean that this wide range of staff can be empowered to deal with issues which have so far been the provenance of specialists; for example, credit transfer, vocational guidance and complex decision-making on course choice across a rapidly increasing range of qualifications.

The OU, with its guidance and support for all aspects of teaching and administration, will reside wherever it has a staff representative. It will no longer be what it now is for most of its students – the most distant higher education institution in the UK; it will be the most local university and the one which, through the modularity of its curriculum, provides the greatest versatility in terms of study and qualifications of any higher education institution in the UK. Its human resource strategy and localised service, made possible through new technology, appropriate forms of initial and in-service staff development and good management, will ensure competitive advantage.

References

Peters, O. (1973) 'Die didaktische Struktur des Fernunterrichts, Untersuchungen zu einer industrialisierten Form des Lehrens und Lernens', *Tübinger Beiträge zum Fernstudium* 7, Weinheim: Beltz.

Sewart, D. (1993) 'Student support systems in distance education', *Open Learning* 8(3): 3–12.

16

STAFF DEVELOPMENT ISSUES IN INTEGRATING DISTANCE EDUCATION MATERIAL INTO ON-CAMPUS TEACHING

Jo Osborne

There is an increasing tendency within tertiary institutions to utilise course-ware, originally developed for distance education students, for on-campus teaching and learning. Teaching and tutorial staff need to be provided with staff development and research findings that will help them to be responsive to individual student preferences and to ensure that these materials are used appropriately and effectively (Jevons and Northcott 1993; National Council on Distance Education 1996: 6).

This chapter draws upon research conducted in one Australian dual-mode university into the methods employed by individual lecturers in applying off-campus materials to on-campus resource-based learning and the relative acceptability of these methods as expressed by the students in their classes. It uses these to recommend some appropriate procedures for educators who may wish to exploit the opportunities presented to both the deliverers and receivers of learning by the flexible use of such existing resources.

Using distance education materials as an on-campus resource

Arguments for cost-effectiveness, resource efficiency and economies of scale are commonly used in tertiary institutions to underline the perceived benefits of utilising distance education resource materials more widely. Such a strategy is proposed as a consequence of the managerialist and economic forces that now impact on the universities and colleges, the suggestion being that using existing distance education materials may enable larger classes to be taught without increasing staffing levels. Individual lecturers may perceive benefits in using study guides to cope with larger classes and greater student diversity: they may, for example, use the time saved for the research and writing which are now so central to institutional judgements on their academic performance.

157

There is also increasing awareness of the pedagogical benefits of resource-based learning. Advocacies for such practice range from 'allowing campus-based students greater flexibility in choosing from a range of resources and strategies for learning' (Kelly 1987: 175), to encouraging a shift in focus from teaching to student learning (Nunan 1994) and generating a more active and independent learning in the student (Day 1995). Taylor and White (1991) report that the use of study materials specifically designed for teaching flexibly on- and off-campus was recognised at the Darling Downs Institute of Advanced Education (now the University of Southern Queensland) as capable of reducing lecturing hours whilst emphasising the development of self-directed learning and enhancing participation in classroom activities.

Because of their tangible and essential nature as learning resources for off-campus students, distance education study materials have frequently undergone more rigorous development and peer review than the equivalent classroom-based teaching. Being aware of the potential economic and pedagogic benefits of utilising well-designed distance study materials in parallel on-campus classes at my own university, the University of Tasmania, I was intrigued by a report of the Australian National Board of Employment, Education and Training (NBEET) which concluded that '[a] very large amount of material which could potentially serve as resource materials in on-campus teaching is not being used because of the uncertainties that surround this way of using them' (National Board of Employment, Education and Training 1994: 166). On further enquiry, it transpired that any guidelines which had been developed lacked a studied appreciation of the students' experiences of working in this mode.

Teaching staff at the University of Tasmania have been using their distance education materials as on-campus resources since the mid-1980s, and by 1994, this had become common practice in some departments. In all cases, the materials had been developed by 'expert teams' of content specialists, instructional designers and production staff whose aim at the time of development was to prepare quality learning resources for use by off-campus students. No methodological advice had been proffered through staff development or had even been expected by lecturers in regard to the subsequent adaptation of these materials to on-campus teaching. I therefore decided that it would be instructive to undertake a study into this emergent flexible teaching approach, to interview some lecturers about their intentions and expectations and to research their students' experiences and perceptions of the process. My aim was to identify some examples of the 'successful' integration of such materials, with the intention of developing some guidelines for their future use. My study (Osborne 1995a; 1995b) focused on four subjects (two taught in the Faculty of Commerce and two taught in the Faculty of Humanities), the four lecturers responsible for teaching these programmes, and one tutorial group from each of their on-campus classes. All four lecturers expected their on-campus students to purchase the sets of print-based distance education study materials, which were made available at cost. The observations and guidelines that follow derive from this study, and have been substantiated by previous and subsequent observations in my experience as an instructional designer.

My observations and the staff and student feedback through interviews and questionnaires confirmed the findings that '(resource-based learning) is not simply a matter of taking a set of distance teaching materials and dropping them into a face-to-face teaching situation' (National Council on Distance Education 1996: 1). The findings are summarised in Table 16.1. The experience enabled me to develop a set of guidelines for use in my and others' staff development programmes about integrating distance education material into on-campus classes.

The summarised primary reasons given by the four lecturers for using these materials in an on-campus setting were as follows:

- the materials provided core content which the students needed to read in preparation for their classes, thus freeing up class time for practical work or enrichment activities;
- the materials were a source of practical examples and exercises which were missing from the textbooks and gave the students practice in problem-solving;
- the materials were a supplementary resource to the lecture material, and were particularly useful in assignment preparation.

Guideline 1

Staff development programmes should assist lecturers in understanding the potential of resource-based learning in fostering independent learning.

Whilst two of the lecturers stressed the importance of students using the study materials as a preparation for classwork, only one gave any hint in interviews that independent learning might in any way be an aim: 'I'm one of those people who believe that students learn rather than being taught – an extra resource for them to work from is beneficial.'

Guideline 2

It is important to advise the on-campus students on how they should use the distance education study materials, especially if lectures and tutorials do not follow the same structure and content as the study guides.

The study found that the students find supplementary study materials to be very useful when the lectures and tutorials follow a similar structure. This holds true even when the lecturer does not refer students directly to the materials on a regular basis. Students can easily become confused, however, when the lecturer does not comment on, or does not appear to be following, the structure and content of study materials. To take one example, an anthropological unit was being tutored by a sociologist who was using resource materials written by an

Table 16.1 Using distance education materials on campus: a summary of the findings

	Unit A (study guide only)	Unit B (study guide only)	Unit C (study guide + reader)	Unit D (study guide + reader)
Lecturers' perceptions of the materials (interview)	Providing core content Allowing more practical work in contact time The best option, given the reduced teaching time	Supplementing texts/poor library resources Compensating for lack of tutorial time Improving teaching effectiveness Allowing for enrichment in lectures Improving teaching effectiveness	Providing core content Providing easiest access to scarce resources Preparing students for tutorial discussions	Outlining the topics A resource for research/discussion No improvement in teaching effectiveness
Lecturers' advice to the students (observation)	Important to prepare from the materials for each week's class	Use as a resource for practice Particularly helpful for assignments/tests	The materials are the main resource (No mention of the study guide)	Use the reader to start investigating the topics
Comment on context (observation)	Informal lecture style Tutorials centred on practice and open discussion Participative climate	Formal lecture style Tutorials centred on discussion of prepared exercises A markedly 'academic' climate	Informal lecture style Tutorials centred on discussion of prepared exercises and issues A climate of serious discussion	Relaxed lecture style Tutorials centred on prepared individual presentations A climate of relaxed discussion

Student perceptions of the lecturer's use of the materials (questionnaire)	The lecturer makes regular/weekly mention of the study guide	The lecturer makes occasional mention of the study guide	The lecturer mentions the study materials several times a week	The lecturer makes occasional mention of the study materials
	Most students are satisfied with the study advice given	Students are satisfied with the study advice given	Students are satisfied with the study advice given	Students are significantly dissatisfied with the lecturer's use of the materials
Student use of the study materials (study diary)	Averaged 1½ hrs/week	Averaged 2½ hrs/week	Averaged 2½ hrs/week	Averaged < ½hrs/week
	3 hrs/week before a test	No change in test week	No test	No test
	Study patterns very varied	Study patterns mostly regular	Study patterns mostly regular	Negligible use of the materials
Student perceptions of the materials (questionnaire)	Very useful	Vital/very useful	Vital	Very/occasionally useful
	Used because they usefully summarised the topics and formed a good basis for revision	Used because the exercises helped the learning, they usefully summarised the topics and they helped the overseas students	Used because they formed a good basis for revision and increased the learning	Used because they helped in assignment preparation and in tutorial preparation
	Not used more because time was limited and we could cope without them	Not used more because the lecturer did not refer to them much and other references were more useful	Not used more because time was limited and they were most useful for revision purposes	Not used more because the lecturer didn't refer to them much and they were only useful for assignments

(Continued)

Table 16.1 (Continued)

	Unit A (study guide only)	Unit B (study guide only)	Unit C (study guide + reader)	Unit D (study guide + reader)
Students' expected use of materials for revision (questionnaire)	A major focus or useful additional resource for revision	A major focus or useful additional resource for revision	A major focus for revision	A major focus or useful additional resource for revision
Students' comments (interview)	The study guide was most useful. It provided a concise review/revision resource	—	The study guide and reader were used as a major resource throughout the semester and for revision	The study guide and reader were useful in parts There was some confusion regarding the lecturer's advice

historian. A requirement of the students was that they should integrate both sources of knowledge, but this was too large an expectation because neither the lecturer nor the material gave them a framework for comparison.

However, even with a comparable class and content schedule, it was shown that the learners may not make the best use of the available resources unless prompted and guided by the staff member, especially if the concept of self-study is new to these students. Nor is it generally sufficient merely to provide general instructions in an introductory meeting. Unless direct reference and use of the content is made in the subsequent classroom discussions and activities, the distance learning resources may simply be disregarded by the students. Making students more responsible for their own learning does not absolve tutors from their responsibilities. They need to become facilitators and, to facilitate learning in a flexible environment, there is a need to guide learners towards a useful application of the relevant resources.

Guideline 3

If students are to be encouraged to exploit the study resources, it is advisable to make regular use of, or reference to, these in class. This need not involve direct reference but might be in the application or utilisation of techniques introduced in the materials.

One lecturer I observed made the most of the available contact time with the students by relying on the distance education materials to deliver the detailed content and condensing his formal lectures, thereby making more time available for extended interaction in tutorial sessions. However, whereas the study resources had included thought-provoking, in-text learning activities designed to help the out-of-class students interpret and apply the theory, the lecturer told his face-to-face students to ignore these activities, saying that he would consider these in his tutorials. As a consequence of this, many students decided that they could survive in class without background reading, assimilating the theory or developing the capacity to apply the knowledge. By contrast, the most lively and focused discussions that I observed in another lecturer's tutorials were promoted by the prior setting of two or three questions chosen from the distance education in-text activities and linked to available references in the prescribed reading.

The exercises and activities in well-designed distance education materials are intended to prompt reflection and application at optimum stages in the learning process. The first lecturer was missing the chance to help his students use all of the available resources to prepare for the tutorial sessions. If he had helped the students to structure their thinking before each session and consider the activities in the materials in advance, he could have helped the students with their essential prior learning and then provided them with a useful focus for further exploration within the tutorials, thus encouraging deeper learning.

Since conducting this study, I have discovered that editing distance education study materials for on-campus use – typically by the removal of embedded exercises – is practised by other lecturers too, even when they are the authors of the original material. Such actions may be motivated by a desire to demonstrate the need for the lecturer to be present, but they undermine the promotion of self-directed learning for meaningful understanding through engagement with materials.

Guideline 4

Recognise that the 'usefulness' of a learning resource is not necessarily to be equated with regular use. Students may prefer to reserve the study materials for specific purposes and in accordance with their individual study strategies – for example, for revision or assignment preparation – and this may result in irregular usage.

Two questions that I have stumbled over quite a few times in my role as an instructional designer are these. How can we tell if the learners find the study resources useful? And can 'useful' be defined in this context? At the outset of my research I hypothesised that the amount of time on-campus students spent with the distance education materials, particularly on a regular weekly basis, would give me some indication of their perceived usefulness as learning resources. However, this turned out not to be the case. I collected regular weekly study diaries which recorded the amount of time various students spent working with the study resources available to them. The students were grouped according to the different study patterns displayed: 'regular' users tended to spend a similar amount of time most weeks; 'sporadic' users' use fluctuated considerably over the semester, 'starve and binge' individuals never touched the materials until the week before an assignment or test was due, and 'no use' learners at most glanced over the materials once or twice. At the end of the semester, all of these students were invited to complete questionnaires which asked them to rate the usefulness of the distance education materials to their studies. They were asked to rate these materials as being 'vital: I could not manage without them', 'very useful', 'occasionally useful' and 'of little use'. These criteria may lack precision, just as 'usefulness' is a subjective term, but during the piloting of this questionnaire, these terms presented no apparent difficulties for the students.

Overall, 80 per cent of the returned questionnaires classified the distance education materials as 'vital' or 'very useful' to study. It emerged that students displaying a variety of study patterns (regular, sporadic or starve and binge – sometimes within the same tutorial group) found the materials useful, *because they had chosen to use them in different ways.* It transpired that the students were variously using the materials for the purposes of summary, overview, practice, assignment preparation or major revision, according to their learning styles and needs. This is a particularly important consideration for staff providing a range of alternative learning resources just as the librarian needs to recognise that even if a particular library book is not constantly out on loan, it may still comprise a vital part of the learning mix.

Guideline 5

Consider how the provision of distance education materials to internal classes may assist overseas students with their understanding of the language.

It is important to consider whether there are any sub-groups within the class for whom the supplementary study materials might be particularly useful. The non-Australian students involved in this study were notable for their regular study patterns. Four students identified themselves through the questionnaire as coming from overseas and having English as their second language, and two of these indicated that the distance education materials had helped them overcome difficulties of understanding. This was corroborated by another survey of overseas students at the University of Tasmania, which reported that problems arising from lecturers' delivery styles (such as strong accents, speaking fast, colloquial expressions and unclear diction) could be significantly offset by the provision of clear lecture outlines and printed notes (Kingston 1995).

Guideline 6

Lecturers should be aware that learners studying from a variety of resources may recognise distance education materials as important revision aids. It is therefore recommended that lecturers should encourage this if previous students have found them useful, or provide alternative advice if a different revision strategy is more appropriate.

On-campus students frequently elect to use the prescribed distance education study materials as a major revision resource prior to examinations, even if not so advised by their lecturers. Student interviews suggested that this may be because the students perceive the materials as providing a more concise overview of the content than the textbooks or lecture notes, or because there are no other easily accessed 'authoritative' resources. I found this to hold true in each of the four classes that I studied, even the one in which students experienced a dissonance between the two modes of content delivery. However, a warning note must be sounded at this point. The provision of concisely packaged study materials may give the students an undesired and undesirable sense of security – a hidden message to the effect that this particular content is all they really need to know for their examination. Indeed, it was illuminating to find the following unbidden comment in one of the students' questionnaire responses explaining the use of the study materials as a revision resource:

> Because they are for external students, you assume the exam questions will be based on this information as this is all external students have available to them . . . if information is mentioned in the lecture that is not mentioned in the study guide or prescribed text, then you assume this information will not be examinable.

At the University of Tasmania, on-campus and off-campus students study the same units and complete identical assessment components. This student's comment suggests that some of these students are developing an expedient, surface-learning approach. The frequency with which many students use their distance education study materials as revision resources calls into question the learning approaches that may be reinforced by their availability. This raises questions that warrant further investigation.

Guideline 7

Be wary of making assumptions about the staff and student understandings and uses of flexible learning.

The study showed that students form and follow their own opinions of distance education materials and do not necessarily use them as the lecturers expect or intend. It also revealed that lecturers have different perceptions of, and attitudes towards, the use of distance education materials in their on-campus classes, have differing expectations of their students and use a range of strategies in such contexts. These various teaching strategies appear to affect the students' use of the study resources, but the learning strategies the students adopt are largely dependent upon individual student factors and attitudes.

Conclusion

To simplify matters of comparison, all of the distance education materials used in the units in this study were print-based. However, the observations and recommendations above may be applied to courseware in any media providing a few principles are adhered to. For instance:

- A set of audiotaped lectures expressly designed by one lecturer to integrate with printed study guides for a distance education unit could usefully be referenced by another lecturer with on-campus classes. The students could benefit from hearing an alternative interpretation of the subject matter, especially in regard to their assignment topics.
- A videotape and workbook prepared for laboratory, clinical, studio or fieldwork by off-campus students could be a useful tool for on-campus students who have failed to grasp the procedures in class and would like further practice in their own time.
- Print-based materials could be adapted for the Web, to facilitate learning by both on-campus and off-campus students.

Reid (1996: 42) suggests that as a practical necessity more courses need to be less campus-based and more campus-based courses need to be less rigid in their modes of delivery. From his experience at the dual-mode Deakin University more than a decade ago, Jevons (1984: 27) perceived that distance education materials and methods had strengths which could be exploited in on-campus study. It is now possible to say that a growing number of students are coming to appreciate these strengths, provided that it is made clear to them how their content and activities integrate into the overall teaching and learning plan. In discussing the benefits of using distance education materials for internal teaching, Kelly (1987: 190–3) suggested that on-campus students might find independent study more difficult, demanding and time-consuming. To date, economically driven institutional policies and sheer conjecture have largely prevailed in the multiple use of distance education resources, and as a consequence, such materials have often been under-utilised because of uncertainties about the best ways of using them in on-campus settings.

Although it cannot be confidently stated that the guidelines above will ensure success in all on-campus flexible learning situations, the underlying principles are underscored by acknowledged teaching strategies. Writing on flexible learning, Reid (1984: 79) suggests that

the very nature of the pedagogic contract that goes with these arrangements seems more likely to encourage active and intellectually independent learners; instead of being the sole initiator, a teacher can combine the roles of a *resource specialist*, who puts the learners in contact with usable information, ideas and techniques, and a *response specialist*, with whom the learner can negotiate and test particular communications.

An *ad hoc* approach to the flexible use of existing study materials cannot produce such an optimum learning situation. Staff developers and teachers engaging in such flexible learning can foster sound, student-responsive delivery by conducting research into the role of the teacher and the ways in which students choose to engage with the materials to advance their understandings.

References

Day, I. (1995) 'Independent on-campus learning: case studies in flexibility', in F. Nouwens (ed.), *Distance Education: Crossing Frontiers*, papers for the 12th Biennial Forum of the Open and Distance Learning Association of Australia, Central Queensland University, pp. 141–7.

Jevons, F. (1984) 'Distance education in a mixed institution: working towards parity', *Distance Education* 5(1): 24–37.

Jevons, F. and Northcott, P. (1993) 'A culture of teaching excellence', in National Board of Employment, Education and Training (1994), *Costs and Quality in Resource-Based Learning On- and Off-campus*, Commissioned Report No. 33, Canberra, Australian Government Publishing Service.

Kelly, M. (1987) 'Barriers to convergence in Australian higher education', in P. Smith and M. Kelly (eds), *Distance Education and the Mainstream*, London: Croom Helm.

Kingston, A. (1995) unpublished Bachelor of Education project, University of Tasmania.

National Board of Employment, Education and Training (1994) *Costs and Quality in*

Resource-based Learning On and Off Campus, Commissioned Report No. 33, Canberra, Australian Government Publishing Service.

National Council on Distance Education (1996) *Resource-Based Learning: Report of a Working Party on NBEET Report 33*, Toowoomba: University of Southern Queensland.

Nunan, T. (1994) *Flexible Delivery: A Discussion of Issues*, Adelaide: University of South Australia.

Osborne, J. (1995a) 'The emergence of convergence: how distance education materials are used in on-campus classes', in D. Sewart (ed.), *One World Many Voices*, 17th World Conference for Distance Education, vol. 2, International Council for Distance Education and the Open University, pp. 167–70.

—— (1995b) 'Using distance education materials on-campus – ask the grass roots', in *ODLAA Papers* 2 (August).

Reid, I. (1984) *The Making of Literature: Texts, Contexts, and Classroom Practices*, Adelaide: Australian Association for the Teaching of English.

—— (1996) *Higher Education or Education for Hire? Language and Values in Australian Universities*, Rockhampton: Central Queensland University Press.

Taylor, J. and White, V. (1991) *The Evaluation of the Cost-effectiveness of Multi-media Mixed-mode Teaching and Learning*, Canberra: Australian Government Publishing Service.

Part III

STAFF DEVELOPMENT IN ACTION

17

STAFF DEVELOPMENT FROM AN ACTION RESEARCH PERSPECTIVE

David Kember

Models of staff development are initially considered from the perspective of positivist, interpretative and critical paradigms. The positivist model, which has been prevalent in both conventional and distance education, is considered problematic in that it takes a deficit view of academics' teaching and fails to address the issue of implementing organisational change.

A case is therefore advanced for educational action research projects as a form of staff development activity. A justification for this mode of staff development is drawn from a synthesis of interpretative and critical epistemological positions. In such projects, participants examine and seek to improve aspects of their own teaching which they themselves have selected as being of interest or concern. The projects proceed through cycles of planning, action, observation and reflection. Regular meetings allow for perspective transformation through discourse. Gathering interpretative data provides evidence to share with departmental colleagues. The aim is to empower participants to reflect upon, monitor and take responsibility for improving their own teaching.

Instructional design

I went to Hong Kong about ten years ago as someone who was best known as a staff developer in distance education. I am still a staff developer, but the bulk of my activity is now concerned with face-to-face teaching. Making this transition has been an interesting experience since the predominant methods of staff development in the two modes of education are so different and operate under very different assumptions. These are, to a large extent, tacit rather than well-articulated in the literature. It is surprising that there are such differences since both deal with improving the quality of teaching and learning and both deal with academics and indirectly students – and often the same academics and students.

If there are staff developers in distance education, they are usually graced with the title 'instructional designer', though many of these do not appear to consider staff development to be a primary aspect of their role (Allen 1996). Allen's survey of ninety-nine staff working in this field in Australia found that sixty-six had the title 'instructional designer' and that no other title featured in significant numbers. Those concerned with conventional education have more diverse titles, with 'educational developer' being the most common. That distance education staff developers have chosen to be called 'instructional designers' suggests that the predominant model for their work has been derived from the instructional design literature.

Reigeluth, one of the best-known instructional designers, deals with the nature of instructional design as follows:

> The result of instructional design as a professional activity is an 'architect's blueprint' for what the instruction should be like. This 'blueprint' is a prescription as to what methods of instruction should be used when for that course content and those students.
>
> (Reigeluth 1983: 7)

Technical rationality

Much instructional design is based on a technical-rational approach (Schön 1983). Schön argued that the predominant paradigm in professional schools in universities was the logical positivist paradigm of the pure sciences. In these, practice was often taught as well-defined procedures. The models of instruction provided by such writers as Reigeluth (1983) are clearly based upon this underlying technical-rational paradigm.

Schön, though, argued that the technical-rational approach to professional practice ignored its characterisation as having to deal with messy and ill-defined problems. One professional may examine a case or situation and define the problem in a particular way, whereas another might see quite different problems needing to be tackled. Therefore, issues need to be approached with a view to problem-framing or problem-posing rather than problem-solving. This implies that professionals face multifaceted issues with many variables to be taken into account. Furthermore, the aspects of an issue are likely to belong to several traditional disciplines. Even if some measure of agreement can be reached over the nature of the problem and the aspects involved there will not be an ideal solution. There will often be conflicting tensions – a solution can have positive consequences for one aspect of the problem but negative repercussions upon others.

Translating from the general case of professional practice to the specific practice of teaching, it is easy to see the relevance of Schön's work simply by envisaging a single classroom. The complex array of personalities, issues and events are surely better envisaged as a messy problem than an arena to which neat prescriptions apply. If this applies to an individual classroom, a distance education programme is surely a veritable jungle.

172

Deficit assumption

Implicit within the instructional design approach is a deficit model of teaching. The instructional designer is seen to be an expert in instruction who is able to design the necessary blueprint. There are even examples in the literature where the deficit assumption is quite explicit. For example: 'With the emergence of instructional design, it has become increasingly evident that subject matter experts in the various disciplines do not know how to teach' (Shaw and Taylor 1984: 279).

If attitudes like this are prevalent, it is hardly surprising that many of the instructional designers in Allen's 1996 survey felt that academics had a negative perception of their role or were uncertain of, or misunderstood, their role.

What instructional designers do in practice

These uncertainties or misunderstandings are perhaps not surprising in that instructional designers themselves still seem to be engaged in much debate about their role (see Parer 1989), and what many appear to do in practice does not seem to match the widely accepted definitions of instructional design. The seven most frequently performed activities reported to Allen were as follows:

- defining instructional goals and objectives;
- determining instructional strategies;
- editing;
- designing layout and appearance of material;
- proof-reading;
- managing materials development; and/or
- designing assessment items.

It is noteworthy that four of these seven top-rated items are activities which have nothing to do with the accepted definitions of instructional design, but are tasks normally associated with editors. In a detailed study of a smaller number of instructional designers through qualitative case studies by Murphy (1995), it was confirmed that much of the time of instructional designers is devoted to editing tasks. Further, that two of Allen's top ranked items are not perhaps as design-orientated as they might seem and that the first and last items on the list are better described as writing objectives and in-text questions into draft materials where the authors have not included these. Murphy also concluded that much of the work of instructional designers made little use of any educational theories.

What is of particular interest in Allen's findings is that only three of the ninety-nine instructional designers mentioned staff development in the open-ended part of the survey on perceptions of the role of instructional designers. This is possibly because instructional design's prescriptive and deficit assumptions are hardly suited to staff development.

Divergence

There clearly appears to be a divergence between what instructional designers are doing in practice and the nature of the role implied by the title. This divergence has presumably motivated the growing literature on the role of the instructional designer.

As well as the examinations of what instructional designers do in practice there have been several attempts to describe the role in terms of metaphors. In a book which largely sets out to explore the role of the instructional designer in distance education (Parer 1989), the contributors suggest such diverse metaphors as 'the amicable guerrilla' (Carl 1989), the 'editor' (Jenkins 1989), 'the Continental Op' (Haughey, 1989), and the 'engineer' (Fenwick 1989) to portray the role of the instructional designer. No wonder that Arger's (1989) chapter is entitled 'The developer's identity crisis'.

What is surprising, in view of the confusion, is that the founding framework has not been questioned more. There are those who have questioned the applicability of instructional design theories and particularly the prescriptive assumption (for example, Meacham 1989; Lentell and Murphy 1993) but it is hard to find any calls for alternative paradigms. If instructional design does not provide an appropriate framework, a more fruitful line is likely to be that of exploring alternative theoretical bases.

Educational development

It is interesting that those involved with staff development in conventional education do not call themselves 'instructional designers'. More significantly, the discipline of instructional design has not been adopted as a founding framework and has had little or no influence upon them.

Until recently there has been little in the literature on the theoretical framework for educational development. However, there is now a growing literature with several alternative emerging paradigms. One writer (Webb 1992; 1996) provides a useful base for the discussion by analysing educational development activities in terms of positivist, interpretative and critical epistemologies. He asserts that positivism has been the dominant paradigm for educational development activities. A scenario typical of this pretext might be a personal counselling session, workshop or short course delivering advice on good teaching practice. The advice would typically be based upon research which followed a positivist educational psychology paradigm.

This position shares similar behavioural origins to the instructional design literature and, therefore, suffers the limitations of the technical-rational hypothesis. It assumes that there are universally applicable recipes for good teaching. However, because students are so varied, institutions idiosyncratic and teachers heterogeneous, universal remedies have not proved to be a cure-all solution. Even when lecturers do receive soundly based advice in workshops or courses they often find it very difficult to implement their new-found wisdom in the swampy ground of the classroom. They invariably have greater difficulty still when changes impinge upon their departmental colleagues, as they normally do. In essence, the positivistic paradigm for staff development fails to address the vital issue of implementation.

Student approaches to learning

The dominant influence within the interpretative paradigm has been the research tradition of student approaches to learning. This is a version of the constructivist theories of learning, according to which the student is the one who constructs meaning, not the teacher who imparts it. The movement is probably best known for its characterisation of learning approaches into deep and surface (Marton and Säljö 1976). For educational developers this dichotomy has proved to be a construct which is readily understandable and useful in interpreting a wide range of educational issues.

An important point about learning approaches is that the issues focused on depend upon the students' perception of the course and the teaching and learning environment. A range of variables such as high workload, didactic teaching, content-orientated assessment and a fact-filled syllabus have all been consistently associated with the less desirable surface approach. Examination of learning approaches has provided educational developers with readily inter-pretable evaluation tools which are sensitive to the context of the department or the individual lecturer.

The limitation of the interpretative framework, though, is that there is no inherent mechanism for moving beyond interpretation. It can provide a means of analysing a teaching scenario and suggesting the reasons for any perceived deficiencies. However, if the paradigm is followed, the investigation rests at the level of interpretation. There is no mechanism for moving on towards remediating the identified problems.

Critical theory

While in other paradigms it is problematic if the investigator perturbs the subject, critical theory positively embraces change. The mode of research associated with critical theory – action research – therefore provides a suitable foundation for educational development because this is inherently a process of seeking change in teaching and learning. The characteristics of action research discussed below have been distilled from a number of accounts representing the major typologies (Carr and Kemmis 1986; Elliot 1991; McKernan 1991; McNiff 1992; Stenhouse 1975).

Action research is applicable in situations in which participants wish to improve their own practice. The mode has been called 'participative' action research, indicating first that it is normally a group activity involving those affected by the topic being investigated. There may well be an attempt to widen the circle of involvement to include others involved in the practice. Many would consider it essential that action research be conducted by a group. Others, however, accept that it can be an individual problem-solving activity or an individual reflecting on his or her practice.

The term 'participative' is also indicative of the importance placed upon the participation of practitioners themselves. A distinction has been made with other paradigms where it is more common for expert researchers to conduct enquiries and hand down their findings and recommendations to those in the field.

The roles of the practitioner and expert researcher also influence the subject matter of action research. It has been claimed (Carr and Kemmis 1986; Stenhouse 1975) that educational researchers following other paradigms commonly concentrate upon theoretical issues which are of little interest or relevance to teachers. By comparison, in action research, it is the participants or teachers who decide upon the subject or topic for research. It can be something they feel is interesting or important or it can be a problem they want to solve.

Perhaps the clearest distinction between action research and other modes lies in the attitude towards changes to what is being researched. Other paradigms tend to avoid perturbing the subject of their research. Action researchers set out with the avowed intention of improving their practice. Action research is perceived as a cyclical or spiral iterative process involving planning, acting, observing and reflecting. It is normal for projects to go through two or more cycles; improvement is brought about by such cycles, each incorporating lessons learned from previous cycles.

It should not be thought that action research is a soft or imprecise mode of research. Rigorous, systematic enquiry is as integral to this as for other research paradigms. The action research cycle incorporates systematic observation and evaluation. Outcomes of systematic enquiry are made public and subjected to normal criteria for scrutiny and acceptance. Action research thus contributes to both social practice and theory development. Its advocates also claim that it brings theory closer to practice.

Action research applied to educational development

In its application as a mode of educational development, the major action research initiative described later in this chapter, the Action Learning Project, has adopted the following characteristics for the fifty projects it supports (Kember and Gow 1992; Kember and McKay 1996; Kember and Kelly 1993):

- project teams are composed of small groups who share a similar interest or concern;
- the topic for the project is chosen by the participants to fit within the broad aim of investigating and improving some aspect of their own teaching;

- project groups meet regularly to report observations and critique their own practices;
- projects proceed through cycles of planning, action, observation and reflection. At least two cycles are normally necessary to implement and refine any innovatory practices;
- evidence of the effectiveness of teaching practices and their influence on student learning outcomes are gathered using a variety of evaluation methods;
- the evidence gathered can be used to convince departmental colleagues, not originally participating in the project, that they too should change their practices and the curriculum; and
- lessons learned from the projects can be disseminated to a wider audience through publications. Participants are, therefore, eligible for rewards through the traditional value system of universities.

The role of the staff developer

There is an element of dichotomy, almost of contradiction, between the characteristics of action research and those of staff development. Action research is based upon collaboration, participation, democratic decision-making and emancipation through critical self-reflection. Staff development, however, implies some element, at least, of external involvement and/or direction setting.

The relationship between the researcher and teacher in school-based action research programmes has been discussed by Stenhouse (1975). He concludes that the most promising way of overcoming the social and psychological barriers to teacher participation is through mutually supportive, cooperative research between teachers and full-time researchers. Others (Carr and Kemmis 1986) feel that the relationship between researcher and teacher is important. The researcher should become a 'critical friend', helping the insider to make wise judgements in the process of educational transformation. Stenhouse believes that proposals should be presented as provisional specifications to be tested rather than as unqualified recommendations. This orientation or approach seems highly appropriate for staff in educational institutions who are often sceptical of didactic pronouncements.

The approach or status of the facilitator and his or her relationship to the participants will clearly influence the nature of the action research. Once a project has started, the facilitator needs to maximise support while minimising manipulation. In this context one observer (Habermas 1974) points to the paradox between the intervener, who acquires a superior knowledge status, and the concern of action research with enlightenment through democratic critical reflection. As mentioned before, the adoption of a critical friend orientation seems to help in avoiding, or at least minimising, the effects of this snare.

The action learning project

The action research projects under discussion here were originally based solely at the Hong Kong Polytechnic University, but, through the Action Learning Project, came to involve all other Hong Kong tertiary institutions. Their role is to organise the project and to provide staff development and support for the fifty project teams.

The Action Learning Project has itself been an action research project into how best to provide this support. The critical friend role performed by the coordinating team has evolved into a multifaceted role. Important facets of this role include the financier; the project design consultant; the rapport builder; the coffee maker; the mirror; the teaching consultant; the evaluation adviser; the research adviser; the resource provider; the writing consultant; the match-maker; and the deadline enforcer. The orientation or attitude of the critical friend is quite different from that of a traditional instructional designer doing something which at face value may seem similar. In illustrating this role, I shall concentrate on the thirteen projects that have been concerned with developing multimedia packages as these fit most comfortably with most people's understanding of the term 'flexible learning'.

The involvement of the coordinating team varies from project to project, and defining the role has been an evolving process. The coordinating team suggests an initial meeting with the project team to negotiate the level and type of involvement. However, the project teams are not required to meet with, let alone use the support of, the coordinating group. Those who feel confident about conducting their own projects are free to proceed on their own. In the event, all but three or four groups have wished to have an initial meeting with the coordinating group and most chose to maintain some form of relationship thereafter. The level and nature of involvement of the coordinating team vary considerably from project to project.

An important underlying principle in the relationship is that the project teams own the project. All development work is done within their departments. Grants have been given to most of the projects for research assistants or programmers so these are employed by the team's department and located in that department. There is, therefore, a sense of ownership and a development of expertise and interest within these departments. This rarely happens when the development work is carried out by distance education unit staff in some centre away from the teaching departments.

The idea for each project comes from the participants themselves but they may need help in planning it, so this brings in the 'project design consultant' facet of the role. It should be noted that the plans are not devised in accordance with the rigid blueprints of instructional design. Action research is an iterative process so plans are changed and refined as the cycles progress. Hardly any of the projects in the Action Learning Project stuck closely to their original plans, and many participants seemed surprised that they were allowed and encouraged to deviate from them.

Establishing a viable relationship with a team brings in the facet of 'rapport builder'. Once a relationship is established, this needs to be developed into an on-going relationship of mutual respect and trust which has been christened the 'coffee-maker' facet of the role.

The topic for the projects comes from the participants, so they are clearly regarded as having expertise and interest in teaching rather than 'not knowing how to teach'. Advice on teaching is not then a major facet of the role but the 'teaching consultant' does play a part in passing on advice from appropriate educational research to be tested in the particular context of the project.

Reflection upon practice is an essential component of action research for it is through this that lessons are learned from initial cycles which can guide practice in future ones. It is also through critical reflection that attitudinal change can occur. The 'critical friend' can play the role of 'mirror' by asking questions, prompting and challenging the teams while they are engaged in their critical discourse.

The most significant facet of the role has been found to be that of the 'evaluation and research adviser'. It is important that appropriate evaluation is conducted during each cycle so that lessons can be drawn for future practice. The orientation here has been that of helping the participants to develop the necessary expertise rather than carrying out the evaluation for them. In this way, the teachers can become equipped for on-going monitoring and improvement of their own teaching. The research element typically arises because most teams want some means of 'proving' that they have achieved what they had set out to.

The initiatives are treated as akin to research projects, so the staff can benefit from the traditional reward structures of academia by publishing the outcomes. Some participants have sought advice from the 'writing consultant', as they were unfamiliar with writing papers in an appropriate format for educational research.

The Action Learning Project has encouraged teams to share lessons learned with other teams and with academics not involved in the projects. This started in an informal way with the 'matchmaker' putting participants in touch with those working in similar areas. As the Project developed, Interest Group Meetings were held around themes such as multimedia development or problem-based learning, or within disciplines such as English language teaching. In these meetings, progress reports were given and discussed. In this way, the participants become resources and sources of expertise for one another. The instructional designer is not the sole expert.

It may be noted that with each facet of the role, the emphasis is on equipping the participants to perform each aspect of the development role themselves. The aim is to help the staff to develop the expertise and desire to continue to evaluate, reflect upon and improve their teaching long after the project is completed. In the 'critical friend' paradigm, empowerment through staff development is to the fore. This is quite different from the instructional designers in Allen's survey who ranked staff development equal tenth in the frequency of types of activities performed. Here, staff development ranked alongside checking references but behind checking copyright issues and well behind proof-reading.

References

Allen, M. (1996) 'A profile of instructional designers in Australia', *Distance Education* 17 (1): 7–32.

Arger, J. (1989) 'The developer's identity crisis', in M.S. Parer (ed.), *Development, Design and Distance Education*, Churchill, Vic.: Centre for Distance Learning, Gippsland Institute.

Carl, D.R. (1989) 'The amicable guerrilla, working in a traditional university', in M.S. Parer (ed.), *Development, Design and Distance Education*, Churchill, Vic.: Centre for Distance Learning, Gippsland Institute.

Carr, W. and Kemmis, S. (1986) *Becoming Critical: Education, Knowledge and Action Research*, Brighton: Falmer Press.

Elliot, J. (1991) *Action Research for Educational Change*, Milton Keynes: Open University Press.

Fenwick, J. (1989) 'Defining educational development in distance education', in M.S. Parer (ed.), *Development, Design and Distance Education*, Churchill, Vic.: Centre for Distance Learning, Gippsland Institute.

Habermas, J. (1974) *Theory and Practice*, London: Heinemann.

Haughey, M. (1989) 'The critical role of the educational developer', in M.S. Parer (ed.), *Development, Design and Distance Education*, Churchill, Vic.: Centre for Distance Learning, Gippsland Institute.

Jenkins, J. (1989) 'Working with writers', in M.S. Parer (ed.), *Development, Design and Distance Education*, Churchill, Vic.: Centre for Distance Learning, Gippsland Institute.

Kember, D. and Gow, L. (1992) 'Action research as a form of staff development in higher education', *Higher Education* 23 (3): 297–310.

Kember, D. and Kelly, M. (1993) *Improving Teaching through Action Research*, Higher Education Research and Development Society of Australasia (HERDSA), Green Guide No. 14, Canberra; HERDSA Publications.

Kember, D. and McKay, J. (1996) 'Action research into the quality of student learning: a paradigm for faculty development', *Journal of Higher Education* 67 (5): 528–54.

Lentell, H. and Murphy, D. (1993) 'Neats and scruffies: approaches to quality in open learning and distance education', presented at the Cambridge Conference on Student Support in Distance Education, UK.

McKernan, J. (1991) *Curriculum Action Research*, London: Kogan Page.

McNiff, J. (1992) *Action Research: Principles and Practice*, London: Routledge.

Marton, F. and Säljö, R. (1976) 'On qualitative differences in learning, outcome and process I', *British Journal of Educational Psychology* 46: 4–11.

Meacham, D. (1989) 'The role of developers and designers in distance education', in M.S. Parer (ed.), *Development, Design and Distance Education*, Churchill, Vic.: Centre for Distance Learning, Gippsland Institute.

Murphy, D. (1995) 'Chaos rules: an exploration of the work of instructional designers in distance education', Doctoral thesis, Deakin University.

Parer, M.S. (ed.) (1989) *Development, Design and Distance Education*, Churchill, Vic.: Centre for Distance Learning, Gippsland Institute.

Reigeluth, C.M. (ed.) (1983) *Instructional Design Theories and Models: An Overview of their Current Status*, New Jersey, Lawrence Erlbaum.

Schön, D.A. (1983) *The Reflective Practitioner: How Professionals Think in Action*, New York: Basic Books.

Shaw, B. and Taylor, J. (1984) 'Instructional design, distance education and the academic tradition', *Distance Education* 5 (2): 277–85.

Stenhouse, L. (1975) *An Introduction to Curriculum Research and Development*, London: Heinemann Education.

Webb, G. (1992) 'On pretexts for higher education development activities', *Higher Education* 24: 351–61.

—— (1996) *Understanding Staff Development*, Bristol, PA, and Buckingham, UK, Society for Research into Higher Education and Open University Press.

18

STAFF DEVELOPMENT

An enabling role

Neil Haigh

As an academic staff developer, I encourage colleagues to adopt ways of teaching that increase the potential for open and flexible learning and try to model them in my own practice. More recently, I decided that I should commit myself to making greater use of these approaches and to extending my repertoire of associated skills. Two factors account for this decision. First, I became aware that a gap was opening up between what I was advocating and the reality of my own practice. Second, for the first time initiatives were being proposed within my university to encourage and help teachers to adopt these approaches. As a result, I could anticipate a substantial increase in requests for support from colleagues who were beginning to explore them.

In keeping with a commitment to reflective practice, I decided to observe my own learning closely as I revisited the assumptions and concepts of open and flexible learning and set about acquiring some new skills. I hoped that this would provide insights that could inform my development work. The outcome has been both reinforcement and further development of my views about appropriate ways of helping colleagues when they begin to engage in the same learning. These views are summarised in this chapter.

Getting under way: personal practical knowledge and the meaning of open and flexible learning

Some of what I have come to know about open and flexible learning is *public general knowledge* – acquired as I read the literature and listened to and talked with expert practitioners in this area. Some of what I now know is *personal practical knowledge* – constructed when I reflected on my own experiences when engaging in open and flexible learning and arranging opportunities for others to do the same. I value both forms. Whereas the value of personal, practical knowledge finds support (see Schön, 1983; 1987; Argyris 1982) and is shared by most teaching developers (for example, Boud *et al.* 1994), I recognise that it is not shared by all of my colleagues. Many perceive public general knowledge to have greater validity and enduring value, particularly in academic learning situations. In my staff development role, I endeavour to challenge this perception by explicitly valuing and drawing on their personal practical knowledge and helping them develop it more.

An appropriate occasion for doing this arises when I begin to work with colleagues who have expressed an interest in open and flexible learning. I offer them a self-directed learning package of activities that both concern and embody features of these forms of learning and which are intended to help them recognise that they already have related personal experiences and practical knowledge to draw on as they

- identify defining features of open and flexible learning;
- assess the extent to which their existing courses incorporate these features; and
- distinguish the pros and cons of a commitment to changing courses so that they are more open and flexible.

What are some of the specific ingredients of the package? The beginning activity prompts them to reflect on circumstances and events associated with a recent occasion when they have learned something (unrelated to their teaching and research roles) that they valued. For example:

- Why did you set out to learn this?
- When did you do your learning?
- Where did you learn?
- How did you learn?
- How did you decide how you would learn?
- Who was involved in your learning?
- How did you know that your learning was complete and successful?

They will be prompted to then compare these circumstances and events with those experienced typically by students in their courses.

This analysis reveals that everyday, non-formal learning characteristically embodies opportunities to (learn how to) make decisions about what to learn, how to go about learning, when to learn, where to learn, as well as learning the criteria for judging the success of learning and how to express and apply what has been learned. In these terms, learning is open and flexible. Most teachers consider these features to be positives in the context of their personal day-to-day learning, but conclude that they are not strongly represented in the course-based learning that their students engage in.

This sets the scene for further activities that provide an opportunity for them to encounter some of the basic assumptions, concepts and language associated with open and flexible learning (for example, by reading excerpts from Derek Rowntree's text *Exploring Open and Distance Learning*), to learn about the motives and efforts of some of their colleagues who have set out to develop courses that are more open and flexible, and to consider the potential of open and flexible learning in their own courses. Throughout they are encouraged to reflect critically on, record and share their response to suggested learning activities as well as emerging ideas and feelings about the subject matter.

This learning package has proved an appropriate and effective way of helping colleagues to begin to venture into this territory. It is also a convenient test-bed for my own exploration of the skills that I continue to develop. I choose to work face-to-face, however, when helping them explore a further set of concepts and issues that I believe should be addressed when such approaches are being considered.

Establishing a context: concepts of effective and educative teaching

I invariably share my own assumptions about the nature of effective teaching and the purposes of higher education with colleagues when beginning to help them develop their teaching. I do this both to prompt them to reflect on their own assumptions and to account for the agenda that I propose for exploring particular approaches – including those associated with open and flexible learning.

A core assumption is that teachers who are best equipped to facilitate their students' learning have the following general attributes:

- a rich repertoire of teaching methods and skills;
- sensitivity to factors that make particular ways of teaching more or less appropriate;
- good control of specific teaching skills;
- willingness and capacity to 'research' their own teaching;
- awareness that the choices they make concerning teaching and learning objectives and approaches are shaped by their beliefs about the primary purposes of education. They can make those beliefs explicit and teach in ways that 'fit' these purposes. In this sense, their teaching is 'educative'.

(Haigh and Katterns 1984: 23–7)

An agenda for teaching development based on these criteria includes extending repertoire, increasing sensitivity, gaining control, undertaking research and examining assumptions about teaching and learning. How does this agenda unfold as I continue to help my colleagues explore open and flexible learning?

I observe that the terms 'open' and 'flexible' learning have been variously associated with views about:

- the purposes of education;
- accessibility of learning/education opportunities;
- the appropriateness of particular learning and teaching approaches.

When commenting on the first of these conceptions, I draw my colleagues' attention to the similarity between this and the New Zealand legislation that defines the primary purpose of university education as 'concerned with more advanced learning, the principle purpose being to develop intellectual independence' (New Zealand Education Amendment Act 1990: 33). We then tease out what it might mean to be intellectually independent, review the case for giving this purpose priority and identify some ways of facilitating independence (Haigh 1994). In turn, this allows me to emphasise the relevance of the extensive literature on open and flexible learning to tertiary teaching and learning.

When observing that this legislative mandate is compatible with the first conception, I also prompt them to examine it critically. Is independence valued universally? Are there any other higher-order outcomes that might be valued equally or more highly by some groups? Are other valued outcomes compatible with or antagonistic to independence? For example, when working with Maori colleagues, we have explored the concept of intellectual *interdependence* as well as independence. The former acknowledges that individual lives – including learning lives – are inextricably bound into those of others. Maori values concerning cooperative, communal behaviour mean that the sensitivities and skills required for learning and working together are given very high priority. In addition, learning goals determined by a wider reference group may be given precedence over personal learning goals.

The internationalisation of tertiary education has also helped to increase awareness of the differing views about teaching and learning that students can hold. For example, more teachers now appreciate that, for some Asian students, the expectation that they will wish to (learn how to) take responsibility for aspects of their learning conflicts with a cultural viewpoint that teachers have the responsibility to determine such matters; recent research on teacher and student conceptions of learning and teaching provides further insights. While concepts of open and flexible learning that emphasise flexible adjustment of objectives and approaches can accommodate such contrastive views, it may also require a reappraisal of the place that a 'becoming independent' agenda has in associated programmes.

From my experience, raising these issues with colleagues produces several important dividends. First, their response to advocacy of open and flexible learning is more likely to be a balanced and 'critical' one. They are less likely to become either 'instant converts' who want to step off the stage of face-to-face teaching immediately and become the authors of self-directed learning packages delivered through the Internet, or 'rejecters' who see such approaches as a fundamental threat to their continuing role and status as teachers. Second, they are more likely to understand why some of their colleagues and their students will almost inevitably hold views about the merits of open and flexible learning approaches that differ from their own. Finally, it opens up an opportunity to encourage them to talk with their students about the purposes of higher education and the rationale for adopting particular teaching and learning approaches. Teachers usually need to be presented with a coherent and persuasive case for changing the way they do things. I suggest that their students are entitled to the same.

We move on then to consider open and flexible learning conceived of in terms of distinctive learning (and teaching) approaches and discuss the following agenda for becoming effective in their use.

Considering the repertoire of methods, skills and tools that can be used to facilitate open and flexible learning

I draw the teachers' attention to the extensive body of relevant literature, and identify colleagues on site who are a further rich repository of valuable personal practical knowledge as well as technical skill. Their stories, which are likely to deal with difficulties they have encountered or even failures as well as successes, provide an important adjunct to book-based information which tends not to dwell on the former. With this in mind, the university's Teaching and Learning Development Unit has begun to publish narrative-type accounts of the initiatives of some of these teachers and is preparing a directory of staff who are prepared to work with their colleagues in this way.

Exploring actions that should be taken into account when drawing from this repertoire

I indicate potential sources for such insights (for example, their own 'action research', formal research findings, colleagues' accounts).

Becoming competent and confident in the use of particular techniques and tools

I emphasise that practice and fine-tuning will often be prerequisites to this.

Researching their own programmes and methods

I observe that such research or piloting has always been strongly advocated by proponents of open and flexible learning. Again, I alert my colleagues to guidelines, and my own requests for their feedback on features of the introductory learning package serve as a further occasion for considering this aspect. This discussion also provides the opportunity to consider ways in which I might continue to support their learning on an individual or team basis; for example, by

- helping them devise an appropriate agenda for learning new skills and for beginning to use these;

186

- encouraging them to reflect on the experiences that they begin to have and prompting such reflection;
- locating and offering additional resources and examples, as their experience grows and they embark on specific design projects; and
- sharing my own experiences and insights.

My decisions about ways of supporting staff when they are clearly beginners are influenced by my own reflections on the experience of being a novice and the insights offered by theory and research concerning changes in the mental life of people as they journey from being a novice towards being an expert.

Helping teachers journey from novice towards expert

My understanding of the nature of this journey has been helped by recent scholarship on expertise. I have found one particular model (Dreyfus and Dreyfus 1986) of skill acquisition to be particularly illuminating. This model differentiates performance status according to the individual's perceptions of the task that they are learning and their modes of decision-making when performing the skill. Five stages are differentiated along the route from novice to expert: novice; advanced beginner; competent; proficient; expert. Dreyfus and Dreyfus also make recommendations for the teaching and learning approaches that would be more appropriate for learners at different stages. Here are some of the defining features of the novice and expert stages which have particular relevance to this commentary.

Novice

The novice:

- has no experience or has limited experience;
- has trouble deciding the relevant facts, features, actions;
- needs to learn to recognise a limited number of elements of situations relevant to certain actions;
- needs context-free rules to guide their actions so that they know that if (this feature) occurs, then (that action) is needed;
- often applies these rules regardless of what else is happening around them;
- suffers from severe limitation of capacity to talk or listen to advice because exercise of skill requires so much concentration;
- judges how well they are doing by how well they are following the rules;
- needs support while they generate their own experience to learn from.

Expert

In the case of the expert:

- their skills are part of them;
- when things are proceeding normally, they don't solve problems and don't make decisions – they just do 'what normally works';
- they use intuition and deep understanding but cannot always provide convincing, rational explanations for their 'know-how';
- they recognise things holistically, have great perceptual acuity and zero-in on the real problem very quickly and accurately;
- when time permits and outcomes are crucial, they deliberate before acting – their action is not analytical, rather it involves critical reflection on their intuitions; their thinking is only analytical if absolutely necessary;
- with expertise comes fluid performance: things happen unconsciously, naturally, automatically.

What implications has this model had for the type of support that I endeavour to provide?

Setting a modest agenda

First, the model has helped me to recognise that the learning agenda often needs to be a relatively modest one. So I help the teachers identify some general-purpose routines or skills that they could learn and can use. I observe that 'getting practical experience' needs to be a priority when we are novices, because it is from experience that we will learn many of the important things to do with using skills well. Often I need to resist my inclination as an enthusiastic teacher to overwhelm them with a surfeit of 'good ideas that they could try out' – particularly ideas that will not be fully meaningful when they lack experiences to relate them to.

Providing experiences appropriate to beginners

Second, the model has helped me refine my ideas about the types of experiences that the teachers may need as beginners and that I can help provide. Some experiences will involve trying out and polishing particular skills or techniques. Often they can do this initially in the context of existing programmes and materials (for example, describing anticipated learning outcomes; writing self-assessment questions and feedback; using a conversational style of written language; and giving readers signposts through materials). Other experiences will provide opportunities for learning about what can be involved in selecting and integrating these skills in order to complete a significant practical task – the process that Phil Race has referred to as 'stitching the bits together' (Race 1994:

114). My own experiences and observations suggest that it is uncertainty about how to manage the process of thinking about all of the bits that often accounts for teachers not moving from knowing about to actually doing.

What strategies might we then use to help them learn what can be involved? Sometimes it is appropriate to guide the teachers through a carefully selected and staged series of activities that cumulatively provide a representation of what it can be like to engage in a design activity. We can make it clear that this approach doesn't represent a prescriptive model for doing the activity or that this is all that can be involved. Colleagues who have just moved beyond beginner status can provide retrospective, 'warts-and-all' accounts of what particular planning episodes actually involved. There are some published versions of such accounts (Wright 1994; Cubitt et al. 1994). Michael Parer has compiled some 'tales from the mud' (Parer 1989) which capture in similar fashion what this process can involve when an academic developer helps a teacher stitch the bits together. Phil Race (1994) helps his readers out by suggesting an overall 'strategy for writing open learning materials'. He builds a convincing case for trying out the strategy by sharing the personal experiences and observations that underpin it and that a beginner is likely to relate to; others (Rowntree 1994) provide similar 'route maps'.

There are also experiences that provide an opportunity for the beginner to recognise, for themselves, when situations are the same or are different, the relative importance of different features and whether other ways of doing things need to be learned. As these insights are gained and adjustments are tried out, the teachers are beginning to move away from rule-guided 'knowing that' to experience-based 'know-how' (Dreyfus and Dreyfus 1986: 19). We can help out here by gradually exposing them to more variants of open and flexible learning approaches and prompting them to consider similarities and differences when contrasted with those already encountered.

Enabling experts to teach novices

Third, the model has also helped me account for, and to some extent address, difficulties proficient and expert people sometimes have when trying to teach beginners. The very nature of expertise can make it difficult, if not impossible, for the expert to recognise what their expertise actually constitutes and, in turn, to articulate it to others. This applies in particular to the thoughts and thinking that are a crucial component of most skills. Expert teachers are not immune to this potential difficulty. There are some techniques that we can use to help accomplished performers recognise and reveal the character of their 'know-how'. They include stimulated recall, talk aloud protocols, stream of consciousness records. These are techniques that I am exploring in the context of my staff development work. Dreyfus and Dreyfus (1986) caution, however, that although they are useful for capturing the know-how of competent people, such techniques may provide a very impoverished or distorted representation of what is really involved in proficient or expert performance. For example, when asked to describe what they are doing, experts often revert to stating the rules that they learned and applied as a beginner but manifestly are not using now.

Developing realistic plans

Fourth, I have also introduced the model to beginners to help them understand the nature of the journey that they are embarking on and then to assist them to develop realistic plans for it. Sometimes this is an occasion for talking about handling the 'don't knows' and uncertainties that will inevitably be experienced as well as the 'getting worse before getting better' phenomenon that is integral to learning that transforms ways of doing things. And at times, the conclusion is reached that it makes more sense for them to draw on the expertise of other people rather than set out to develop it themselves. I observe that this has been recognised by many who have accumulated experience in the development of open and flexible learning resources and are strong advocates for team-based development.

Acknowledging context: institutional teaching and learning culture

While I have experienced great satisfaction and some success working closely with colleagues who have wanted to learn more about facilitating open and flexible learning (Scott *et al.* 1997), I have recognised that the time–cost effectiveness of this work can be questioned in the absence of an explicit and tangible institutional commitment to encouraging, supporting and rewarding the efforts of these teachers. Until recently, such a commitment was not apparent in my university. However, several recent developments have signalled that such commitment has been given and a more pervasive shift in the teaching and learning culture may well be under way. Two developments in particular provide evidence for this. First, the implementation of a strategic planning process during the last few years has led to the adoption of institution-wide teaching- and learning-related objectives as well as strategies and criteria for their achievement. Some objectives concern the adoption of open/flexible learning goals and approaches, for example:

- encouragement of the flexible delivery of courses and programmes;
- ensuring that courses provide opportunities for independent learning; and
- encouragement of diverse and innovative styles of learning and teaching, including interactive computer-based material.

The second development is the Vice-Chancellor's Initiative in Teaching and Learning (or VITAL), which confirms a commitment at the highest level of management to promote innovations in teaching and learning. This represents one of the key strategies for achieving the strategic plan objectives noted above. The specific objectives are to

- establish an institution-wide awareness of these approaches and associated technological applications;
- help academic and support staff acquire the knowledge and skills required to use these approaches and associated technology effectively;
- identify the most appropriate models for a team-based approach to development; and
- make a costs/benefits analysis of the use of these approaches and tools for both the university and the students.

A wide range of strategies is being used to achieve these objectives – including support, monitoring and publicising of a number of projects which involve the (re)development of courses so that they are more open and flexible and, where appropriate, make greater use of information technology.

Understandably, as a staff developer I have been greatly heartened and motivated by these moves. In response to them, I have continued to give priority to building my own repertoire, sensitivity and control in respect to the skills and tools available for facilitating open and flexible learning. The gap between my advocacy and practice is closing and as it does, my capacity to help my colleagues address the same agenda grows.

References

Argyris, C. (1982) *Reasoning, Learning and Action*, San Francisco: Jossey-Bass.

Boud, D., Keogh, R. and Walker, D. (1994) *Reflection: Turning Experience into Learning*, London: Kogan Page.

Cubitt, J., Hodgson, T. and Norman, E. (1994) 'A flexible learning strategy for design and technology students', in W. Wade, K. Hodgkinson, A. Smith and J. Arfield (eds), *Flexible Learning in Higher Education*, London: Kogan Page.

Dreyfus, H.L. and Dreyfus, S.E. (1986) *Mind over Machine: The Power of Human Intuition and Expertise in the Era of the Computer*, Oxford: Basil Blackwell.

Haigh, N.J. (1994) 'Promoting intellectual independence: a legislative catalyst', paper presented at the Annual Conference of the Higher Education Research and Development Society of Australasia, Canberra.

Haigh, N. and Katterns, R. (1984) 'Teacher effectiveness: problem or goal for teacher education', *Journal of Teacher Education* 35(5): 23–7.

Kember, D. (1991) *Writing Study Guides*, Bristol: Technical and Educational Services.

Kolb, D. (1984) *Experiential Learning: Experience as the Source of Learning and Development*, Englewood Cliffs, NJ: Prentice-Hall.

New Zealand Education Amendment Act (1990) Section 162 (4), p. 33.

Oliver, R., Herrington, J., Herrington, A. and Sparrow, L. (1996) 'Developing an interactive multimedia package for tertiary teaching: processes and issues', paper presented at the Annual Conference of the Higher Education and Research Society of Australasia, Perth.

Parer, M.S. (ed.) (1989) *Development, Design and Distance Education*, Churchill, Vic.: Centre for Distance Learning, Gippsland Institute.

Race, P. (1994) *The Open Learning Handbook: Promoting Quality in Designing and Delivering Flexible Learning*, London: Kogan Page.

Rowntree, D. (1992) *Exploring Open and Distance Learning*, London: Kogan Page.

—— (1994) *Preparing Materials for Open, Distance and Flexible Learning: An Action Guide for Teachers and Trainers*, London: Kogan Page.

Schön, D.A. (1983) *The Reflective Practitioner: How Professionals Think in Action*, London: Temple Smith.

—— (1987) *Educating the Reflective Practitioner*, San Francisco: Jossey-Bass.

Scott, J., Buchanan, J. and Haigh, N. (1977) 'Reflections on student centered learning in a large class setting', *British Journal of Educational Technology* 28(1): 19–30.

Wade, W., Hodgkinson, K., Smith, A. and Arfield, J. (eds) (1994) *Flexible Learning in Higher Education*, London: Kogan Page.

Wright, I. (1994) 'A distance learning programme for design engineers', in W. Wade, K. Hodgkinson, A. Smith and J. Arfield (eds) *Flexible Learning in Higher Education*, London: Kogan Page.

19

THE DYNAMICS OF DISTANCE TEACHING

Voices from the field

Liz Burge and Jennifer O'Rourke

Among the legacies of the industrial models of distance education are the views of faculty development as a process of orientating newcomers so they 'learn the ropes' of an established system as quickly as possible. Implicit in this approach are two assumptions: that teaching at a distance is sufficiently different from classroom teaching to require acquisition of a new set of specialised skills; and that distance teaching is so consistent in practice across all disciplines and contexts that the mastery of a few simple universal principles should be all that is needed.

Fortunately, these views have been challenged by practitioners' observations that teaching at a distance, like all other forms of teaching, requires continuous reflection and learning by instructors as well as learners. Those directly involved suggest that on-going, peer-supported learning about effective distance teaching practice is more in keeping with the principle of respecting the individuality of the learning process; a principle widely espoused by distance educators (Lentell 1994; 1996; De Vries *et al.* 1995; Malnarich and Gunn 1996). This approach is in contrast to the model of faculty development in which instructors new to distance teaching are imprinted once and for all like a bar of mint rock.

Franklin (1992: 26–9) suggests that a highly structured and systematised approach to staff development reflects a production model of instruction, whereas a supportive approach is more in keeping with a growth model of learning. The growth model is a holistic process that can prompt gradual rethinking of prior beliefs and habits as it cultivates a new repertoire of attitudes and skills. The process involves two intrinsic drives to human action: *competence* – the skills, knowledge and attitudes to operate autonomously; and *connectedness* – the sense of belonging in rewarding relationships (MacKeracher 1996). Such a model provides a focus for considering faculty development.

We may ask to what extent does any activity, planned or unplanned, promote competence and connectedness? And how does the growth model operate in practice? Using a qualitative approach to talk directly with five teachers, we heard thoughtful reflections and responses to these questions.

The teachers

Our five teachers were chosen for their range and diversity of teaching experience. All teach courses for the University of New Brunswick (UNB), where distance courses are offered by means of various real-time conferencing technologies – audioconferencing, audiographics and videoconferencing – complemented by course materials. A set of questions explored three aspects of these teachers' experience:

- the origins of their distance teaching – kinds of help sought or received, feelings and needs;
- the present situation – things enjoyed and not enjoyed, any changes made in teaching styles; and
- the future – any professional development needs, and how they might help their peers to teach at a distance.

The comments of these five teachers indicate that instructors need to devise their own ways of learning about distance teaching, in the same way that they develop different teaching approaches for other contexts they encounter. This individuality does not mean that they should be left on their own, but that they should be able to determine the pace, timing and manner in which they learn what they need to know in order to be effective distance educators. Ideally, there is appropriate support available for them whenever they need it, and there are opportunities for on-going discussion and reflection among peers and instructional resource staff. As well, promoting the sense of continuity between good teaching practice in the face-to-face classroom and good teaching practice at a distance provides a sense of greater competence and confidence: instructors realise they are simply adding new strings to their bows, not changing instruments.

Their voices

Lesley is a professional librarian new to teaching. She is completing her Master's degree in Adult Education and became the part-time coordinator of a distance programme in 1995; she also received a grant to adapt the course to an audiographics mode. She did not seek out nor expect much help in the early stages, except to consult the prior coordinator whose professional judgement she trusted, and two adult educators whose distance teaching experience she respected.

Now in her second year of teaching, she has addressed some of her initial concerns. 'How do I establish contact [not the technical kind], feeling some connection? It's a compromise. . . . A face-to-face workshop early in the course helps strengthen connections among members of the group.' Lesley now also feels more confident to encourage students to use their own experience, to use higher levels of thinking.

> I make a connection with each student in the first half hour of class to confirm they are present and engaged in the topic under discussion. Prompting each student to join in at the beginning of class promotes student-to-student discussion as the evening progresses.

She identifies other developments in her teaching abilities.

> I feel I develop a rapport with my students, both on-site and at a distance. I know how they want to learn and the pressures they are under. My confidence and experience have grown to allow me to act quickly on my feelings about how a learning activity is working, and I've established my own ways of doing things.

As the programme expands to include advanced courses, Lesley is now interested in learning more about course design and development of effective course packages, but she adds, 'What I am doing is working well.'

Judith has taught twelve audioconferenced courses and four videoconferenced courses since 1991. She learned how to do it 'by the seat of my pants' with some help about equipment operation and support about distance teaching from colleagues who reassured her that distance education does work. She felt she needed most to learn about 'how to help students connect – how to make them feel part of a group'.

Her teaching style focuses on learner discussion rather than lectures, on helping learners express developing insights and transforming perspectives, so an early concern was 'How much of a transformative process can distance education be? How can I hear the light bulbs going off in their heads?' Using her usual facilitation strategies she most enjoys distance students' willingness to share their experiences and respond to her prompting questions. 'I walk in with a set of questions, not a set of lecture notes.'

Judith comments that distance teaching did not require a major re-orientation: 'I didn't have to break bad old habits.' But she knows that after teaching sixteen courses, she has gained a lot of confidence as a facilitator, especially in her ability to 'see' unseen students as individual personalities. In particular, she has learned to trust students to pull out the salient points to be learned and discuss them in some depth (MacIntosh 1993).

Judith usually sees herself as calm, cool and collected under the pressures of malfunctioning technology. However, distance education changes the scheduling of her workload: 'August is a busy month because all the materials have to be prepared in advance.' Travel is an added demand when, to 'connect' with students, she visits sites across the province once per term. Her approach is practical: '[I] use teaching strategies appropriate to what I'm trying to teach, and then pick the technology to suit.' Her advice for novice teachers is: 'You don't need the most expensive technology to do a good job.' She would also say: '[Get] information about the technology and get it out of the way; sit in on a few classes – attend to the role-modelling and interaction management; and read some articles.' In common with colleagues in distance teaching, she likes the idea of getting the student view, especially 'to experience what it's like to be at a distance'.

Peter had had a twenty-year teaching career before his recent move into part-time teaching of adult education degree courses. He has used audioconferencing for one of these courses and audiographics conferencing for the other. He consulted with people who had taught the course before and people who had used audioconferencing, and believes that '50 per cent of my learning came from just talking, and 50 per cent from reading'. Talking, reading and sitting in on a live class showed him the essential logistical procedures and organisation of the course. He did not expect formal help from UNB but relied on learning as the need arose: 'As you stumble, you look for resources; [and] it didn't look that complex [anyway].' His biggest concerns were the 'lack of visual clues' in audioconferencing sessions because he had seen instances where learners at a remote site talked on their own and made jokes while the guest speaker talked on his own topic. Peter needs to see the learners' reactions to what he does.

How did Peter deal with the problem of distance?

> I had to dive in and try . . . after twenty years [of teaching], I felt I could wing it without the visual cues. [But] after a while, I ended up using the [learners] in front of me as representatives, as resonators of how the whole class may be feeling [out there].

When the time came to teach his second course, he was asked to use audiographics. And here he reflected on a sudden insight about his role *vis-à-vis* the technology:

> I was scared because I had to prepare all my graphic slides ahead of time. . . . I thought I had to change my teaching style because of the technology. Then one day a student called asking how the technology would work, and I found myself saying that I'm going to use the graphics software just as a blackboard [during live discussions]. I would make the technology fit me, not me fit the technology. It was like a paradigm shift.

Another turning point was his strong reaction to a disk containing clip art: he found the images and the assumptions behind the production of such a disk 'abysmal and demeaning'. He rejected it outright. He uses audiographics only to enable everyone to make notes and summaries in written, essential or pictorial

196

form, rather than using it more formally for prepared lectures and detailed visuals. However, he believes that the 'little improvement' the technology gives him (for publicly visible note-making) is not balanced by the extra operating costs of audiographics technology. Peter's experience so far of teaching one course by audioconferencing and one by audiographics has clarified the impact of the technology: 'I've de-toxified a dragon – the dragon [technology] is a pussy cat. It's not as complex or as difficult as one is led to believe when all that jargon about it is used.'

He most enjoys the fact that distance teaching enables learners to get access to the course: 'Before I started teaching [by audioconference], I had a really negative attitude, but then one day a student told me about the joy she felt in being able to take the course, in the comfort of her sitting room, with several other learners.' Peter has learned that the real learning about how to 'do' distance teaching is 'not from advice from others; it's from how you adapt in the situation and learn from experience'. He feels the quality of the audioconference and audiographics classrooms to be 'ephemeral – sound structures aren't the same as visual structures; sound is based on memory', so he believes an effective teacher needs rapid response skills and close attention to the immediate moment.

To help a colleague learn to be a good teacher, he would encourage them to be a student in an audioconferenced or audiographics class and experience the positive and negative conditions of the class as any student might. And he says: 'Don't lose your judgement, or sense of who you are – don't be awed or intimidated by the technology.'

Elaine had taught for six years before beginning distance teaching three years ago. UNB had encouraged her faculty to become involved in distance teaching and apply for government funds for the development of distance mode courses. For her, the initial experience was not a positive one. She had no prior formal training in instructional design, and because little help on the use of audiographics was available, she had to find experienced colleagues and resource materials herself. Her immediate needs were for criteria and strategies for generic course design, followed by attention to the equipment and audiographics software. She says: 'It still comes back to basic and good instructional design.' Indeed, her feelings are strong on this point, 'I don't believe there's any difference in teaching [by audiographics]: it's the process of becoming an effective teacher.'

She treats the audiographics context as a small group discussion, one in which she explains particular concepts interactively for fifteen minutes, then has the students discuss them and solve problems. The style is somewhat similar to her face-to-face class style but there are more demands and opportunities for group dynamics than on campus, where lecture theatres limit group interaction. She has honed her listening skills, and can rely on her ability to check on students' understandings, especially now that she has local students with her in the room. The process feels to Elaine as if 'we're all in the same boat, but I'm steering'.

She has learned that preparedness is a relentless requirement of audiographics: 'It takes me four times as long to prepare for audiographics as it does for my face-to-face class.' The technology prompts another frustration: every class that uses audiographics results in a loss of about fifteen minutes at the outset for set-up. But her students cannot come to class unprepared or 'hide' in the audio-based speaking medium because they have to meet the responsibilities of small-group work and respond to real-time questions.

Despite her less-than-positive initiation and having to learn distance teaching skills on the job, Elaine has reassuring advice for novice distance teachers. 'You need to be enthusiastic, and feel excited and challenged. With that attitude it's not hard to do. Talk to those who have used audiographics. . . . Networking is very important. If [your basic] design is good, the conversion to the technology is easy.' In her view, the key task for university administrators is to address a key fallacy – 'they think we're all good teachers' – and ensure that faculty receive adequate training in how to teach effectively. Only by building on this is training in instructional technology relevant.

Peggy Holt has twenty-three years' teaching experience. After teaching two adult education courses by audiographics and one course by audioconferencing, she has become an enthusiastic distance teacher. But there were some initial reservations. 'I read two articles that stressed how lonely the teacher can be. . . . I felt I'd have to be more structured than I like to be in a face-to-face class: it might get boring with every activity already planned. . . . I worried about not being able to see them.'

Peggy received valuable initial help from experienced colleagues who reassured her that her existing teaching skills were transferable, who explained how the printed course manuals were designed to work, and who helped her find answers to problems. Support staff also provided operational and logistical help.

After teaching three distance courses, Peggy identified some key issues from reflecting about her experience: 'You can't ramble. . . . I didn't use my listening skills as much in the [face-to-face classroom]. . . . I now speak more clearly [pronunciation] and slowly. My voice is my instrument.'

She values being well-organised, and comes to class physically rested: 'It's a performance.'

Why does she 'love' teaching by audiographics? Because the students are forced to become self-responsible learners, and the technology enables the production of creative graphics to explain concepts and integrate the students into a whole: 'We colour code the sites as they write on the screen.' She now appreciates the silences in the predominantly audio classrooms: 'I now feel more confident – I don't have to fill every second with talk; I can wait for the answer . . . [actually] when you give them time to think, you get a better response.' She is attentive too for 'the things that people won't say out loud'.

Peggy is adamant about the need to recognise three skills essential to use on-line time effectively: 'Organisation, presentation of self, and anticipation. . . . It's like shooting pool: when you set up the shot, you need to know where the ball is going. . . . If you're always catching up [repairing mistakes], you're wasting time.'

Peggy is equally clear about four adult learning principles that need to be applied by faculty new to distance teaching:

- know how to help students take responsibility for their learning;
- promote collaborative learning;
- help students reflect on and use their prior life experience; and
- be creative and non-verbal to represent ideas and theories.

To help in such learning, and to reduce novices' fears about technology, she encourages them to be assertive in asking questions and insistent on finding answers.

Commentary

The comments from these teachers reveal how individual is the process of learning about teaching. One person wants a clear picture and pre-planned strategies before embarking on the process; another wants to try it out and then consider what works best; yet another wants to have opportunities for reflection at various stages in the teaching process; while another prefers to have a general idea of the territory and a sense of others' experiences before starting out. Despite their differences in preferred timing and approaches to their own development, there are common elements in what they value: experience as a learner in distance education; support and insights from peers; self-awareness and confidence in one's personal teaching style; and timely access to people who can help with technology and demystify its use.

All the teachers convey a sense of the purposeful use of technology, trusting in their own judgement about what is appropriate and useful. They recognise that they have maintained their teaching style while they have adapted their teaching strategies to deal with the reality that they were not in direct face-to-face contact with learners. Their observations about the changes in teaching techniques required for using audioconferencing and audiographics show that it is possible to allow for spontaneity, reflection and learner responsibility, even though teaching at a distance also demands a considerable amount of pre-planning, advance preparation of learning material, and enhanced attention to class dynamics.

The distinction between teaching style and teaching strategies is important. For those whose teaching style is already highly interactive, the move from an interactive traditional classroom to a conferenced situation is not dramatic. But for someone accustomed to a transmission model of teaching, it can be much more stressful to use a technology that is predicated on interaction. The teachers indicated that their adaptation was one of procedure, rather than a transformed conceptual approach.

Conclusion

To enhance distance teaching skills entails distinguishing between the more static course elements usually planned well in advance with attention to clarity and structure, and the more fluid dynamics of real-time interaction in distance teaching, requiring timely, focused interventions. The relatively static elements, particularly course materials, have been discussed extensively and often prescriptively in the literature, because they are the permanent and visible component of the course. The relatively fluid elements are discussed to a much lesser extent, perhaps because they are the unpredictable, ephemeral and invisible building blocks of learning, or possibly because they are regarded as the same as traditional classroom dynamics, which are assumed to be familiar to all teachers.

Just as skilful distance teaching requires balancing the static and fluid elements of a course to suit the content, context and teaching style, effective faculty development requires balancing the emphasis on each of the two elements. Placing too much emphasis on the planning and preparation of the static elements, the course materials, can intimidate prospective distance teachers, especially if there are limited support systems and resources. And ignoring the importance of the fluid elements, the interaction, can place teachers in a position where they feel unprepared, fall back on one-way communication, and risk losing the attention of the students.

The question of balance between the static and fluid elements is essential whether a particular institutional framework places more emphasis on a prepared course package (complemented by print, telephone or computer interaction) or on the interactive sessions (complemented by prepared course materials). Support for faculty in distance education has to offset any institutional bias towards either one of these elements by addressing faculty learning needs about both preparation of resources and about facilitating an interactive teaching/ learning process. Planning is essential for both elements: '[planning] is crucial to good facilitating, even if you hope to make your facilitating strategies spontaneous' (MacKeracher 1996: 256).

Using facilitation techniques that support a sense of continuity and connectedness, a skilled instructor can weave together a 'class' of responsive learners, whether they are dispersed individuals whose contact is by print, phone or computer messages, or groups connected in real time by conferencing technologies.

Prospective distance teachers can be encouraged to look for that balance and to identify what they need to learn about both the static and fluid elements of distance teaching. They can find out more about the interpersonal element by taking a distance education course as a student, as our interviewees indicated, and as other experienced educators have noted (Haag 1992). For faculty, being introduced to the receiving end of technology while in a more relaxed role as learners and observers helps develop a sense of its appropriate use without the pressure to master it immediately. They can consider which strategies will work well for particular teaching and learning goals and which techniques will need some adaptation.

Despite enthusiastic claims that the technology is 'transparent', experience shows that the technology appears transparent only when a teacher has skilfully adapted strategies to work with a particular medium. For example, audio-conferencing requires much more careful attention to sound and silences, to feeling and thinking. Experienced distance teachers know when to intervene and when to stay quiet, when to encourage expression and when to encourage reflection. Down-playing the need to learn how to use a given technology appropriately, not just operate its controls, can result in frustration and dis-appointment, or even a resolve to give up distance teaching. On the other hand, portraying the technology as a specialised medium only for expert use can result in talented teachers missing an opportunity to expand their repertoire of skills.

Balance is an appropriate concept for summarising this chapter. Keeping one's balance means 'not being distracted from the fundamentals of good teaching' (Haag 1992). Balance means giving equal attention to our existing values and reflective experience and our emerging values and reflection-in-action as we try out new techniques and technologies. Balance implies that the teacher is a connoisseur of learning, not merely an uncritical user of others' recipes. Balance is about, finally, managing that delicate dynamic between the stresses of taking on new teaching contexts and the comforts of maintaining old habits. In short, balance is about competence and connectedness.

References

Burge, E.J. (1996) 'Inside-out thinking about distance teaching: making sense of reflective practice', *Journal of the American Society of Information Science* 47(11): 843–8.

De Vries, L., Naidu, S., Jegede, O.J. and Collins, B.A. (1995) 'On-line professional staff development: an evaluation study', *Distance Education* 16(1): 157–63.

Franklin, U. (1992) *The Real World of Technology*, CBC Massey Lectures, Toronto: CBC/Anansi Press.

Gunawardena, C.N. (1992) 'Changing faculty roles for audiographics and online teaching', *American Journal of Distance Education* 6(3): 58–71.

Haag, S. (1992) 'Speaking personally', *American Journal of Distance Education* 6(3): 72–6.

Landstrom, M. (1995) 'The perception and needs of faculty in distance education courses in a conventional university', *Canadian Journal of Educational Communication* 24(2): 149–57.

Lentell, H. (1994) 'Staff development in distance education: who says it is a good thing?' *Open Praxis* 1: 29–30.

—— (1996) 'Professional development: pertaining to recipes and cooks', *Open Praxis* 1: 40–1.

MacIntosh, J. (1993) 'Focus groups in distance nursing education', *Journal of Advanced Nursing* 18, 1981–85.

MacKeracher, D. (1996) *Making Sense of Adult Learning*, Toronto: Culture Concepts Inc.

Malnarich, G. and Gunn, J. (1996) 'Weaving learning webs: redefining the partnerships – instructional technologists and faculty developers', presented at Connections '96, Vancouver, BC (May).

Soules, M. (1996) *Enhancing Capacity: Videoconferencing at Malaspina University College*, report to the British Columbia Ministry of Education.

20

THE CATALYTIC STAFF DEVELOPMENT EFFECTS OF A CD-ROM PROJECT

David Murphy and Ross Vermeer

This is not a chapter about staff development activities that have the acquisition of multimedia skills as a spin-off. Rather, it is about a multimedia development project that acted as a catalyst for staff development (Race 1989). Essentially, the project involved combining the existing skills of Open University of Hong Kong (OUHK) staff with those of an outside consultant to design and develop a CD-ROM package for a course dealing with the history of Hong Kong. The project gave the OUHK staff the chance to be pathfinders in a technology-based development that could enhance their skills in a variety of ways which are discussed in this chapter.

A context for staff development

You may recognise the following scenario. A notice is circulated by the Staff Development Unit listing all the forthcoming workshops, seminars and conferences. About half-way down is the announcement of a 'hands-on' workshop in the computer laboratory for the latest version of 'Become a multimedia developer in a day'. The applications flood in and a couple of extra sessions have to be organised. Meanwhile, the seminars on 'Identifying students with learning disabilities' and 'Using evaluation to improve learning materials' are cancelled due to lack of interest.

The multimedia workshop is a great success. The demonstrations are riveting and it is amazing just how quickly the participants can learn to import and combine a variety of media – print, audio, video, the excitement is palpable, and everyone goes away simply itching to produce their course on CD-ROM.

Over the next few weeks, various members of staff can be seen inviting their colleagues into their offices to view their on-going developments. Snippets of images float momentarily across screens, and the erstwhile authors enthuse about what will come next, and how great it will be when it is all finished. Six months later, everything is back to normal. Nothing of substance has been produced or utilised. The only evidence that anything had ever happened is the odd file of sad and sorry efforts at the multimedia game left on some computers. Was the lesson learned? One suspects not, judging by the huge number of applicants registered for the upcoming 'Become a Web page designer in a day' workshop.

We have all experienced situations such as this and will probably continue to do so. However, there can be progress, and this chapter describes a relatively modest foray by the OUHK into multimedia development using CD-ROM technology. In particular, it outlines the particular facets of the project that relate to staff development. The staff development we refer to here is that of the course design and development team within the OUHK's Educational Technology and Publishing Unit (ETPU). These staff had plenty of experience in the development of materials using the more traditional media, but required first-hand involvement with new technologies in order to enhance their skills.

As at most distance education institutions, OUHK courses are largely print-based, although many of them also use audiotapes and videotapes. Resource use is quite flexible, in that much of the production work is contracted out, including most of the printing. Recently, through the advent of OUHK Research and Development funding, the opportunity arose to apply new technology to an appropriate course. A central issue was, of course, an assessment of how much relevant skill existed at the OUHK, how much would need to be imported, and how much skill improvement could be achieved. The question of which skills the OUHK needed to develop further was also addressed.

Harnessing new technologies

Much has been claimed in regard to the new and emerging technologies in recent years, though not a lot of this is strongly research-based. We are all well aware of the over-zealous claims made for such technologies, even within reasonably conservative journals and magazines, and thus welcome more reasoned assessments of their power and potential (Bates 1994; Laurillard 1993). As Laurillard has explained:

> It is not feasible to ensure effective teaching through multimedia methods by promulgating prescriptive guidelines on how to design materials, or what to use these methods for. Our use of IT-based media over the last twenty years has been prodigious but it is not matched by our understanding of it, because the emphasis has been on development and use rather than on research and evaluation.
>
> (Laurillard 1993: 223)

Laurillard's contribution to the debate on the relative merits of a variety of educational technologies is instructive because she takes to task some of the more extravagant claims made for these, particularly in the area of hypermedia. Thus, though acknowledging the strengths of hypermedia, such as controllability by the reader and making the structure of a topic completely explicit and highly accessible, she challenges assertions of much stronger benefits, observing that information bases are not the same as knowledge bases, that hypermedia is neither adaptive nor reflective, that the inter-activity of multimedia databases is limited, and that they cannot offer stand-alone teaching:

> They only enable students to explore large quantities of data, making them the equivalent of a small library. None the less, the multimedia database has several advantages over print:
>
> - it can make available the data from which the supporting evidence for a new thesis might be selected;
> - it offers wide margins for annotations, enabling the student to describe their own conception as it relates to items in the database.
>
> (Laurillard 1993: 129)

Part of the power of Laurillard's text is that it places educational technology in context, and addresses the system-wide issues that need attention in order for large-scale technology enterprises to take hold in an institution. Staff development is discussed, albeit briefly (Laurillard 1993: 244–5), but at least there is recognition of the integral role this must play. Laurillard sets forth a framework for development that locates staff development within the 'implementation and student learning' part of the necessary infrastructure.

Staff development with respect to educational technology has in general endured a chequered history in recent decades. Typically, the advent of a new 'educational toy' has meant that someone in an educational technology unit has taken a particular interest in, and developed a measure of expertise with, this technology. This person is then able to run a seminar or workshop to introduce the technology to other staff, and a few are inspired to incorporate it into their teaching. The simpler a technology is to use, the more likely it is to take hold – the now indispensable photocopier is the prime example. The computer is still appreciably more difficult to use, and we are all familiar with staff members within our own institutions who steadfastly refuse to bow to this technology that most of us shudder at the thought of having to do without. Naturally, the staff development we are here interested in involves significantly more than simply enabling staff to use a computer – our interest is in developing skills in the judicious and creative choice and application of technology to the course design and development function.

What does seem to achieve a relative amount of success is the educational technology project that receives recognition and resources from institutional leaders. Further, the relaxing of normal institutional restraints to allow innovation and speedy decision-making add to the possibility of successful outcomes. As will be explained later, these and other factors were instrumental, especially in a staff development sense, in the success of the particular project under discussion.

More particularly, what the project we outline here exemplifies is that quality multimedia development is possible from a relatively modest resource base, provided that the resources can be used flexibly. The OUHK, although it had the requisite instructional design skills, did not have the programming and other related expertise needed to bring the project to fruition. The ability to contract in external expertise meant that the small OUHK team was able to succeed in completing a logistically difficult project with the added benefit of developing their own professional skills.

The project

An internal OUHK survey carried out in 1994 showed that only thirteen of its courses had a computing component, and – much more telling – that all of these computing software packages were externally produced. We decided to leap into the fray of multimedia development and produce an inter-active multimedia (IM) program delivered on CD-ROM, since we had a likely basis for such a project, a newly developed Hong Kong history course. The CD-ROM program was developed under the auspices of a staff research project by a small team, headed by Ross Vermeer, from the ETPU. The project also enjoyed the collaboration of the original course writer, Dr David Faure of the University of Oxford, who wrote additional explanatory text and guided the selection of visual materials. The project offered a direct opportunity to help ETPU staff develop their expertise for future non-print media projects while experimenting with new and more effective ways to deliver teaching materials to the students.

The project, although intended to produce a useful tool for students, was configured as a staff development exercise. This model was born of necessity. The OUHK had no staff with the necessary programming and interface design experience, so we had to seek an external producer. Through an open tendering process involving bids from both educational institutions and commercial producers, the project was awarded to a team of specialists in multimedia development from the Centre for Applied Learning Systems (CALS) at the Adelaide Institute of Technical and Further Education in South Australia. This international cooperative effort gave the project a unique dimension, but it also caused some difficulties: having the support of an educational institution, CALS, strengthened the project in terms of educational input and design, but may have hindered its timing.

Project execution

The work was carried out to a simple, flexible development model for commercial CD-ROM development and design published in *New Media* magazine (Strauss 1994). This model comprises four stages: research, design, production and testing. The OUHK researchers sought and acquired textual and visual resources, managed the project as whole and contributed to the general program design.

The staff from CALS provided additional project management, graphic and interface design, and coding – just what a commercial production house might have provided. OUHK staff will complete the final program testing and evaluation, based primarily on data collected from students using the program, in 1997.

The program features text extracts, photographs and extensive video footage; most of these resources were selected from Hong Kong government sources with very low copyright clearance costs. They are arranged and accessed through what has turned out to be a quite elegant interface. The program's visual design is perhaps its strongest quality; this is of a high standard and is certainly comparable to that in commercial products costing many times the budget for this project.

In its final design, the program comprises four main sections:

- a time-line, conceived as a dragon, showing key events in Hong Kong's history and a pictorial history of the development of Hong Kong's famous harbour and skyline;
- a large section covering a wide range of historical themes and comprising 100 textual extracts, hundreds of photographs and about 20 video clips describing Hong Kong's economic, industrial and political development and its experiences in World War II;
- a map/menu-driven section on towns and districts in Hong Kong and the changes in Central, Kowloon, Shatin and other locations over the years;
- a section which focuses on the ways in which the majority of Hong Kong's people have lived their lives over the years.

Overall, the program contains hundreds of text articles, photographs and other graphical images and over thirty minutes of video footage. A word-search engine gives users immediate access to any part of the program that appears as a search result.

On the whole, the primary project objectives – developing staff experience, using a new technology, and of course developing a useful learning tool for our students – were achieved. Financial constraints imposed through the bidding process did have some effect: accepting the lowest bid impeded the full development of some proposed program features, but not to an extent that rendered it of less value to the researchers or the students.

Staff development implications

How can this multimedia development project be assessed in terms of its contribution to staff development? One way is to reflect on it using a framework developed by Lindquist (1978) as an adaptive development model of innovation (Smith 1992). Lindquist identified five factors as critical ingredients for success: linkage, openness, leadership, ownership and rewards. These are discussed below.

Linkage

If linkages are about getting two sides together, and crossing boundaries, this staff development project did just that. The project was made possible through access to research and development funds specifically designated to cross boundaries and create links among academics. At the OUHK, course development is usually pursued through a closely structured process, due to accreditation and temporal restraints. The funding this project drew upon allowed an escape from the normal OUHK procedures, not by bypassing the need to assess the program's content, but in terms of enacting a new and more flexible development model.

The project also crossed significant institutional and geographical boundaries, linking two quite different institutions in two countries. It was shown that this cross-cultural model for IM development has much to offer. Both sides brought unique experiences and need sets to the process. The Hong Kong team members had access to a wealth of textual and visual resources and had significant experience in designing the print-based course that this IM program is designed to accompany. They lacked the necessary knowledge and skills in IM development. The CALS team from South Australia brought programming, IM development and management skills to the project; not surprisingly, they had no prior experience of work on Hong Kong history.

Both OUHK and CALS staff were therefore 'developed' through this linkage. Working on a project that brought together the skills and experiences of disparate institutions and cultures was found to benefit both institutions in their attempts to serve students better in the increasingly international Pacific Rim.

Openness

Several levels of analysis are appropriate in this regard. First, among the project participants, the novelty of working on a relatively new technology, and in an unusual institutional arrangement, fostered a sense of openness in trying new things and testing out new skills, and this was a strong incentive for staff development at the individual level.

Second, institutional openness was also reflected in the model of staff development that this project encouraged. That is, few restraints were placed upon the researchers once their project was approved; nearly all of the decisions regarding the design and management of the project were left to them. Without this openness, the project would not have been an effective staff development exercise, as true control would have remained out of the investigators' hands, diminishing their chances to learn. For the project to serve as a catalyst for staff development, undetermined possibilities had to pre-exist; this open situation enabled the reaction to take place.

Finally, the OUHK showed openness in making a significant financial investment in something new. Distance education institutions are often committed to researching and developing new technologies, but the relative newness of the OUHK, coupled with its financial constraints (it does not receive regular government funding) have generally discouraged too much expenditure on 'unproven' technologies and the university places heavy reliance upon print. Without an open institutional pocket, therefore, the project could not have gone forward.

Leadership

The project leadership can also be analysed at several levels. First, the impetus for the project as a whole was provided by former Director of the Open Learning Institute (prior to it being renamed the Open University of Hong Kong), Professor Gajaraj Dhanarajan, who led the Institute's research interest in this area. This follows the pattern identified by Bates (1994), in which senior-level managers are the most frequent instigators of the often expensive forays into developing new educational technologies. In this case, OUHK's senior management encouraged and supported a form of collaborative staff development in which the principal investigator was able to develop his capacities as project leader through a model which placed the greatest onus on him as the leader.

The contract between the OUHK and CALS, which clearly specified the latter as a service provider, eliminated the possibility for leadership to be obfuscated between the two institutions: the OUHK team led the project and made all substantive decisions. A more equal 'partnership' between the two institutions could have severely limited the opportunity for the OUHK staff to develop leadership skills, in that staff from CALS, the institution more experienced in IM design, might have been able to assume *de facto* leadership roles.

Ownership

Project ownership in regard to the CD-ROM is difficult to assign to any one person or institution. At the institutional level, the collaborative arrangement between the OUHK and CALS gives ownership to both, although in different senses. CALS now owns a project completed for an international client. This represents a new achievement for them; their previous clients had all been Australian institutions or organisations. The OUHK has gained ownership of an instructional tool that will help them promote the university's image as a leader in educational technology in Hong Kong. There is some pressure for the OUHK to lead in this area, since its methods are demonstrably distinct from those of other local tertiary institutions.

Within the OUHK, the ETPU's ownership of the successfully completed project places the unit in a leadership role within the university, and demonstrates that it is not necessary to be wholly dependent upon in-house knowledge, skills and resources in upgrading staff expertise.

At the personal level, 'owning' the project encouraged the researchers to take their training opportunity seriously: failure to do so would likely have meant the diminished success – or perhaps failure – of the project. New skills and strategies learned were acquired on the job and quickly applied; this ownership of learning made for rapid, and sometimes quite intense, staff development.

Rewards

Managing this fairly large-scale IM development project constituted the core of the principal researcher's staff development. Having direct control over such a major CD-ROM development project forced him not only to manage the project, but also to evaluate the very worth of this project. This is a crucial distinction; being granted such a high degree of autonomy in this project improves vision, in the sense that responsibility is borne for all decisions made. Making hard decisions about which features could or could not be included in the program provided excellent opportunities for learning project management skills.

The evaluative perspective gained through first-hand experience was a unique opportunity for staff development for the course designer. He may not have learned to write code to drive multimedia applications, but he did gain an experiential framework for evaluating technological education tools, an equally valuable skill. Such project management skills fill a significant gap in the world of multimedia, the Web and online education: there are programmers and there are content experts, but there is not always an individual capable of bringing these experts and the elements of the program together in the most effective ways. With the continually rapid pace of change in technology, such a person will in essence be engaged in 'staff development' all of the time, as he or she tries to keep up with new developments and new challenges. As this person gains in experience, judgements improve and potential projects can be better discriminated. This project gave the researchers an excellent opportunity to start out on this road, and being granted such responsibility and opportunity was a major reward in itself.

Managing a Web project should also be a rewarding staff development exercise, since an individual new to the field can more quickly adopt a 'do-it-yourself' approach to a project, and a great deal less money is needed. Such development can also be done more incrementally, with results posted and usable as the process proceeds. CD-ROM-delivered IM programs are by definition harder to test and alter once development has begun. Certain fundamental decisions taken early in the process are virtually unalterable, so any mistakes made are manifest or even magnified in the final version.

At the departmental and institutional levels, more experienced staff are another obvious outcome of this project. The project participants are better equipped to handle projects and manage these creatively with limited resources. Proving this model of staff development to be successful also provides the incentive for others to undertake similar projects under the auspices of staff development.

Conclusions

From the above analysis, it is apparent that, from a staff development perspective, our ETPU CD-ROM project has been a success. It has been a catalyst for moving the OUHK along the multimedia development path and it has provided a firm base for future staff development and technological innovation. We now have a much clearer picture of the strengths and weaknesses of this particular technology and have enhanced our understanding in ways that will help us work more effectively with our colleagues.

To refer back to the illustration at the beginning of this chapter, what we have argued here is that it is not necessary to develop the skills of staff in every regard when undertaking projects involving new technologies. This is especially true for an institution with relatively limited resources. Rather, the key to success is to determine which are the skills worth developing, and if necessary, contract out the rest of the work. Will the OUHK become a major producer of educational CD-ROM material? This seems unlikely. However, those charged with developing multimedia applications have completed a useful project and developed understandings and competencies that stand them in good stead for future work in this area.

References

Bates, A.W. (1994) *Technology, Open Learning and Distance Education*, London: Routledge.

Laurillard, D. (1993) *Rethinking University Teaching: A Framework for the Effective Use of Educational Technology*, London: Routledge.

Lindquist, J. (1978) *Strategies for Change*, Berkeley, CA: Pacific Soundings Press.

Race, P. (1989) *The Open Learning Handbook*, London: Kogan Page.

Smith, G. (1992) 'The innovation of decentralized staff development at Birmingham Polytechnic', *Educational & Training Technology International* 29 (4): 316–20.

Strauss, R. (1994) 'Budgeting and scheduling a CD-ROM Project', *New Media* 4 (2) (February): 99–101.

21

STAFF DEVELOPMENT WITHIN
A FLEXIBLE AND OPEN
LEARNING COURSE

Cathy Gunn and Mary Panko

If people can be brought beyond the mechanical to the visionary
by necessarily developing a whole new set of relating and doing
skills . . . then the shaping of learning environments that stretch
the limits of our vision can begin.

(Cooper 1991: 89)

Trends to raise institutional status and standards through quality assurance
place heavy demands on teaching staff in tertiary institutions in New Zealand.
The expectations are that they will teach more students with fewer resources
by embracing innovative teaching methods and technologies. At the same
time, they are required to gain higher-level qualifications and add research and
publication to their already excessive workloads. This chapter describes a staff
development initiative aimed at promoting greater efficiency in course design,
delivery and management through progress towards the wider adoption of flexible
and open learning.

Staff development as a catalyst for change

Our experience of teaching in tertiary institutions in New Zealand leads us
to believe that the key to successful staff development in the 1990s is the
empowerment of teachers through an understanding of, and the capability to
generate ideas and solutions for, organisational change and appropriate applications of educational principles and new technologies. Such an approach also
supports the development of the requisite skills for the acquisition and creation
of appropriate and innovative resources. Equipped with this comprehensive
knowledge and skills base, such staff should be able to create optimally supportive
learning environments which make efficient use of limited resources.

This view of staff development as a transformational process underpinned the
recent design and delivery of an accredited course in Flexible and Open Learning
offered by UNITEC Institute of Technology in Auckland. This course is based

on the principles of experiential learning and focuses on the relationship between contemporary models of learning and the development and integration of technology-based learning.

The course development concepts

Cooper (1991) presents a teacher-centred model of staff development which we adopted as an underlying philosophy for the Flexible and Open Learning course. This model defines the role of a teacher as an agent of change who is empowered to challenge the political, social and economic forces that shape educational systems and to turn visions of innovation into accepted educational practice through detailed action plans. Another model we referred to was that of inter-active staff development (Griffin 1991), which is defined as a constantly moving, mutually affective relationship of teachers, social perceptions, beliefs and events towards the achievement of desirable ends. In the case of the Flexible and Open Learning course, the desirable end was an extension of the concept of formal education provision to reach a broader range of individuals within the community, facilitated by the capabilities of new technology to support accredited educational programmes through flexible delivery and in non-traditional settings. These objectives are clearly tempered by the current climate of financial constraints, increasing competition and decreasing government support.

With these concepts in mind, we devised a course which we hoped would allow the participants to delineate the opportunities and problems of open and flexible learning and develop their own repertoire of new educational under-standings and technology-related skills through engagement in the practical experience of an open learning environment.

The resulting course, Flexible and Open Learning, was designed to be part of a 120-credit Graduate Diploma in Higher Education programme which aims to enhance the educational effectiveness and understanding of lecturers, managers and support staff in universities and polytechnics. The course therefore has the direct and tangible benefit of providing a pathway to additional qualifications, which New Zealand polytechnics in particular are expecting of their staff. The course is primarily studied in flexible mode with materials provided for self-study interspersed by tutorial sessions and work on practical assignments.

The course

The participants in the first offering of this course, who were all practising tertiary teachers, initially explored the key theoretical concepts of open and flexible learning. They were then encouraged to focus on the practical issues of course development and selecting suitable methodologies. Ethical and equity issues and the resourcing of flexible learning were concurrent themes pursued throughout the course.

The participants came to recognise that 'openness' and 'flexibility' are characteristics which exist somewhere along a continuum between total structure and control and absolute flexibility and autonomy. The degrees of flexibility or control in delivery, support and assessment may vary according to the desired level of learner independence as well as to various practical considerations such as budgets, quality standards and resource availability. Our experience suggests that, currently, the majority of New Zealand lecturers and teachers have little or no experience in making choices related to course design and management for this mode of learning and our student population is also largely unfamiliar with the concept of self-management in learning. Consequently, raising awareness of the choices and constraints becomes a priority consideration.

The participants were led to recognise that the degree of freedom to choose modes of delivery relies upon a number of factors. Questions have to be asked about the options that are available, and why a particular mode may be more suited to the characteristics and learning objectives of the target group. It was also shown that, whereas in principle technology provides opportunities for an almost infinite range of choices, in practice, it is the limitations which typically prove to be the decisive factors. A local example of this may be seen in the unique nature of Internet access pricing in New Zealand where both the provider and the user pay for connections. Consequently, the prospect of enrolling large numbers of students on Web-based courses simply to reduce contact hours, and demand for classroom space is not as desirable, equitable or cost-effective as it might at first appear. It is also currently unrealistic to expect that all learners will have Web or Internet access or that those who do will be using equipment which delivers sufficient bandwidth to run even quite basic programs at acceptable speed. Despite cost and maintenance issues, CD-ROM delivery may be a more practical option for some New Zealand applications, while for others, video, audio and print currently remain more appropriate.

It was important for us to stress that educational technology is a delivery mechanism and a vehicle for providing support resources, rather than an answer in search of a problem. We aimed to encourage :

- consideration of the possibilities for increasing the flexibility of any study programme being designed or developed;
- investigation of the management of learning support relevant to different modes of study; and
- consideration of a variety of delivery techniques and the possible advantages and disadvantages of any method or combination of methods for particular contexts and target groups.

In their two major assignments, the participants were asked to consider the implications of education technology for teachers and administrators of conventional, distance and open learning and the potential impact of technology on the curriculum and on society in general.

Throughout the course, the various methodologies were explored and assessed from the perspectives of the individual participants without any definitive answers being offered by the facilitators. The individual needs and potentials varied enormously. For example, one participant was involved with a post-graduate course in project management for practising architects in Asian countries which both demanded and justified the high development costs of electronic media resources and the essential multilingual capabilities. By comparison, another participant was concerned with the more conventional distance delivery of a junior floristry course throughout New Zealand which could comfortably continue to rely upon the more traditional mix of text, video and attendance at residential school.

It was pointed out to the participants that course delivery using print and audiovisual material is a well-established means of providing distance education and that simply attempting to give a course a more 'up-to-date' feel by using a new technology such as CD-ROM does not guarantee any improvement in the learning. It was posited that the concept that the 'medium is the message' (McLuhan 1967) might hold true in the world of advertising, news media and entertainment where people initially respond more strongly to symbolism than to content, but that such impressions were short-lived where the appealing image is not substantiated by something more solid in terms of educational content, pedagogy and learning outcomes. Media applications have to be totally tenable in these times of constrained educational resources and budgets.

The participants considered the most suitable methodologies and delivery mechanisms for specific groups of learners both in terms of their learning needs and the resources to which they might have access. They quickly learned that compromises would be necessary until longer-term strategies could be designed to promote positive structural change.

We then invited the participants to examine some existing course material so that they might become more familiar with the range of technologies commonly used in open and flexible learning, identify their key characteristics and consider the instructional strategies they made possible. The applications were selected to provide as broad a view as possible and included professionally developed videodisks, CD/i programs, inter-active material prepared by local teachers, and videotape, audiotape and CD-ROM materials from various educational and training sources.

The educational applications of telecommunications technologies were also examined. These were considered from two perspectives: delivering course material and providing on-going student support and interpersonal communications. It was shown that there is a considerable overlap between these two forms of provision and that, as teaching and learning become increasingly flexible and more interactive, there will be a greater blurring of any distinction. It was shown that even the most traditional, lecturer-directed study could be augmented by additional communication strands between staff, students and the wider academic community. Indeed, it was argued that such a course has a greater need

215

than most to enhance the diversity, richness and flexibility of its delivery and communications channels.

It was stressed that where programmes are designed to rely heavily upon the Web, the mere transfer of existing text to the screen or basic competence in Web-page creation are insufficient and can all too easily result in nothing more nor better than electronic page-turning exercises. It was shown that levels of search, interactivity and two-way communication must be planned for from the start to encourage and support deeper forms of learning, discourse and enquiry. The participants were helped to see that text-based communication systems such as 'Chat and Talk' could allow learners to share experiences and concerns synchronously and that such dialogue could be further extended and enhanced by means of room- or desktop-based videoconferencing systems such as CUSeeMe, while for those unable to brave the sometimes banal world of instant online text and presentation, electronic mail provides the safety net of time delay associated with asynchronous communication. Here, the reflector can ponder while the theorist practises in the safety of his or her own space. Participants were encouraged to recognise that synchronous and asynchronous delivery systems have their own strengths and that either of these can accommodate a range of learning styles.

For most of the participants it should have come as no surprise that flexible and open learning gains the greatest benefits from a mixed-media base for resource presentation and student participation. The individual learning styles of different participants can be supported by a variety of media and interactive methods. It is argued (Honey and Mumford 1992), that defined activists can immediately engage with the material at a pace and in a sequence that they find most valuable. Such learners come into their own in multi-way, synchronous communications but their sheer exuberance may create difficulties for the more reflective type of student. This is but one of many areas wherein the mediating skills of the tutor are needed, and we found that practice in running teleconferenced tutorials was a vital developmental step for the participants. Several key delivery issues were highlighted by this:

- planning supervision to minimise the effects of dominant or obstructive end-user behaviour;
- maintaining control of the dispersed group when tutorials are conducted by teleconferencing, for example, by charting participants' names and reactions;
- ensuring that tutorials are not used as information dumping sessions but are inter-active;
- establishing personal contact between learner and tutor; and
- firmly fixing the 'virtual campus' in personal reality.

We then encouraged application of the insights provided by research into multimedia and diverse learning styles (see, for instance, Montgomery 1995) to real-life flexible learning situations.

Their examination of media and methods led the participants to realise that courses might make little use of high-end technology but could still be totally open and flexible and that, by contrast, some Web-based programmes required the participants to work in accord with set programmes and prescribed time-lines and were thus more 'closed' or 'controlled'. They thus came to appreciate that the teaching–learning possibilities range along the open–fixed continuum regardless of the technologies employed.

It took a while for some of the participants to appreciate fully the wider implications of flexibility in learning but in time most became enthralled with the range of delivery possibilities. However, all too frequently, their next reaction was to reject these approaches out of hand as being too difficult or too expensive to implement. This highlighted the importance of managers and teachers being enabled to identify the issues and gains associated with alternative learning strategies, the ways in which these link to the characteristics of various learning media, and practical solutions to achieve the necessary change.

Having explored the ways in which these various technologies could be used to assist learning in a general sense, the participants then discussed their potential for appropriate educational applications from their own particular professional perspectives. In many cases, they began to look at their existing teaching methods through fresh eyes, attracted by the possibilities of enhancing courses and making them more open and flexible through the use of technologies such as audiographics, audioconferencing and the Web. Finally, we asked them to prepare a learning resource in a field or application which was familiar to them and which made effective use of the key characteristics of the medium or media they had previously identified as most appropriate from the providers' and the users' points of view. They were also required to submit a description of how this learning resource would be integrated into the overall learning programme and to define the minimum hardware and software requirements. The resources they set out to develop took a number of forms, including video or audio, home experiment kits, sets of Web pages and computer-based learning software.

In carrying out their practical assignments, the participants learned something of the quirks and pitfalls in such work. However, this resource development activity turned out to be the major problem on our new course. We had expected the teachers to be able to work with a high degree of autonomy, but in practice many of them did not have the skills to develop their own resources without considerable instructional design and technical support. Because of this, a gap developed between the desired model of empowerment and the reality of many participants being frustrated and needing more support. From this experience, we all learned much about the constraints imposed on teachers involved in open learning development within the current institutional structures.

In retrospect, it would have been wiser to have addressed this issue from day one by more strongly emphasising the deliberately experiential and developmental nature of the course and securing additional technical services and support for the participants. However, until the course was actually trialled in its first year of operation, there could be little realistic anticipation of some of the difficulties faced by the participants.

Course evaluation

The evaluation of the course at the end of its first year of operation was conducted in a fairly relaxed and informal manner by an independent researcher. It took the form of a group discussion after which all participants were asked to complete a short questionnaire. The questions in both cases were designed to gauge:

- the participants' perceptions of the theoretical/practical orientation of the course, since the intention was for it to be mainly practical with just enough theory to provide support for the design decisions;
- any changes in the participants' perception of their roles and responsibilities as teachers and agents of institutional change;
- whether anything significantly new had been learned by the participants and, if so, what conditions they considered necessary for this to be successfully applied to their professional practice and contexts in the short and the long term.

The course providers needed to know whether the participants felt that the course had offered practical solutions to the development and implementation issues across the range of subjects that they were responsible for teaching (these ranged from traditional Maori flax-weaving to boat-building and business management). They also needed to be able to assess whether the participants felt confident and competent enough to apply successfully the principles and methods they had learned during the course, both in terms of course and materials development and the promotion of organisational change.

In the event, most of the participants displayed a reasonable degree of understanding of structural changes necessary if they were to move to more open and flexible learning and proficiency in course development techniques. Given that the course was of such short duration and that the levels of previous academic achievement and technical knowledge were so varied, it could be judged to have been an overall success in these regards.

Generally speaking, the course was also considered to be effective in broadening the participants' understandings of the teachers' role in contemporary higher education and in encouraging them to reconceptualise their roles and objectives as teachers. Most reported that they had acquired a number of completely new ideas about teaching and learning and that subject to existing limitations (of which they now felt more fully aware and capable of challenging), they intended to work on changing the ways in which they designed and delivered their courses. However, the participants did indicate that more opportunity to explore the practical aspects of education technologies would have been appreciated (we were able to point out that there are in fact other courses available for this purpose).

One perceived negative aspect was the limited amount of information and advice that was made available on the requirements of the practical assignment. This had left some participants unsure of their ground. Some concerns were also expressed about the apparent lack of structure to the course, the unfamiliar and high degree of self-directed learning required in the work and the limited amount of tutor time assumed within the course. However, on reflection it was recognised that this experience successfully modelled the sometimes confusing experiences of autonomous learners when they are exposed to learning environments with less structure than they are accustomed to, and the evaluation revealed that most of the participants found their first-hand experience of the realities of open learning from a student perspective to be a valuable element of the course. Such reflection on the problems of independence and self-management may help these participants to be more sensitive to this important issue and generate practical solutions in their future course design for open and flexible delivery.

At the same time, the providers will ensure that in the future they will make more explicit the purposes of the experiential learning on the course and the nature and requirements of the assignments so that the learners can work towards these goals throughout the semester. It is also seen that all future courses should give more focus to the contact and support elements that need be built into flexible course design to overcome student feelings of isolation.

Another important issue which emerged through the course and the participants' discussions of their experiences was the cross-cultural ramifications of open and flexible delivery. Such is the broad ethnic diversity of the New Zealand student population that all teachers must be capable of dealing with a number of educational philosophies and styles of learning. The majority of the resident population comprises Maori, Polynesians and descendants of European settlers, but there are increasing numbers of South African, Indian and Asian immigrants and their descendants. The overseas student population comes mainly from Asia – Japan, Taiwan, Malaysia and Indonesia. Such a multicultural society means that variations in socio-educational culture, philosophy and style and language barriers frequently have to be addressed. In the case of Maori students, the cultural requirements are reinforced by government directives.

For some of these ethnic groups, studying in isolation on an open learning course is such an alien concept that it has been shown to be significantly less effective than more conventional, face-to-face teaching and learning. The participants became aware of the fact that unfamiliar degrees of autonomy and flexibility could give rise to concern on the part of students from all ethnic backgrounds and that this required an imaginative 'fix' in the design of future technology-supported learning environments. For example, such feelings of isolation might be offset by the unique capabilities of multimedia technology to model the oral and visual traditions associated with learning in some cultures.

Other changes will be made to the structure of the Flexible and Open Learning course as a result of this initial experience and feedback. Longer-term evaluation will be conducted to see if changes to course development and delivery actually result from such learning and to discover what institutional and contextual barriers continue to block the implementation of new technologies in course development. Ultimately, the Flexible and Open Learning course will be judged by how well its graduates contribute to institutional planning for change and are willing and able to apply their knowledge and skills in widening access to higher education. If students are to take more charge of their learning, then so too must the managers and teachers of their programmes.

References

Cooper, M. (1991) 'Stretching the limits of our vision', in *Staff Development for Education in the 90s*, A. Lieberman and L. Miller (eds), New York: Teachers College Press, p. 89.

Griffin, G. (1991) 'Interactive staff development: using what we know', in *Staff Development for Education in the 90s*, A. Lieberman and L. Miller (eds), New York: Teachers College Press.

Honey, P. and Mumford, A. (1992) *The Manual of Learning Styles*, 10 Linden Avenue, Maidenhead, Berks SL6 6HB: P. Honey and A. Mumford.

McLuhan, H.M. (1967) *The Medium is the Message: An Inventory of Effects*, New York: Random House.

Montgomery, S.M. (1995) *Addressing Diverse Learning Styles through the Use of Multimedia*, http://fairway.ecn.purdue.edu/asee/fie95/3a2/3a22/3a22.htm, University of Michigan.

22

UNIVERSITIES LEARNING
The lure of the Net

Anne Forster and Lindsay Hewson

It is ironic that universities and other educational organisations which support teaching, learning and research are so apparently resistant to change and, unlike the 'learning organisation' described by Peter Senge in his book *The Fifth Discipline*: '[where] people continually expand their capacity to create the results they truly desire, where new and expansive patterns of thinking are nurtured, where collective aspiration is set free, and where people are continually learning how to learn together (Senge 1990: 3). In higher education, increasing differentiation has resulted in more competitive marketing of institutions and programmes with information technology identified as a core capability. Many institutions are investing heavily in upgrading their technology infrastructure and developing applications which will give them a competitive advantage.

This chapter is a response to the need for educational institutions to adapt and respond to the changing environment, in particular through developing the capacities of their staff. It focuses on the development of skills around the use of the Internet and how this process is in itself a means of developing a learning organisation, one which enables the flow of ideas and actions from all of its staff through participative management processes. Internet applications such as the Web provide both a mechanism and a metaphor for staff development strategies which will assist educational institutions in their efforts to reframe themselves for survival in the twenty-first century.

The lure of the Net

The Internet has been promoted and commercialised primarily around its value as a distribution medium and publishing instrument. In education, the access to information databases, online catalogues and entire instructional programmes has been the driving application. This lure of the Net is a potential trap, likely to reinforce the most didactic models of teaching and learning wherein information transmission, with the teacher in control, predominates.

[P]rofessors are fired up by the idea that all the world can access their ideas, their research, their wisdom through the World Wide Web – a passion to widen access to their teaching. This is not always accompanied by a similar passion to improve the quality of their teaching, as can be witnessed very easily by surfing their Web pages.

(Bates 1996: 6)

The Internet with the application of the Web provides an effective space for teaching and professional support staff to develop networked communities for sharing staff development practice and knowledge building. The inter-active features of the Internet for conferencing and collaborative learning require instructional methods such as problem-solving, games, multimedia and simulations to be developed for networked learning groups.

Knowledge communities, or communities of practice, facilitate social interaction between staff developers who are learning how to be effective agents of change. But practitioners of the new media require new metaphors – why is it that the most common metaphor selected by designers of virtual classroom software has been the building, with rooms and doors? Negroponte (1995) makes some challenging statements which require creative responses from designers of learning spaces:

being digital allows the process, not just the product to be conveyed. . . .

Thinking about multimedia needs to include ideas about the fluid movement from one medium to the next, saying the same thing in different ways, calling upon one human sense or another. . . .

The harmonising effect of being digital is already apparent as previously partitioned disciplines and enterprises find themselves collaborating not competing.

(Negroponte 1995: 224, 72 and 230)

The key element of the new metaphor has to be participation, not just information or communication. It needs to be multidimensional and suggest the fluid movement from one medium to the next. The Internet itself is the metaphor, but only if it is understood and conveyed as the rich space it is. There is a new generation of Internet interfaces and browsers under development which tries to create a new aesthetic and new metaphors for the building blocks, processes and relationships of the virtual community. SUN Microsystems (SUN 1996) have developed a network-based virtual space for learning. This distributed classroom allows several users to move about in a 2-D space (called 'Kansas'). Users can scroll their viewpoints across the vast surface, causing their rectangles to overlap in order to collaborate, or can move away from others to work alone. Similarly, Apple™'s Hotsauce MCF and the Information Visualiser from Xerox™ (Hearst 1997) provide a 3-D space in which users develop and impose their own structures (meta content formats) on the Web according to their purposes and interests. The time will come when intelligent interfaces will do that for users by monitoring and learning user preferences and pre-empting needs – but these tools will only be possible when we can fully identify and express the processes, values and needs of the online learning community.

Developing knowledge communities: two examples of practice

Ways of modelling a staff development knowledge community are illustrated by two examples: a virtual conference and a course leading to a formal qualification.

The virtual conference on the virtual university was run as part of Tele-Teaching 96 (TT96), an IFIP conference (Forster 1996). It was designed to address the question 'Can the virtual university deliver real learning?' A panel of international experts and discussion leaders addressed this question and this initiative demonstrated how it was possible to create a 'virtual learning community', and link practitioners at various levels of expertise, across the globe. Each listserv had well over 100 members from all over the world. Most of these were silent members, receiving all postings but not participating actively, but this rate of participation mirrors the reality of large face-to-face groups. In addition, visitors to the Web site could read the archives of the discussions without subscribing. The virtual conference represented a staff development process wherein visitors could visit demonstration classrooms, read through course outlines and notes, view student projects, read position papers, explore student support services, network with other practitioners and participate in discussions ranging over a myriad issues.

For two months prior to the on-site conference, this virtual conference presented international best practice through the Virtual University Web site. Topics included strategies for change, new technologies, pedagogy and the re-engineered classroom, support services for students, research into collaborative learning and knowledge building, lessons learned and academic staff development.

Each topic was represented by a Web site developed by one of the invited presenters. Each Web site included a position paper and links to demonstration sites of online courses, resources, technologies and research. Participants were invited to explore the issues raised by the presenters by visiting the specially developed Web sites and then joining listserv discussion groups. These discussion groups were the source of questions and issues put to the panellists by the facilitators. The facilitators, like the presenters, were all invited specialists, with both research and practitioner experience. The international representation and high quality of these invited contributors was widely recognised and provided a world class event for TeleTeaching 96. The design effort and time commitment required to build the individual sites and to link relevant sites to the conference home page was supported by Opennet Pty Ltd. Opennet continues to maintain the site, which remains a rich source of pedagogical and theoretical resources for anyone searching the Web for ideas on the virtual university.

A more formalised example of the application of the Internet to staff development is found in the Information Technology for Teaching and Learning component of the Master's in Higher Education at the University of New South Wales PDC (UNSW). In this case, low student numbers, limited staff availability and a belief in the technology led to the creation of a different approach to the development of IT skills in university teachers. The Master's-level course was designed to be offered only online, and in so doing, to demonstrate the implications of this environment for both teachers and learners. The learners (all university lecturers) have to acquire the skills and attitudes to function online so that they can access the courseware. The package integrates Computer Mediated Communication (CMC) and a locally authored technology named WebTeach© which provides for Web-based distribution of course notes, resource directories, online seminars, chats and quizzes, online submission of assignments and the publishing and sharing of projects within the group. The assignments involve a discipline-specific evaluation of Web sites for teaching, and the development and evaluation of a prototype inter-active teaching package. With student consent, all quality outcomes are archived for future groups to build a rich Web-based resource for staff development. Learners experience the medium from the perspective of both learner and teacher and are left with a dynamic resource to support them in their ongoing applications of IT to teaching. The success of this approach has led to the building and hyperlinking of similar resources in related areas of learning theory, educational technology and course review to address an increasing demand for staff development, and to model new methods of teaching.

More examples of the building of knowledge communities and their application to learning can be found at Betty Collis's site in the Netherlands and at several US sites, such as the Institute for Academic Technology and Hamline University. The distinguishing characteristic of these initiatives is their public, collaborative nature and their demonstration of networked staff development. The universal resource locators (URLs) for these and other sites are provided at the end of this chapter.

Competencies for building knowledge communities

So, what specific skills and competencies will people need in order to be effective staff developers and effective and confident members of the online learning community? Given the collective inexperience with this teaching environment, there are no proven methods for development. We can, however, begin from basics and identify the skills, knowledge and attitudes that will be necessary and recognise the prior learning of staff from which to build such competence.

Using language acquisition as an analogy, 'net literacy ' can be expressed as a continuum of skills and understandings ranging from pre-reading and reading, through to writing, and competency in authoring. Most would-be users need an agent to guide them through the acquisition of online literacy. However, it is not just the mastery of the language or the technology skills which determine effective use of the Web. These basic skills enable users to participate in a new social space. Once there, high-level competencies are required in the development of the content and the design of the communications to suit particular purposes.

Staff developers themselves must become competent authors or capable of serving in a competent authoring team if they are going to design and deliver programmes and know how to select and manage the appropriate training activities, presenters and technologies for this purpose. These specific network skills and knowledge will be in addition to the traditional instructional design skills needed to diagnose staff needs, identify competencies and prior learning, and match these to appropriate levels of training. Staff developers will also need to have the technical and pedagogical capacities to participate actively in the design and delivery of online staff development. Equally importantly, they will need to develop attitudes towards online learning that can sustain them in the dynamic of a shared, collaborative medium.

Technical skills are necessary for the implementation of teaching strategies and day-to-day functioning within the environment. Technological competency will change as the physical form and functionality of the network evolves, and so the approach to the development of these skills needs to be flexible. In general, however, progress in hardware, software and interface design will effectively reduce the technical demands on users of the network and competency will be more easily acquired, maintained and updated.

Pedagogical skills represent a more fundamental set of competencies needed for the effective design of learning. With origins in instructional design, cognitive science and distance education, competencies are needed to bring learning theory to bear on the goals of achieving deep, self-directed learning and producing independent lifelong learners.

Attitudes that are needed to operate in such a global environment include a commitment to develop strategic networking skills, cultural awareness and reciprocal responsibility. Teachers, students and staff developers have to avoid being seen as cultural raiders or Internet pirates, out to loot the best sites and the most responsive classes. Users of the Web need to be sensitive to the issues involved in forging links with other groups and institutions, to the loads placed on the learners and to the need to integrate this work with other classroom practices and schedules. Other sensitivities required in this new environment might include:

- acceptance of responsibility for a network presence ('netiquette');
- ownership of intellectual property and copyright in a collaborative system;
- issues of censorship, privacy and the right to know; and
- willingness to collaborate and contribute to group processes.

Progressive development strategies

The majority of users need staff development strategies that recognise progressive levels of competence. These categories of staff technology competence have been variously labelled as *novice* > *expert* (Yetton and Associates 1997), *aware* > *conversant* > *confident* > *competent* (Tinkler *et al.* 1996) and *naïve* > *knowledgeable* > *sophisticated* (Longstaffe *et al.* 1996). It can be argued that the lower end of the continuum constitutes core competencies essential for any user, while at the higher end a smaller number of users are able to author original instructional processes and be responsible leaders in the new environment. A range of staff development strategies are needed to identify and target these constituent groups and match provision to the immediate needs of each group. In her paper on resistance to computer use in tertiary institutions, McNaught (1995) suggests strategies for traditional 'institution-based' staff development that range from general awareness-raising activities, skills workshops and user groups through to detailed policy development processes. She advocates a mix of centralised, faculty-based and individual developmental activities. She also suggests the use of technology such as the Web and E-mail to provide self-access mechanisms supplementing the 'contact' strategies. These ideas suggest approaches for staff development for networked teaching.

Returning to the language acquisition metaphor, it is possible to conceive a staff development hierarchy of four levels of net literacy: *awareness* (pre-reading); *conversance* (reading); *confidence* (writing); and *competence* (authoring).

Awareness

At the awareness stage, would-be users have heard about the technology and are interested in its potential application. They want to see it working and want to ask questions of others. At this stage, the staff developers seek to create interest and motivation, demonstrate the advantages of the medium and provide basic information in non-threatening and entertaining ways. Exhibitions, workshops, demonstrations, newsletters, datasheets are all appropriate strategies.

Conversance

At the conversance level, the user has acquired the basic technical skills in the operation of equipment (client and server terminals), and has learned about the physical form of the network (how these units are inter-connected), the types of synchronous and asynchronous communication available to the teacher and learner (Internet, FTP, E-mail, CMC, listservs) and the functionality provided by these protocols (hyperlinking, searching, communicating, collaboration, inter-activity). The user is now familiar with the jargon.

The user requires access to the technology, guidance in the acquisition of skills to explore, navigate, store data, and examples of, and experience in, configuring browser plug-ins, FTP applications, E-mail, search engines, listservs, and Internet relay chats.

Confidence

The confident user has begun to produce material for the network, design interaction with users, and integrate the network's functionality into all aspects of teaching and learning. Specifically, they have developed competencies in

- Hyper Text Markup Language (HTML) writing skills for the creation of network sites or the use of Web publishing software;
- instructional design and assessment;
- computer conferencing;
- using online audio and video; and
- using CGIs (Common Gateway Interfaces) to link Web sites with traditional computer software, such as databases, simulations and spreadsheets.

The user requires access to 'fellow travellers' through user groups, special interest groups and newsgroups, and opportunities to collaborate with peers in sharing skills and knowledge, participate in Web-based learning, and create network products and processes within the safety of a developmental environment.

Competence

At this highest level, users have been enabled to design and author total educational packages, analyse and evaluate networked products and processes and contribute critically to the processes of networked staff development. Specifically, competent users have acquired skills in

- the design and establishment of network servers;
- the operation of listservs and groupware;
- producing online audio and video;
- inter-active authoring;
- acquisition and management of copyright;
- interface design;
- evaluation of network sources;
- project management;
- construction and specification of CGIs; and
- technical maintenance.

The user is afforded appropriate support for the design, creation, development, management and implementation of networked teaching and learning.

Competency can be at the individual or at the group level (a team of people with complementary expertise). The Web is a complex electronic and social domain employing multimedia, and so specialist skills such as interface design are not expected of staff developers. However, awareness of the characteristics of interface design, and the ways in which it can improve or impede effective interaction with the site, is a necessary understanding for competent authoring. Competence to judge when a specialist skill is required is one of the highest levels of achievement and, as with all published material, a team approach to Web development is the most likely to result in marketable, error-free and accessible documents and interactions and so competencies in teamwork are also called for.

Managing change

The 'learning organisation' has the capacity to adapt to lead, and benefit from change, because its management processes assist all staff to have the necessary competencies. By contrast, while the application of technology to teaching and staff development can be driven by enthusiasts at the grassroots level, this will achieve little if management does not provide the vision, leadership and commitment. Staff development can target and address staff needs using a variety of traditional and online strategies, but there is a need simultaneously to influence the mind-set of managers to create the necessary policies and procedures and facilitate corporate moves into this networked model of staff development. The managers must be convinced of the imperative to transform the organisation and the ways in which it prepares its staff for their enterprise. Staff developers must begin by interpreting the institution's vision and its implications for the staff. The lure of the Net and its effective use as a component of institutional change can be much more powerful if there are rewards and incentives to motivate people to participate in staff development programmes.

Conclusion

The Internet and the Web are a powerful mechanism and a vital metaphor for transformation. Through these, universities and other institutions can learn how to adapt to the changing external and internal environments. They can empower intra-organisational communication and knowledge communities and inter-organisational exchange and alliances. Universities which learn how to develop a 'collective aspiration' will achieve the results they desire. Understanding how to harness this new technology as a tool for organisational transformation requires that individuals are assisted, encouraged and eventually obliged to act. However, widespread literacy and application will not occur without substantial commitment, resources and support to address the currently high percentage of IT-illiterate and resistant individuals. Investing in staff development strategies which enable the powerful application of the Internet and the Web to teaching and in organisational growth and development is a low-risk strategy.

There is still much that we do not understand about the new technologies. The Internet is a new medium which requires analysis, reflection, trial and retrial. TV was first described as radio with pictures; the Web has been described as a distribution medium for multimedia. More importantly, it is a new space for a new community wherein new kinds of relationships and interactions are possible. It offers a vast range of resources and opportunities which must be managed within a framework that values the learning intention, defines the proposed outcomes and provides the design blueprint.

The lure of this technology lies in the fact that it is so easy to use. Its technical brilliance and potential can certainly lead to superficiality and inefficiency, but used well, the technology can provide the means of transforming staff development, creating previously unachievable relationships and activities and helping universities and colleges not only to be great places to learn, but also great learning organisations.

References

Bates, A.W. (1995) *The Future of Learning: Minister's Forum on Adult Learning,* Edmonton, Alberta, http://bates.cstudies.ubc.ca/

—— (1996) 'The impact of technological change on open and distance learning', keynote presentation, *Open Learning: Your Future Depends on It,* Queensland Open Learning Network Conference, Brisbane, Australia.

Forster, A. (1996) 'A virtual conference on the virtual university', unpublished presentation to *Universities in the Twenty-first Century: Education in a Borderless World,* a Colloquium organised by IDP Education Australia and the British Council (13–14 August), Singapore. WWW reference: http://www.openweb.net. au/TT96University/

Hearst, M. (1997) 'Interfaces for searching the Web', *Scientific American* 276(3): 60–4.

Longstaffe, J.A., Whittlestone, K.D., Edwards, J.D., Williams, J. and Hammond, P.M. (1996) *Supporting Learning Technology in Higher Education,* Educational Technology Service, University of Bristol.

McNaught, C. (1995) 'Overcoming fear of the unknown! Staff development issues for promoting the use of computers in learning in tertiary education', in E.A. Pearce (ed.), *ASCILITE '95– Learning With Technology,* University of Melbourne, pp. 410–16.

Negroponte, N. (1995) *Being Digital,* Sydney: Hodder & Stoughton.

Senge, P. (1990) *The Fifth Discipline: The Art and Practice of the Learning Organisation,* London: Random House.

SUN (1996) *Kansas: A Distributed Classroom,* SUN Microsystems Academic and Research Computing, http://www.sun.com/edu/events/progs/kanas.html

Tinkler, D., Lepani, P. and Mitchell, J. (1996) *Education and Technology Convergence* (Commissioned Report No. 43), National Board of Employment, Education and Training, Canberra: Australian Government Publishing Service.

Yetton and Associates (1997) *Managing the Introduction of Technology in the Delivery and Administration of Higher Education,* Report for the Department of Employment, Education, Training and Youth Affairs, Canberra: Australia.

Universal Resource Locators (URLs)

HEPROC	http://rrpubs.com/heproc/index.html
IFIP	http://www.acs.org.au/ifip96/tele.html
ISWorld Net	http://www.isworld.org/isworld.html
Hotsauce MCF	http://mcf.research.apple.com/
Kansas (SUN)	http://www.sun.com/edu/events/progs/kanas.html
Virtual University	http://www.openweb.net.au/TT96University/
PDC (UNSW)	http://www.pdc.unsw.edu.au/pg/
Betty Collis's site	http://www.to.utwente.nl/user/ism/collis/home.htm
Institute for Academic Technology	http://www.iat.unc.edu/
Hamline University	http://www.hamline.edu/

23

THE ROLE OF WORKSHOPS IN STAFF DEVELOPMENT

Derek Rowntree

This chapter begins by mentioning various approaches to helping staff develop the knowledge, competencies and dispositions they will need in open or flexible learning (OFL) and suggests that these approaches need to be integrated into an overall strategy. The main body of the chapter focuses on the workshop as a key means of staff development, offering some ideas as to its distinctive character and sharing the author's experience of what makes a successful workshop for staff who are new to OFL.

The staff development context

OFL projects are often set up in a hurry and with a view to economising on staff time and other costs. The time-scale may seem too short to prepare people in advance. And the powers-that-be may not see much necessity for briefing or training. Or they may hope that staff will pick up whatever new skills they need as they go along. In any case, staff may be given no time off from normal duties to prepare for their new roles.

All this can spell danger. Few newcomers realise how much they may need to learn. For example, designing an OFL course can be quite different from planning a classroom course. Writing appropriate learning materials can be very different from any kinds of writing the teacher has done before. Tutoring and supporting open and flexible learners may be quite different from working with class-based learners. And a move into new technology can present any of us with a daunting learning curve. Staff may need to acquire new knowledge, new competencies and, in many cases, new attitudes or dispositions.

My experience suggests that every OFL project should have a *strategy* for staff development. This strategy should be thought about as soon as the project is mooted and *evolve throughout its life*. Here are some possible components of such a strategy:

- a needs analysis, to determine the insights, dispositions and competencies that roles within the project will demand of staff;

- an appraisal of *all* individuals involved (teachers, administrators, librarians, media specialists and others) to identify where each one might need help in preparing for their role;
- briefing and debriefing sessions and information packs, together with explicit job descriptions;
- workshops, seminars, networking and visits to other OFL providers;
- encouragement for staff to enrol as OFL learners themselves;
- newsletters, conferencing and other means of sharing colleagues' experience and keeping them updated;
- working with an external consultant;
- internship – assisting a more experienced colleague;
- supervision and mentoring by experienced colleagues;
- keeping a reflective diary or building a portfolio;
- accreditation (for example, through S/NVQs in the UK) for new competencies as a tutor, developer or manager of OFL courses;
- a staff appraisal system that reinforces continuous staff development;
- a rewards system that – whether through extra money, promotion or enriched opportunities – makes it worth people's while; and
- a management that ensures that someone is responsible for *integrating components* like those mentioned above and thus making it all happen.

I have given this lengthy list to indicate that I do not see workshops as the be-all and end-all of staff development. They are one component among many; but I do see them as an essential one.

What are workshops?

In this context, the term 'workshops' means something different from lectures, presentations or even seminars. In my opinion:

- their purpose is to develop not merely the participants' knowledge but also their vocational competence (participants should emerge better at doing some aspect of their jobs);
- they are based on carrying out activities (the 'work') rather than listening to a presenter;
- such activities will have much the same purpose as those in an open learning text – but the feedback will come not from the 'author' but from fellow learners and the workshop leader;
- workshops focus on the experience (either recalled or here-and-now) of the participants rather than on the knowledge of the workshop leader;
- they are not a vehicle for the transmission of information but for the thinking through of ideas or practising of competencies and for the sharing of individualised feedback;
- participants will be doing much more talking than the leader – perhaps two or three times as much;

- participants can expect to learn as much (or more) from one another as they will from the workshop leader;
- the workshop leader can expect to learn as much from the participants as they do from the leader;
- the leader (to use a well-worn but still worthwhile cliché) does not so much teach as arrange for learning to take place; he or she is a facilitator, not the fount of all wisdom, not the 'sage on the stage' but the 'guide on the side';
- in a workshop, the objectives and priorities of the participants are at least as important as those of the workshop leader.

Might your less experienced colleagues benefit from this kind of approach in their staff development? If so, and if you are new to teaching this way yourself, you may be interested in the following suggestions drawn from my own experience of running workshops over the last thirty years.

Planning your workshop

1 If you have any choice, aim to have *around twelve participants*. With fewer than eight, the pool of experience may be insufficient to fuel the learning (or create a social 'buzz' within the group); with sixteen or more, participants may be frustrated by lack of time to air their ideas and get satisfying feedback.

2 Find out what you can about participants in advance – especially their prior experience and what they expect of the workshop. If you can't ask them directly (face-to-face or by questionnaire or on the telephone) you may want to ask their line managers or other people who have worked with them.

3 Be realistic about participants' likely level of motivation. For some, the workshop may be compulsory and they may resent having this extra demand on their time when they are already hard-pressed. Some may even resent being required to embrace OFL. Any such feelings may need to be discussed, at, or preferably before, the workshop.

4 Write out and make public the proposed *aims* of your workshop. What are the competencies you hope to help participants develop? This should help you in deciding on appropriate activities around which to structure the event. It will also help participants to focus their own expectations and, if they wish, to negotiate for rather different aims.

5 Allow scope for participants to *modify* the proposed aims – for example, by arranging a pre-workshop discussion or by asking for and responding to participants' 'expectations' at the very beginning of the workshop. This should enable participants to have a greater sense of 'ownership' of the workshop and hence be more committed to learning from it.

6 If you want participants to discuss an issue, consider the possibility that more of them will get involved, and to better effect, if you first ask them to think about the issue individually (or talk about it in pairs) before the general discussion begins.

7   Get participants to examine specific examples rather than abstract generalisations. For example, don't ask them to talk about 'The problems people have in learning' (general), or even 'The problems you have in learning' (slightly less general problem(s)), if you can say: 'Think of the last time you tried to learn something; what kinds of problem(s) did you have?' (specific). The general principles can then be drawn out of people's reflection on a variety of specific situations.

8   Design your workshop around participant *activities*. Ask yourself what activities the participants will need to engage in if they are to improve in the competencies embodied in the aims. Ideally, these activities should relate directly to concerns and tasks the participants are facing in their work; for example, developing a course specification, drafting learning materials, counselling students.

9   Ensure a reasonable *variety* of activity – such as individual work, whole-class discussion, work in pairs, syndicate work (three or more people), reporting back by groups or individuals, brainstorming, role plays, simulation of work situations, demonstrations, brief (five to ten minute) presentations by the leader or other participants (perhaps using video/audio), and so on.

10 Develop activities that articulate the themes and issues of the workshop (and thus make them concrete) through the *experiences* of the participants. For instance, if the theme is 'bias in teaching materials', don't bombard them with examples from your experience followed by your analysis and your conclusions from that experience. Instead, form syndicates and ask them to come up with examples from their own experience which they can then analyse and draw conclusions from. These can then be compared with yours. Alternatively, you might give each syndicate a set of materials exemplifying various kinds of bias for them to use as a trigger for their discussion.

11 Plan to *debrief* such syndicate discussions (and any other individual or syndicate activities) by allowing plenty of time for feedback to, and comment from, the whole group. In the desire to avoid lecturing it is easy to go overboard for activities so much that one omits to allow adequate time for sharing and reflecting on the implications of those activities – for instance, a five-minute role play might fuel twenty minutes of group discussion.

12 If you want to ensure breadth of coverage without sacrificing depth of discussion, consider arranging for *division of labour* within the group. For instance, if you want the group to consider, say, the possible benefits of OFL to their organisations, to their learners and to the teaching staff, ask one syndicate to make a list of benefits to the organisation, another the benefits to the learners and a third the benefits to staff. Then get the syndicates to report back so that each syndicate can consider and comment on the others groups' deliberations.

13 Prepare suitable *resource materials* in print or other media. Decide what is essential 'pre-read' material before people come to the workshop (be realistic) and what is optional and/or can be used for reference after the

workshop. Prepare handout material for use during the workshop. Consider whether this is to be given to participants all at once or handed out piece by piece as you go along. Are you using similar material on the overhead projector or other presentation media? If so, how will this differ – for example, the main points only on screen with the fine details spelled out on the paper handout?

14 Consider whether it may be worthwhile and practical to set the participants some *pre-workshop* task (such as 'Interview two of your potential learners using the questions set out below . . . ') which they would then be debriefed on or asked to be built upon during the workshop. This device might increase the relevance, ensure a common starting point and save workshop time.

15 Remind participants to *bring with them* any materials they will need to work on during the workshop – such as a draft self-teaching package, plans for an evaluation, problems with which students have sought help.

16 Write a one-page *outline* of the workshop, showing the proposed aims of the workshop, resources needed and what you expect you and the participants will be doing in each of the phases of the workshop (and how many minutes you expect each to take). (For examples, see any of the three manuals by Freeman and/or Lewis mentioned below in the References.)

Running your workshop

17 Check that you have appropriate materials on which your participants can report their discussions in syndicates, and so on – for instance, flip chart sheets or acetates for the overhead projector and the appropriate pens.

18 In running the actual workshop, keep to the overall *timetable*. Start on time (out of respect for participants who arrive on time), and finish on time – out of respect not only for the participants but also perhaps for a colleague who may be leading the next session!

19 Ensure that participants are seated in such a way that they can see one another's faces – namely, in a circle or square rather than in rows. But ensure that this arrangement can be broken up when necessary to form syndicates.

20 Consider beginning with an ice-breaker – this is useful in setting the tone and getting people acquainted if they have not already met. One simple and useful device is to get each participant to interview another and say something to the whole group about that person's background and expectations.

21 Try to learn and use the participants' names. If you haven't met them before, and there are too many to remember from the initial introductions, give them sticky labels and/or put up a 'map' showing who is sitting where.

22 If participants are new to this kind of teaching, you may need to begin by discussing the *rules of engagement*. Help them accept that they will not benefit by trying to fill their notebooks with the pearls of your experience

but that you will help them learn through their own efforts after understanding and from listening to one another. Occasionally there may be signs of discomfort, scepticism or rebellion among some individuals; so be prepared to offer reassurance and support.

23 Beware of talking too much. You will presumably have committed any lengthy exposition to paper handouts. But it is easy to get drawn into giving extempore lectures. Resist the temptation – however satisfying it may be to find that you could talk at length on topics that seem to be of interest to (some?) participants.

24 Think also about your *body language*. For instance, you may decide to stand up (even walk about) while introducing a topic or geeing-up the participants for some activity but to sit down (among them perhaps) while they are reporting back. Relate your body language to the kind of energy you wish to generate and how you wish participants to perceive your role in the various phases of the workshop.

25 When splitting participants into groups, don't automatically do so on basis of whom they happen to be sitting next to. Consider whether groups of relative strangers (or people from quite different backgrounds) might sometimes get more from one another than if they are already acquainted (which is perhaps why they are sitting next to one another). At other times, of course, you will want to group your participants on exactly that very principle of shared interests or similar background.

26 Consider changing the groupings during the workshop, for example, for different kinds of activity, to rotate a 'difficult' participant or to give people a wider variety of alternative perspectives.

27 In giving the syndicates 'instructions' as to what you want them to do or decide, you might need to write the task on a flip chart (or give them a handout for more complex activities).

28 Consider whether to 'visit' syndicates while they are engaged in activities. For brief activities (ten minutes or less) this might be disruptive; but for longer ones you may want to be available to make some input or at least check how things are going and look out for common threads. Resist being recruited as syndicate 'leader' and, again, beware of body language – it is less disruptive to sidle into a sitting position alongside or among the syndicate members than to hover over them!

29 Always ensure each syndicate appoints a scribe or rapporteur to make note of the syndicate's conclusions and to report back to the large group after activities (with time allowed for group comment).

30 You will usually find it is motivating to the participants to *recognise* the syndicates' report-backs by writing up their main points on the flip chart or OHP. Or you may invite the syndicates to present their conclusions on a flip-chart sheet or OHP themselves. Simply listening to what they say may not be sufficient recognition of their work.

31 Where participants have generated materials or substantial ideas in note or

diagram form, consider getting *paper copies* made (very reinforcing) and circulated to all participants as quickly as possible – either for use during the workshop (or a subsequent one) or for reference afterwards.

32 In giving feedback to participants after syndicate discussion, don't imply that the answers they should have been looking for were *your* answers. After participants have been asked, for example, to identify the likely benefits of OFL within their organisation, they might find it alienating then to be told, 'Here is a handout listing all the likely benefits'. Next time you set them an activity they might be inclined not so much to reflect on their own situations as to guess what would be on your next handout.

33 With a 'brain-storming' session – where you get the full group to throw up ideas on the understanding that they will not be commented on or criticised until the flood has dried up – consider asking one of the participants to jot the suggestions down on a flip chart while you sit to one side where you are less likely to be looked to as a referee.

34 Keep reminding yourself of the workshop's *aims*. By all means incorporate new opportunities that you and the group think more worthwhile, but don't allow discussions simply to wander.

35 From time to time, perhaps after each major phase of the workshop, ask the participants if they have any outstanding worries or queries. Their responses can help you link one phase to the next and may also help you evaluate the workshop.

36 Be careful to ensure that questions of interest to only a minority of the participants are not allowed to disrupt the flow of the workshop for the majority. If you are asked questions you can't answer, say so – you can't be expected to know everything; and/or ask the group if anyone else can answer them and/or offer to talk to the questioner afterwards.

37 Consider winding up the workshop by asking participants to reflect (first as individuals then as a group) on their initial expectations of the workshop, how far they have been fulfilled and what new needs have arisen. This may help you to evaluate the workshop as well as help the participants get the most out of the experience.

After your workshop

38 Make an effort to *evaluate* the workshop – for example, with a simple questionnaire asking participants what they liked most and least about the workshop and what suggestions they can make for improving it. Seek post-workshop feedback from participants' line managers or colleagues or other tutors, as appropriate.

39 Reflect on the experience *yourself* and make a note of how you might modify your workshop if you were to present it again to a similar group.

40 Follow up on the workshop. The real learning begins only when your participants get back to their working contexts and try to apply the insights

they arrived at during the workshop. Consider whether you need to make yourself available to participants over the following months – for instance, by telephone, E-mail or computer conferencing or in face-to-face 'surgery' sessions. Do what you can to ensure that your workshops are complemented by other appropriate components from the staff development strategy.

41 One way to follow up on workshops (or substitute for them if you can't get people together as often as you would wish) might be *computer conferencing*. My recent experience (Rowntree 1995) has taught me that the workshop principles I've listed above can still apply even though none of the participants are ever in the same place at the same time. That is, we can still split them into collaborative groups, engage them in activities that relate to their job concerns and enable them to reflect on the issues involved, practise the relevant competencies and discuss the appropriateness of their attitudes.

How far can you go along with the suggestions I have set out above? And, equally important, how acceptable might they be to the staff who will be attending your workshops? Clearly, they are based on my personal beliefs about the most effective learning process and about the appropriate relationship between 'teacher' and 'taught'. You and your participants may not share them. There is no one right way to run a workshop. In the end, you have to work out a way that feels right both for you and for your participants. That is why every workshop can be a staff development experience not just for those attending but also for the facilitator.

References

Three guides to running staff development workshops for colleagues who are new to OFL, with photo-copiable handouts:

Freeman, R. and Lewis, R. (1995) *Writing Open Learning Materials*, Lancaster: Framework Press.

Lewis, R. (1995) *Tutoring in Open Learning*, Lancaster: Framework Press.

Lewis, R. and Freeman, J. (1995) *Open Learning in Further and Higher Education*, Lancaster: Framework Press.

Rowntree, D. (1995) 'Teaching and learning online: a correspondence education for the 21st century?' *British Journal of Educational Technology* 26(3): 205–15.

24

CREATING AN ENVIRONMENT
FOR STAFF DEVELOPMENT

Fred Lockwood

The production of teaching or training material, and its delivery, is often regarded as the core activity of institutions engaged in open and flexible learning. The advice and assistance provided to those colleagues thus involved is typically seen as the central staff development task. While the chapters in this book redress these beliefs and broaden the scope of staff development, many would accept that the production and delivery of such material is a powerful vehicle within which to engage in staff development. A second observation is that, given the opportunity, many teachers and trainers can identify their needs and, cooperatively, satisfy them. I have been fortunate to work with numerous colleagues, within a variety of academic and technical areas, at different levels and in a large number of institutions and countries. I continue to be impressed by how knowledgeable and versatile these colleagues are, how readily they share their ideas and how readily the 'how to produce and deliver the material' vehicle can be utilised. The challenge is to create an environment in which this can occur. This chapter suggests how an environment for staff development activities in open or flexible learning can be created through a board game and how subsequent needs and activities can be identified by the players themselves.

Playing the game

Before an organisation decides whether to invest its resources in the production of self-instructional materials it needs to ensure that there are no existing courses that could satisfy the requirement. The International Centre for Distance Learning (ICDL) database [http://www-open.icdl.ac.uk/] lists over 33,000 courses from nearly 1,000 institutions; a few hours checking the contents of these courses could save considerable time, effort and money.

However, in the event that there are no appropriate courses available, your colleagues are faced with the prospect of assembling a course proposal; one that defines the parameters that are likely to influence its characteristics, assembly and delivery. Unfortunately, assembling such a course proposal is often regarded as a formidable task that may take weeks if not months to complete. Furthermore, in my experience, it is often a cause of considerable tension among staff as they lurch from one unforeseen problem to another, wallow in a morass of detail and try to reach a compromise. As an alternative to the protracted and often bitter arguments that typify the team assembly of course proposals, I offer an environment which typically raises a whole series of questions that staff themselves can address or identify as needing further consideration. This environment takes the form of a board game which requires a minimum amount of pre-reading and is designed to help staff assemble an outline course proposal in an hour or so rather than months. It allows the participants to begin to resolve their problems and flag those areas where they need further discussion or staff development. I have played different versions of this game with teachers and trainers in over a dozen countries and have found it to be enjoyable, energising and capable of identifying the need for further staff development activities. To recreate this environment you would need to

- obtain the pre-reading and specify its purpose (see 'Pre-reading' below);
- assemble the materials you will need (see 'Materials needed' below);
- determine how you could play the game with your colleagues (see 'Playing the game' and 'The rules' below). The rules are minimal and merely designed to keep the game moving and to finish on time. You should feel free to customise the game to suit your particular needs;
- identify emergent issues that can become the focal points for further staff development activities.

Pre-reading

Whenever I play this game, I give the participants fifteen to twenty minutes of self-instructional material to study. This takes the form of a conference paper (Lockwood 1994) which describes, illustrates and analyses five different models of materials production: *Personalised Training, Workshop Generated, Transformation, Independent Comments* and *Wrap Around.* I inform them that the purpose of this pre-reading is to consider the use of these models (and that they may suggest others) for the production of a course of their choice.

Materials needed

The Game board is reproduced in Figure 24.1. This figure can be enlarged to about 420 cm × 594 cm or A2 size. Most photocopiers will allow you to enlarge each half of Figure 24.1 to A3 size and you can then join these together. I aim for between four and six players per board; I find the working group to be less effective when there are more or fewer players.

The Parameter cards (Figure 24.2) indicate a range of amounts for each of the parameters (periods of time, course lengths, support staff available, student numbers, number of contributors and funds available). However, you can vary these to reflect your particular circumstances.

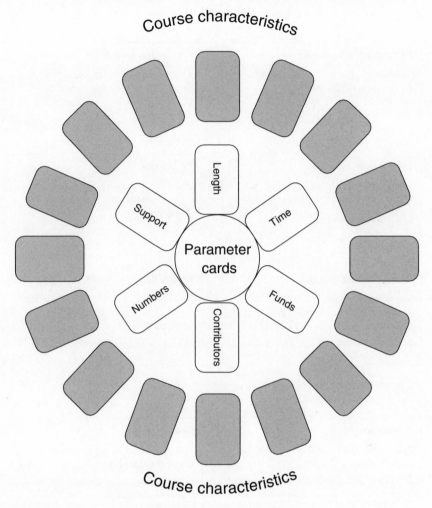

Figure 24.1 Game board for assembling an outline course proposal

I would recommend that you enlarge each of the six sets of Parameter cards onto different coloured A4 sheets so as to differentiate between them. It is possible, with a little care, to position and photocopy 'periods of time', 'course lengths', 'support staff available', 'student numbers', 'number of contributors' and 'funds available' onto the backs of the corresponding sets of coloured sheets and then cut out the individual cards for placement on the positions marked on the Game board. Alternatively, you can print these words on sticky labels and attach these to the reverse of the Parameter cards to indicate which pile is which.

Parameter cards – production time-scale

Production time-scale

You have 1 month to assemble the course material for hand-over to production.

Production time-scale

You have 8 months to assemble the course material for hand-over to production.

Production time-scale

You have 2 months to assemble the course material for hand-over to production.

Production time-scale

You have 10 months to assemble the course material for hand-over to production.

Production time-scale

You have 4 months to assemble the course material for hand-over to production.

Production time-scale

You have 12 months to assemble the course material for hand-over to production.

Parameter cards – course length

Course length

The course will be equivalent to 50 hours of study time.

Course length

The course will be equivalent to 200 hours of study time.

Course length

The course will be equivalent to 100 hours of study time.

Course length

The course will be equivalent to 300 hours of study time.

Course length

The course will be equivalent to 150 hours of study time.

Course length

The course will be equivalent to 400 hours of study time.

Parameter cards – course support available

Course support available

You have (part-time)
1 secretary.

Course support available

You have (full-time)
1 secretary, 1 administrator,
1 media adviser and
1 graphic designer

Course support available

You have (part-time)
1 secretary and
1 administrator.

Course support available

You have (full-time)
1 secretary, 1 administrator,
1 media adviser,
1 graphic designer and
1 educational technologist.

Course support available

You have (full-time)
1 secretary and
1 administrator.

Course support available

You have (full-time)
1 secretary,
1 administrator and
1 media adviser

Parameter cards – estimated student numbers

Estimated student numbers

You expect 50 students to study
the course each year.

Estimated student numbers

You expect 200 students to study
the course each year.

Estimated student numbers

You expect 75 students to study
the course each year.

Estimated student numbers

You expect 500 students to study
the course each year.

Estimated student numbers

You expect 150 students to study
the course each year.

Estimated student numbers

You expect 1,000 students to study
the course each year.

(Continued)

Parameter cards – contributors

Contributors

You have 1 contributor
(part-time) to assemble the
course material.

Contributors

You have 4 contributors
(part-time) to assemble the
course material.

Contributors

You have 2 contributors
(part-time) to assemble the
course material.

Contributors

You have 5 contributors
(part-time) to assemble the
course material.

Contributors

You have 3 contributors
(part-time) to assemble the
course material.

Contributors

You have 6 contributors
(part-time) to assemble the
course material.

Parameter cards – funds available

Funds available

You have £2,500 available (excluding
salaries) to assemble the course
material.

Funds available

You have £20,000 available (excluding
salaries) to assemble the course
material.

Funds available

You have £5,000 available (excluding
salaries) to assemble the course
material.

Funds available

You have £50,000 available (excluding
salaries) to assemble the course
material.

Funds available

You have £10,000 available (excluding
salaries) to assemble the course
material.

Funds available

You have £100,000 available
(excluding salaries) to assemble the
course material.

Figure 24.2 Parameter cards

Course characteristics

Course prerequisites

- What skills, abilities, techniques are needed prior to study?
- What courses are excluded combinations?

Target audiences

- What evidence is there from Training Needs Analyses?
- Will course production be collaborative – if so, with whom?

Access and equal opportunities

- How will access by all potential students be ensured?
- Does the course satisfy the Equal Opportunities legislation?

Assessment policy

- How will continuous and final assessment be made?
- How will academic and technical competence be monitored?

Needs of the disabled

- Will communication-impaired students be able to study the course?
- What restrictions will physical disability make to study?

Learner support policy

- What plans are there for tutors/ mentor support?
- Will a residential component be part of the course?

Financial cost to students

- What will be the cost of course registration?
- What other costs will be incurred?

Design of course

- What will be the order, sequence, alternatives in progress through the course?
- Case studies, project work, worked examples available?

Provision of home experiment kit

- Will practical activities be part of the course?
- What safety, pedagogic and cost implications to consider?

Link to professional body

- Liaison in course construction?
- Negotiations in course accreditation?

(Continued)

Provision of audiovisual media • What playback facilities are needed? • Level of access to appropriate equipment?	**Further courses available** • Future direction/advice to students? • Possible course combinations?
Provision of computing resources • Will computer hardware be provided? • Will computer software be provided?	**Hours of study** • How many hours per week? • Study to a rigid schedule or flexible?
Reproduction method of materials • What methods of print production will be adopted? • Bulk or 'on demand' reproduction?	**Other characteristics?**

Figure 24.3 Course characteristics cards

The Course characteristics cards (Figure 24.3) can also be similarly enlarged onto A4 sheets and cut up into individual cards. To avoid mixing up the cards, I find it useful to photocopy the Course characteristics cards onto a different coloured paper from the other cards. You can also reproduce the words 'Course characteristics' on the backs of these cards to avoid confusion with the other cards.

To set up the Game board, you simply place the six sets of Parameter cards face down on their respective spots in the centre of the board and the sixteen Course characteristics cards face down on the shaded rectangles around the outside of the board. Finally, you need to provide each of the players with the Outline course proposal document (Figure 24.4), advising them that this is their *aide-mémoire* to their discussions and decisions. The participants are now ready to start the game.

Overview

The aim of the game is to enable the players to assemble an outline course proposal and develop a brief report on how they intend to realise it – all within ninety minutes. In completing this proposal they will

246

- agree upon the features associated with Course identification (5 minutes);
- specify or accept the Course parameters within which the course will be designed (5 minutes);
- discuss the Course characteristics and determine their relevance to their Course proposal ($15 \times 4 = 60$ minutes);
- decide upon the model of material production, drawing upon the Pre-reading (5 minutes);
- review the proposal and revise any of the previous decisions to ensure consistency (5 minutes);
- report back to the whole group on the outcome of discussions (5 minutes × number of groups of players).

Playing the game

It is important that the game should be conducted in a jovial but brisk manner. I find that it is very easy for players to become sidetracked and embroiled in detailed discussion which, although fascinating, is better flagged for subsequent resolution and/or staff development activities. It is therefore important that you monitor the progress of the various groups and ensure that they are focusing on the task in hand and keeping to schedule. You will need to decide how much time to allocate to this task. It is possible to complete the whole game and have a report back within an hour. However, I have found that ninety minutes is more realistic, giving the participants the chance to develop their ideas and arguments fully but avoiding the whole process becoming too protracted.

The rules

You may exercise your own judgement on whether to give out all the rules or directions of the game at the outset or reveal them a little at a time. I tend to reveal the rules stage by stage.

Stage 1

Here it is merely necessary to tell the participants that the aim of the game is to assemble an outline course proposal and that each team has to complete the documentation they have been given (Figure 24.4). The challenge lies in the fact that they do not have weeks for this: the proposal needs to be completed in (for example) ninety minutes – otherwise the tea, lunch or whatever will be cold! So the whole game is to be played at a brisk pace and you will keep them on schedule with regular time-checks.

Each team is told that they must reach rapid decisions so as to progress the game but that they will have time to reconsider the implications of their earlier decisions at the end of the process. They will also be allowed to flag issues they have been unable to resolve, or for which they need further information or

Course identification

1 Provisional course title

2 Administering department or faculty

3 New course or remake

4 Academic level

5 Date of first presentation

6 Estimated course life

Course parameters

7 Course length

8 Estimated annual student numbers

9 Production time-scale

10 Funds available

11 Contributors

12 Course support available

Method model of course production

Course characteristics

13 **Course prerequisites**
  • What skills, abilities, techniques needed prior to study?
  • What courses are excluded combinations?

14 **Access and Equal Opportunities**
  • How will access by all potential students be ensured?
  • Does the course satisfy the Equal Opportunities legislation?

15 **Needs of the disabled**
  • Will communication-impaired students be able to study the course?
  • What restrictions will physical disability make to study?

16 **Financial cost to students**
  - What will be the cost of course registration?
  - What other costs will be incurred?

17 **Target audiences**
  - What evidence is there from Training Needs Analyses?
  - Will course production be collaborative – if so, with whom?

18 **Assessment policy**
  - How will continuous and final assessment be made?
  - How will academic and technical competence be monitored?

19 **Learner support policy**
  - What plans are there for tutorial/mentoring support?
  - What residential component will be part of the course?

20 **Design of course**
  - What order, sequence or alternatives in progress through the course?
  - Will case studies, project work, worked examples be available?

21 **Provision of a home experiment kit**
  - What practical activities will be part of the course?
  - What safety, pedagogical and cost implications to consider?

22 **Provision of audiovisual media**
  - What playback facilities are needed?
  - What is the level of access to the appropriate equipment?

23 **Provision of computing resources**
  - Will computer hardware be provided?
  - Will computer software be provided?

24 **Reproduction method of materials**
  - What methods of print production will be adopted?
  - Will bulk or 'on demand' reproduction be required?

25 **Link to professional body**
  - What liaison is needed in course construction?
  - What negotiations are needed in course accreditation?

26 **Further courses available to students**
  - What future direction/advice will be given to the students?
  - Are there possible course combinations?

27 **Hours of study**
  - How many hours per week will be required?
  - Will study be to a rigid schedule or flexible?

Figure 24.4 Outline course proposal

advice; these can give rise to subsequent staff development activities. Finally, you ask one of the participants in each team to act as a rapporteur, recording all of their team's decisions for reporting back to the whole group.

Stage 2

Here you tell the whole group that they have five minutes to decide upon the six course features listed under Course identification (Figure 24.4, points 1–6):

1   *Provisional course title*: whether this relates to a real course or one dreamed up for the occasion, the title needs to encapsulate the content and nature of the course.
2   *Administering department*: the academic or technical base, the potential links with other bodies and the relationship with other courses.
3   *New course or remake*: whether a course structure and teaching sequence already exists, along with evaluative data, or whether this has to be decided upon/collected.
4   *Academic level*: whether the course is to be pitched at diploma, certificate or degree level or is a non-credit offering.
5   *Date of first presentation*: when the course is to be studied and whether it is to fit into a particular term, semester or rolling registration.
6   *Estimated course life*: given the content and nature of the course, how long it will be before it becomes dated and in need of replacement.

A three-minute and one-minute countdown and a reminder that they must reach a decision on all six counts is usually enough to progress these group decisions.

Stage 3

After five minutes, you should ask the rapporteur to ensure that she or he has an agreed list of Course identifiers and then move the team on to the Course parameters. It is worth stressing that while many factors influence the design of a course, it is impossible in the time available to address all of these. As a result, you have identified the six which you feel to be the main ones (Figure 24.4, points 7–12). Alternatively, you can invite the players either to specify their own six parameters (if they are assembling a real proposal, they may already have details of the parameters, the course support available, the contributors and so on), or to shuffle the pack of Parameter cards and derive some or all of the parameters from these. They have five minutes to specify:

7   *Course length*: can the players estimate the hours of study time required to study the course material?
8   *Estimated annual student numbers*: how many students are expected to study the course?

9 *Production time-scale*: how much time is available to assemble the complete course?
10 *Funds available*: how much money is available for the project?
11 *Contributors*: who will be the contributors and will these be full-time or part-time?
12 *Course support available*: what secretarial, administrative, media and instructional design help is available?

Stage 4

After five minutes you should invite the rapporteurs to record the details of their Course parameters on the Outline course proposal (Figure 24.4), and then direct the players to the Course characteristics cards ranged around the outer board. You should explain that they have sixty minutes for this task. You could move to one of the groups and invite a player to draw a card, explaining that their task is to lead a three-to-four-minute discussion on this particular topic. You could repeat the prompts on the card and raise other questions to illustrate how the discussion can be stimulated. For example, if the 'Course prerequisites' card had been drawn, you could ask:

• What skills, abilities, techniques are needed prior to study?
• What courses would be excluded combinations?

And, depending upon your knowledge of the particular course outline the sub-group is developing, you could ask:

• What preparatory materials, if any, would need to be provided before the learners commenced their studies?
• Will the learners need access to particular people, equipment, venues, and so on?

At the end of the four-minute discussion, the group should agree upon how this topic relates to, and should be incorporated into, their course proposal – and/or what other information, help or advice they need. The players are informed every time that the four minutes is up and a different player is invited to draw another card and lead the next group discussion – again with the rapporteur recording the decisions or outcome.

Stage 5

It is important that you keep each of the groups progressing steadily through the game so that when you ask them to review their proposal they have had the opportunity to consider all of the Course characteristics. You can ask any teams that finish ahead of schedule what characteristics they might consider other than those listed in Figure 24.4.

Prior to their reporting back to the whole group, I would recommend that you give all the teams a few minutes to review the proposals they have assembled and to make any changes they deem to be necessary.

Stage 6

Now you invite the rapporteur, or another team member, to describe the main features, parameters and course characteristics of their course proposal to the whole group and how they plan to implement this. They should be encouraged to refer back to the Pre-reading and specify the model they would use to realise the course proposal and deliver the course. Each group has five minutes to report.

Conclusion

Whenever I play this game with teachers and trainers, I am impressed by the variety of courses that are chosen as the focus of the discussion, how completely the participants become involved, and the speed at which they are able to arrive at sound solutions to the problems or identify issues where they need help and advice. It would be totally unrealistic to suggest that a full course proposal can be assembled within ninety minutes, but what the participants will have learned is how to share in resolving problems and identifying areas in need of further consideration. I should stress that the fifteen Course characteristics given in Figure 24.4 are merely illustrative and not exhaustive of the issues worthy of consideration when planning a course and its delivery. Such characteristics can be identified as the focal point for further seminars, workshops, games, simulations and other staff development activities.

Reference

Lockwood, F.G. (1994) 'Effective and efficient production of self-instructional material for teaching and training', paper presented at the *Open Learning '94 Conference* (9–11 November), Brisbane, Australia.

25

A MASTER'S IN OPEN AND DISTANCE EDUCATION FOR UNIVERSITY STAFF

David Hawkridge

The United Kingdom Open University (OU) started up in the 1970s with very few of its staff knowing anything at all about open and distance education. This was as true of the academic staff preparing the materials as it was of the administrators setting up the systems and of the tutors guiding and assessing students. Today, throughout the world, a great many universities whose staff know how to teach face-to-face on campus are trying to attract and teach students through open and distance education networks. Again, few of these staff have any knowledge of what is involved. The rest need to learn fast if costly and painful mistakes are to be avoided and quality is to be maintained. These staff are already graduates. A suitable recognised professional qualification could be a Master's in Open and Distance Education. The OU now offers such a course, available in all countries (except in Australia, by agreement). It is a unique degree, built on know-how accumulated over nearly thirty years, with full use of electronic tutoring and the Web.

Evidence of interest in open and distance education

World-wide, there is substantial general interest in open and distance education among university staff, whether academics or administrators. As a long-standing member of the OU's academic staff, I encounter expressions of interest wherever I go, whether in the United Kingdom or abroad. No traces remain of the hostility and ridicule with which universities greeted the OU's birth in 1969. Instead, I am greeted with friendly curiosity – and the OU is regarded with respect, even admiration. 'How exactly do you do it, this distance education?' they ask. Often they add, 'We're trying to do some ourselves, or soon will be.' If you ask them why they are so interested, you get various replies. On the one hand, the idealists say they want to increase access to higher education for people who, for various reasons, would otherwise be unable to study at that level. On the other hand, academics with a deep interest in their own disciplines want to improve their teaching and exploit new technologies by benefiting from the demonstrated success of distance education in many countries.

Even those who much prefer on-campus, face-to-face teaching say that they are being obliged to take an interest in open and distance education for economic reasons: universities in all countries face financial pressures as governments try to expand student numbers while keeping down costs. For example, Johnston's (1991) estimates of labour force requirements in nine industrialised countries in the year 2000 demonstrate a need, on conservative assumptions, for more than 1,700 new campuses, probably costing over US$600 billion to build, if the money could be found and the building started today. To give but one American example, the state of Florida needs to expand its universities and colleges to serve an additional 100,000 students, over and above the current 200,000, by 2007 (Boettcher and Fell 1996). Even in a wealthy country like the USA, such expansion is extremely difficult without using open and distance education. Or to consider the case of the Mara Institute of Technology in Malaysia (described elsewhere in this book), the government has enjoined the Institute to triple its enrolment to 100,000 students by the year 2000 (Lockwood 1996). No wonder distance learning has its attractions.

Whether at the institutional, national or government level, evidence of this same interest in open and distance education crops up frequently in reports on higher education. Two UK examples come to mind: in Scotland, the MacFarlane report (1992), *Teaching and Learning in a Higher Education System*, and the UK government's *Dearing Review*. MacFarlane, after analysing instructional principles and practice and considering developments in technology-based learning, advocated that students should be able to take distance education courses alongside campus courses. In the USA, the Society for College and University Planning report (1995), *Transforming Higher Education*, advanced a model of teaching and learning remarkably close to that recommended by MacFarlane's team. The Dearing Commission recommendations may well take a similar line, suggesting greater use of distance education in universities, and proposing that opportunities should be created for staff to master the knowledge and skills required to bring this about. But is there a need for a formal qualification for such staff?

Who needs a Master's in open and distance education?

On the face of it, the case must still be made for a formal qualification in this field. University staff in industrialised countries (at least) are already well qualified in the sense of having studied at postgraduate level. Academics are expected to go beyond a first degree, often to a doctorate. Administrators may do the same. It might be expected that they would not wish to bother with a further qualification.

With an eye to increasing quality and efficiency, however, the governments of some countries are considering whether or not to require university lecturers, like schoolteachers, to have some kind of teaching qualification. In the UK context, the Higher Education Quality Council has exerted pressure on universities to provide proper staff development (Crosthwaite 1996), and in 1996, six universities piloted a general accredited staff development scheme aimed at academic, administrative, technical, secretarial and library staff (King 1996). One of these schemes, the Teaching Improvement Project System (TIPS), is designed for experienced but untrained academics (Dennick 1996). In the others, the academics take the Certificate in Teaching and Learning in Higher Education of their particular university. The Teacher Accreditation Scheme of the Staff Education and Development Association (SEDA) is currently the only national scheme of professional accreditation available for university teachers (Beaty 1996), although the Universities and Colleges' Staff Development Agency offers a national programme every year.

Such programmes usually call for only three to ten days a year of the academics' time, although a few require as much as 260 hours of study (Crosthwaite 1996). Rather than these short courses, a much more substantial and demanding Postgraduate Certificate or Diploma may become acceptable or even required. The Dearing Commission asked eleven questions about staff development, one of which was: should there be a nationally recognised teaching qualification for academic staff? UK academics may now obtain the British Psychological Society's Diploma in the Applied Psychology of Teaching, which requires both practical and written work, including a dissertation of 8,000–10,000 words. The Society hopes to upgrade the Diploma to a higher degree. Ultimately, a Master's may be best, though longer and more costly.

Open and distance education do not feature prominently in such schemes. Crosthwaite's (1996) summary of sixty-nine universities audited between April 1991 and April 1994 does not mention the OU. As recently as 1994, there was little or no evidence of interest and demand from individuals or their employers for an MA in this field. However, it does seem as though there is now a pathway opening up for new kinds of professionals who wish to serve in this field. I have been astonished at the number of hits on our Web page for the new international Master's in Open and Distance Education: about fifty people visit the page each day. We have received (as at November 1996) well over 1,000 enquiries from people interested in taking this MA. We asked some of them why they were interested, and the replies show clearly that they perceive a need for such a degree to develop their own knowledge and skills, almost always for use in their own institutions, but in a few cases to embark on an entirely new career. The enquirers clearly see the OU as a, and possibly the, leading exponent and feel they can hardly do better than take the MA through the OU.

Should the Open University teach what it practises?

Within the OU, some staff feel that perhaps the university should *not* teach what it practises; after all, why should its staff pass on their expertise to potential

255

competitors in the market economy created in UK higher education in the past decade? Some OU staff call this 'selling the family silver' – a phrase with interestingly elitist connotations! Critics of the MA within the OU also speculate about who owns the intellectual property rights to the OU's distance teaching expertise, who should be authorised to sell them and in what form – and who should benefit within the OU from such a sale.

I have argued that there is a degree of arrogance, and more than a touch of commercialism, in these attitudes. Conventional universities are dedicated to the pursuit and teaching of knowledge. The OU is no different in this respect. As a publicly funded institution, supported mainly by government grants and student fees, surely the OU has a duty to make available to others some at least of its knowledge and experience?

Over the years, the OU has also gone to considerable trouble and expense to analyse, evaluate and document its research and development activities in this field – and its practice as possibly the foremost practitioner. This work has been done largely but not exclusively through the OU's Institute of Educational Technology. In addition, the Institute houses the International Centre for Distance Learning, with the largest collection in the world of publications and other papers on distance education. Access to such resources adds strength to the case for the OU to teach what it practises.

Nobody would suggest that the teaching should be provided by the OU free of charge, or even at a subsidised rate. For the past six years, the Institute has mounted face-to-face workshops and courses, varying in length from one day to twelve weeks, on a range of topics related to open and distance education. Most of these have had a very practical flavour. The fees charged for these, aimed at covering costs and leaving a surplus for re-investment, have been in line with those for other professional updating courses offered elsewhere.

The MA is similarly funded. The OU in fact requires the MA to be self-financing, not subsidised by the government grant provided through the Higher Education Funding Council for England (HEFCE). The fee charged (£6,750 at 1997 prices) is a reflection of the OU's belief in the value of its own expertise and experience.

Over the past twenty-seven years, the OU has built up considerable, and in some regards, unrivalled, expertise in successfully teaching people at a distance: it now serves well over 200,000 students a year and has more than 125,000 graduates. It is fast becoming truly international: some 25,000 people outside the UK study through its courses and packages every year, and the OU sells complete courses to universities in Singapore and Hong Kong.

OU staff have pioneered methods for teaching a wide range of degrees and academic subjects, including science and technology, and have a high reputation for quality and innovation. If imitation is the sincerest form of flattery, then they must feel very flattered, because roughly 100 new open and distance education institutions have been established in the OU's wake. None of the 'open universities' now operating around the globe is exactly the same as the

OU, but there are similarities, shared concerns and considerable sharing of experience.

The OU is now moving into using computers and telecommunications on a massive scale, at a cost of tens of millions of pounds. More than 30,000 students are currently required to have access to computers for their studies. Most of them are linked into the OU electronically. Each year, thousands more will come on stream as new courses incorporate the new technology alongside well-tried print, television, video, radio and audio. An extensive programme of research and development supports these changes.

It would be a mistake, however, to suggest that the new MA is based entirely on the knowledge and experience of the OU. The OU's international position has given many of its staff opportunities to participate in development of open and distance education in other countries. In my own case, I have enjoyed the challenge of feasibility and evaluation studies in Canada, China, Egypt, El Salvador, Israel, Jamaica, Mauritius, the Netherlands and the USA. Such experiences enable the MA to be truly international, both in content and approach.

The MA in Open and Distance Education

To provide university staff almost everywhere with the chance to gain a postgraduate professional qualification in open and distance education from the OU, and to share what it and others practise, the university launched this MA in Open and Distance Education in February 1997. Among the first group of students, drawn from more than a dozen countries, many are staff in higher education institutions already using electronic open and distance methods or planning to do so. They are studying theory and practice, with a strong emphasis on applications of information technology and modern approaches to teaching and learning. They are encouraged to relate their studies to their everyday work and vice versa.

The degree normally takes three years to complete, part-time. The programme consists of two years of compulsory coursework followed by a third year in which candidates can specialise. They can choose their own time and place to study, and, to some extent, the pace at which they work.

Year 1 is devoted to Foundations of Open and Distance Education. In Block 1, students develop their understandings of major theoretical issues in open and distance education and the theories underlying practice in this field. They are enabled to relate distance education to the wider context by drawing on source material from a diverse range of backgrounds including their own work and experience. Throughout, they are encouraged to reflect critically on their own ideas and experience as a basis for practice.

In Block 2, the focus is on teaching and learning. The students explore the nature of education, and of open and distance education, from different philosophical perspectives that are the key to understanding how to approach teaching and learning in this field. They are introduced to the study environments and the experiences of adult learners at a distance, and they also look at distance education of children, with examples from various parts of the world.

In Block 3, the students learn the skills needed for searching research literature databases by electronic means. For example, they learn how to search online databases and how open and distance education are portrayed in specific classification systems. They acquire a broad understanding of the main areas covered by the research literature, and the sources available. They develop a critical appreciation of the literature in a selected area of open and distance education such as curriculum development, student support or evaluation. They also work with electronic updates, as this is the only way to keep up with developments in this rapidly changing field.

Finally, in Block 4, the students are introduced to social research theory and methods, with particular reference to research in open and distance education. They reflect critically on case studies of research, and acquire the knowledge and skills to design, conduct and report on an exploratory research and evaluation study in open and distance education, under their tutor's supervision. They also acquire the knowledge and skills to undertake reviews of their own and of other research and evaluation studies in this field, and they develop a proposal for either a dissertation or a project for Year 3 of the MA.

Year 2, Applications of Information Technology in Open and Distance Education, is a very different year, focusing on media used in this field. After starting with a broad view of the older media in open and distance education, the students move into teaching and learning online and up-to-the-minute applications such as the Internet, the Web and multimedia. Again, they are expected to take a critical view of the media, new and old, rather than jumping on the latest bandwagon. After experiencing these technologies for themselves, as well as studying and discussing them in detail, they should be in a good position to explain the advantages and disadvantages of the various media in particular contexts, including their own.

Success in Year 2 leads on to the options of Year 3. Here the students have a choice between a project or a dissertation focused on a topic that interests them. Those who take the project also take a half course entitled The Management of Open and Distance Education.

What are the unique selling points of the MA?

These days, academics are expected to be salespeople. So what are the unique selling points of the MA? This is not an ordinary correspondence course. It is not even an ordinary OU course. The students on the course are taught and assessed through a combination of media, from traditional print to the most sophisticated computer and telecommunication technologies. A special feature of the degree is the Electronic Workbook (see Figure 25.1), in which students

[Previous|Next|Forum Top] **Msg #242 of 410; posted 25/2/97 by** **Simonr**

David's group H801 I H801.1.2 I Activity 2.2 I

activity 2.2 ... Eraut's paper on Schon

I was surprised at how enjoyable I found reading Eraut's paper ... not specifically with what he said and how he said it but with what he was discussing - the idea of

```
Reflection IN action -> process of knowledge creation
Reflection ON action
Positive knowledge
Knowing in action ... knowing by doing
Reflection FOR action.
```

The temporal link binding IN action and ON action - when does one become the other? It reminded me of Zeno's paradox (I think it was him) and the story of the arrow that never hits the moving target because at any point in time the arrow has a distance to go and by the time it has gone that far the target has moved a bit ... and so on (I think that's the story - any classical philosopher scholar feel free to correct me!).

I particularly liked Eraut's line on page 13 *"might reflection not lead to perception of a problem rather than be the result of it"*.

In answer the first question: I think Eraut thinks that Schon's analysis is weak in terms of the time scale of the process:

```
(a) problem ... (c) action -> reflection -> (b)
                       ^                     I
                       I_____I
```

whether the reflection is about the process from (a) to (b) or about (a) to (c)?

The whole exercise made me think (again) about the creative process ... how it has rarely been described in such a way as to invest it with the wonder that it deserves. Schon's and Eraut's 'definitions' seem to break it down into such managable chunks that they can be easily dismissed one by one ... but then of course you have dismissed the whole wonderous process. The whole is quite definitely greater than the sum of the little bits.

I guess that the process of installing our workbooks could be broken down into activities that could be grouped under the 3 reflection modes - sometimes I just held my breath and clicked OK to accept what Windows95 was offering, sometimes I reflected on what I had just done and sometimes I reflected on something so that I could do it right the next time.

[**Reply** I Outline I **Parent** I **Jump** I New replies I All in One Page I **History** I **Search** I **Info**]

Moderator Buttons [**Edit** I **Delete** I **Users** I **Conference** I **FlatView**]

Figure 25.1 The Electronic Workbook

record their learning, whether as rough notes or polished paragraphs, and exchange ideas.

The students are frequently in touch with one another and with their tutors via the Internet. They draw on specialised electronic educational resources held on the Web and as CD-ROMs. They also send their assignments to their tutor in electronic form for marking, and comments come back by the same route.

The tutors are from the OU's Institute of Educational Technology, which is top-rated in the UK for its research. They use new software developed by the OU for student assessment, as well as the Electronic Workbook system and electronic mail. Although there are no face-to-face meetings with students, each tutor is in touch with his or her group of ten to fifteen at least as often as on-campus tutors.

As well as exchanging electronic mail with their tutor, students are asked to join others in small conferences on specific topics. For example, they might wish to take part in a conference on the topic of the next assignment, or a more general one in which candidates and tutors pool their knowledge and experience of, say, using audio in open and distance education.

Tutors are also responsible for helping each student to develop a research proposal during Years 1 and 2. On request, the students can receive counselling throughout the programme on study skills and other academic matters.

The MA candidates draw on the wealth of experience in the OU, have access to the latest research in the university, and experience for themselves just what it is like to learn at a distance using the latest resources. The qualification is likely to be of great value to anyone involved in using or developing open and distance education, or who wants to embark on a career in this field. With its leading-edge content and methodologies, it should be of sufficient value to the employing institutions that many staff can obtain support in paying the fees.

The MA allows people to mould the degree to the shape of their lives rather than their lives to the shape of the degree. Once students have successfully completed a course they are not obliged to take another one straight away. If they want to take a year off, they can return without losing the credit points they have gained. If they decide that the MA is not for them, they can leave with a Postgraduate Certificate after completing either Year 1 or Year 2 and a Postgraduate Diploma if they have completed both years. Many students seem likely to continue to Year 3, but with this added flexibility, numbers of applicants are likely to rise.

What equipment is needed?

The students need access to a suitable computer, communications and software. The specification for 1997 was set as low as possible: at least, an IBM-PC, PC/XT, PC/AT or PS/2, or a computer that is completely IBM PC-compatible. Most students will probably be using a more up-to-date machine. It must be able to run Microsoft Windows 3.1 or a later version. The specification for 1998 is higher, to accommodate more demanding applications such as multimedia CD-ROMs. The specification for 1997 was:

- connections to the Internet and the World Wide Web;
- electronic mail software;
- Netscape 2.0 (or a later version) for browsing on the Web;
- a CD-ROM drive that meets the ISO 9660 specification, with Microsoft MS-DOS CD-ROM Extensions software;
- a 486 processor, 8 MB of memory (RAM), a hard disk with at least 10 MB free space after the Windows software has been loaded, and a high-density floppy-disk drive;
- a Microsoft-compatible mouse and a Windows-compatible printer; and
- a monitor with at least VGA graphics (a colour screen that can display thousands of colours is desirable).

Conclusion

In my opinion (but then I am deeply involved and committed), this MA in Open and Distance Education is a stimulating, enjoyable and cost-effective route to a recognised professional qualification. Such a programme is arguably of tremendous potential benefit to the participants. It equips them with essential knowledge and analytical skills, far beyond what they can acquire in short workshops and courses. It enables them to gain an internationally recognised qualification without disrupting their careers, leaving home or losing income. They also stand to gain immeasurably from the world-wide electronic contacts they make with their tutors and other professionals taking the MA. Through the MA, teachers and support staff in countries that do not yet have the infrastructure to set up electronic distance teaching are placing themselves at the forefront of future developments. Those in industrialised countries are gaining valuable expertise in a fast-expanding field.

The institutions can gain substantially too. They do not lose their staff for a year or two as they would if they took a full-time degree. These staff complete MA assignments that often relate to, and stem from, their particular work settings, so from the very beginning they can apply new ideas and skills to their work and seek resolution to workplace problems through their studies. Colleagues can draw on the knowledge and expertise of the new MAs who know how to access enormous and constantly updated educational resources and have established a valuable new network with other institutions, some of which may be in other countries. And these MA graduates can also share their learning with their own students.

Finally, the profession itself gains from a postgraduate programme that is rigorous, soundly based, 'open' in more ways than one, can have an impact at many levels, and helps to raise the academic status as well as the professional standards of open and distance learning.

References

Beaty, L. (1996) 'SEDA and accreditation', *New Academic* 5 (2): 24.

Boettcher, J. and Fell, S. (1996) 'Launching interactive distance learning programs at Florida State University: leading the way', paper presented at the Conference of Florida State University and the Association for Educational Communications and Technology on Distance Learning, Tallahassee (21–23 June).

Crosthwaite, E. (1996) 'Approaches to staff development', *New Academic* 5 (3): 17–19.

Dennick, R. (1996) 'TIPS – the Teaching Improvement Project System in action', *New Academic* 5 (2): 12–13.

Johnston, W. (1991) 'Global Work Force 2000: the new world labor market', *Harvard Business Review* (March–April).

King, P. (1996) 'Accredited development for staff in HE', *SEDA Newsletter* 7: 4.

Lockwood, F. (1996) Personal communication.

26

STAFF DEVELOPMENT FOR PROJECT MANAGEMENT AND QUALITY ASSURANCE

Richard Freeman

Developing staff to run project management and quality systems is the focus of this chapter. It outlines the processes involved in these two techniques and then identifies the skills that are needed. In each case, these skills are matched to staff roles, so creating the starting point for a development plan. Methods for developing these skills are discussed, and the chapter highlights the crucial role of management style and management development in creating an atmosphere in which project management and quality systems can flourish.

Project management

> Project management provides an organisation with powerful tools that improve the organisation's ability to plan, organize, implement, and control its activities and the ways it uses its people and resources.
>
> (Meredith and Mantel 1989: 1)

The above claim is supported by a survey of the use of project management in 400 construction firms which found that 'the majority of organisations using it experience better control and better customer relations' (Meredith and Mantel 1989: 6, citing Davis 1974). None of this, though, refers to the use of project management in education and training, and I have found no evaluative surveys of such applications. All I can cite is my own experience, where I have found that projects using these techniques run more smoothly and deliver, on time and to budget, more consistently than those using less formal methods. This is particularly true of large-scale materials development projects which use large numbers of part-time writers, readers, editors and consultants. Coordinating such projects is a huge task, which is much simplified by the application of formal project management methods.

What is a project?

The term 'project' needs defining since its everyday use is looser than that in project management. A project is an activity which:

- produces a unique thing;
- has identifiable start and end dates;
- has many tasks;
- has tasks which often depend on the prior completion of other tasks;
- is complex; and
- uses multiple resources and personnel.

Table 26.1 illustrates how this definition applies in practice.

Table 26.1 Examples of projects and non-projects

Activity	Is this a project?
One author writing a book	No. It is not a complex activity – just lengthy. Nor does it use multiple resources.
Lots of authors writing a reference book	Yes. This is complex in the sense of lots of tasks and lots of resources.
Running a college	No. There is no clear end date – the job can go on for ever. Particular aspects of running the college (e.g., putting in a new computer network or system) would be a project.
Developing a new Open Learning course	Yes. This involves many tasks and many resources; it also has clear start and end dates.

What is project management?

With this background, it is possible to describe what project management is. It is a formal, systematic approach to

- identifying the tasks in a project;
- identifying the order in which the tasks need to be done;
- identifying when the tasks need to be done;
- identifying the resources needed for each task;
- allocating tasks to people;
- monitoring progress and recording the resources used; and
- adjusting the plan in the light of progress.

Although it may not be obvious from this list, project management produces certain key operational benefits for staff:

- every task is (ideally) allocated to one person;
- each person knows what they have to do and by when; and
- the project manager can see the state of the project at any given time.

In talking about project management, one needs to distinguish between its constituents (the list above) and its methods. There is a huge range of methods, such as Critical Path Method (CPM) and Gantt charts. While *all* projects need *all* of the constituents, *different* projects may use *different* methods. (For an overview of the simpler methods, see Haynes 1989; for an encyclopaedic survey, see Meredith and Mantel 1989.)

Although project management can be done with pencil and paper, more realistically, projects are run using project management software such as MacProject or Project Manager Workbench.

Introducing project management into an open/distance learning (ODL) organisation produces the first development need. Senior staff need to understand what projects are and what project management involves. If these are not understood, the methods will be applied inappropriately and the senior managers will not use the project-reporting aspects of project management appropriately.

Where project management can be used

In ODL, project management can be used to

- develop new courses (especially complex ones entailing multimedia);
- develop and introduce new systems – for example, modularisation or a new tutoring system;
- develop and install new computer systems;
- plan and implement a move to new premises.

The skills required for project management and who needs them

The precise range of skills required in an organisation will depend on the methods which that organisation uses for its projects. Typically, though, there needs to be staff with the skills in column 1 of Table 26.2.

First, the organisation needs senior managers who can define projects clearly; this is a skill that they should already possess. Below the senior managers, each project needs a project manager (although one person might manage several projects); in ODL systems such a person is often a managing editor or a senior tutor. The project manager's task is to deliver the project within budget and to schedule. Working to the project manager, there is generally a project administrator who helps to develop the detailed project plan and coordinates the progress data once the project is running. The project administrator has a special role, requiring special skills: creating and updating the CPM chart, using a computer program. A typical (much simplified) chart is shown in Figure 26.1.

Table 26.2 The skills needed and by whom

Skill	Needed by
Define a project	Senior managers, e.g., director of materials development or director of tutorial services
Manage a project	Middle managers, ODL managing editor
Define milestones	Senior or middle managers
Analyse a project into tasks	Project manager or project administrator, e.g., editorial administrator
Decide the resources needed for each task	Project manager or project administrator, in consultation with those who will carry out the tasks
Order the tasks to produce a CPM or Gantt chart	Project administrator
Record progress on individual tasks	The people who do the tasks
Collate progress reports and update the project details	Project administrator
Re-plan the project as needed in the light of progress	Project manager
Conduct milestone reviews	Senior or middle managers

Once the administrator has created the chart, reports and tables can be generated from it. One of the most important is the Gantt chart (Figure 26.2), which shows each person what they have to do and when.

As the project progresses, the people responsible for the individual tasks report progress to the administrator, who uses this to update the CPM chart. This leads to:

- charts which show which tasks are completed;
- forecasts of problems (for example, time or budget overruns);
- management reports at whatever level of detail has been agreed.

One of the most valuable features of the CPM approach is the speed with which the consequences of problems can be seen. A time or budget overrun on one or more tasks can, within minutes, be followed through to see its effect on the final delivery date and the final costs. Such early warning maximises the time that managers have to respond to problems. For example, in ODL materials development, the early identification of a writer being behind schedule can lead to the early consideration of bringing in a second author. At the technical level, the key to developing project management skills lies in creating and updating the CPM chart. If this is poorly done, or not kept up-to-date, what should be a productivity tool becomes a source of major misinformation. So, unless someone

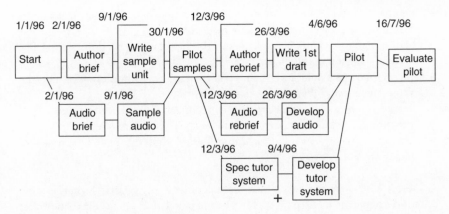

Figure 26.1 An example of a CPM chart

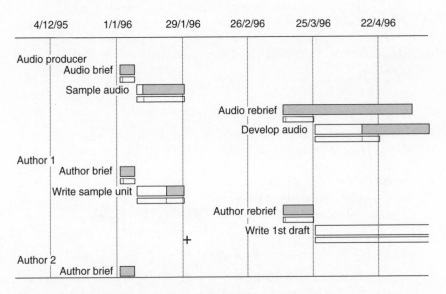

Figure 26.2 An excerpt from a Gantt chart for Figure 26.1

in the project is willing to learn these techniques, formal project management methods will not be of much value.

The heart of the developmental task lies in creating a project management attitude at all levels from senior management to secretaries and administrators. Motivating staff into creating and updating a project plan depends on the plan being seen to be used and to be useful. This requires that

- senior managers take milestone meetings seriously and refrain from inter-fering in the project between these meetings;
- senior managers think carefully about the reports they need from the CPM system and then use them productively;
- project managers take care to find out what information each person on the project needs and then ensure that they get it;
- project managers keep everyone on a project informed about its overall progress, but take care not to overwhelm them with detail; and
- project managers and administrators ensure that the plan is kept up to date.

Project management methods will only flourish in organisations that have an appropriate management philosophy. An approach that leaves everyone to do their own thing will destroy a project management system – it will be out of date and inaccurate within weeks. Equally, an arbitrary, dictatorial management style will issue commands that overrule what the CPM chart says needs to be done – and staff will cease to consult the plan and await the next blast from above. In the ODL context, the people appointed to some of these roles may have teaching backgrounds and be lacking in the skills of planning and coordinating large-scale projects. Identifying this lack can lead to the prompt provision of development opportunities.

Developing project management skills

In planning a development programme for project management skills, it is important to focus on three sets of tasks:

- explaining the rationale and benefits;
- developing project manager skills;
- creating and maintaining CPM chart skills.

Explaining the rationale and benefits

Everyone who will use or come into contact with the system needs to understand its rationale and the benefits that are sought. However, again, these cannot be considered in isolation from the organisation's general management style. For example, there is no point in talking about the benefits of delivering projects to schedule if the organisation repeatedly fails to provide the resources that staff need to do their jobs. In other words, rather than say, 'We are introducing project management to help us deliver to time and to budget,' an organisation needs to say, 'Now that we are all committed to delivery to time and to budget, let's see how project management might help us.' This analysis suggests that the first of the three developmental needs is less a matter of training and more a matter of good organisational development. In ODL, where project personnel may often be part-time and off-campus, such awareness-raising requires particular attention.

The most efficient way of developing awareness of the rational and benefits of project management is to include it as a formal topic in team meetings. This, combined with team-building activities, can help create an awareness of the role and needs of others in the team and an understanding of the interdependency among team members. For example, someone who is arranging the pilot of some new ODL materials can only succeed if the pilot materials are handed over on time. Equally, the writers can only revise materials to schedule if they receive a clear revision specification by an agreed date.

Developing project manager skills

Project managers must have good organisational abilities and excellent interpersonal skills. One would not seek to develop these in order to create project managers, but rather to recruit project managers who have developed these skills in other roles in the organisation. For example, staff who have organised workshops or summer schools would have an appropriate background for becoming project managers.

Assuming such skills to be present, project managers then only need a few days' training in order to acquire the special skills for their new role. Training works best where participants can work on a current or prospective project, since this seems to increase motivation. My own workshops for editorial staff have used one- or two-day sessions with activities such as:

- auditing your own systems (to see what good practice already exists);
- producing a project plan;
- planning changes to your systems;
- putting a project onto a computer.

An example of one such activity appears in Table 26.3. This particular activity asks participants to develop a Gantt chart on paper, even though they will later use a computer to do this. The justification for this approach is that it helps participants gain an understanding of the relationships between tasks, people, costs and time – entities which are central to project management.

A SUGGESTED ACTIVITY-PLANNING PROJECT

Purpose:

- to practise developing the full range of planning documents needed for a project;
- to help you decide the levels of detail appropriate to the projects you run.

Format:

- work in groups of two or three;
- decide whether the group will work on one project or will look at a project provided by each member of the group (ideally you should undertake this work around a project or projects which are in the early planning stages).

Outputs – for each project, the outputs should be:

- a list of goals;
- a budget;
- a milestone plan;
- a project responsibilities plan;
- one single schedule or a master schedule at milestone level plus schedules at activity level;
- activity plans for each milestone stage.

Method:

- use the formats suggested below, or those of your own devising;
- decide the milestones;
- produce a Gantt chart at milestone level;
- break the milestone stages down into activities;
- decide which documents you are going to circulate to whom (for instance, senior manager, project manager, project workers). Does anyone have reports of more than one side of A4? Can you avoid this?

Developing CPM chart skills

There are two sorts of CPM programme, signalling two different training routes. The simpler programmes treat each project in an organisation as a self-contained activity. Thus, if a lecturer is booked to work ten hours in Week 23 on Project A, the chart for Project B does not have access to those data. On the more complex programmes, all the charts have access to each person's overall commitment. Creating the simpler charts can be mastered from the manuals. The more complex systems require more systematic training.

Although the principles behind all CPM programmes are the same, the surface differences are marked, so CPM chart skills are best acquired through a package-specific training course, or by working through the publisher's manual. Some open access courses are provided by training organisations and some programme publishers (such as Hoskyns) offer their own training. Two days' training is typically needed. By the end of the first day, participants will have created a chart for a simple project and perhaps learned to update it. Learning to *use* the chart to manage the project usually needs another day's practice.

Table 26.3 A project management training activity

Milestone planning format

Date	Pathways	Output
		etc.

Project responsibilities

Project aspect (e.g., milestone stage, function, policy aspect)	Person responsible
	etc.

Activity lists

No.	Task and deliverable	Budget	Predecessor task	Duration	Who
					etc.

Quality assurance

Quality assurance refers to the process by which an institution ensures that it delivers its stated aims. Such systems fall into two main types:

- quality assurance management systems (QA systems), such as the British and European International Standard (BS EN ISO9000); and
- total quality management systems (TQM).

QA systems are essentially management systems, setting out procedures for how the organisation and its processes are to be managed. Auditing is a key part of this process, providing management with both a monitoring and a corrective action system. Implementing such systems has been described in many publications – for example, Munroe-Faure *et al.* (1993) and Freeman (1993).

TQM is more of an approach to management rather than a system, seeking to involve all employees in monitoring and improving quality. The approach has been discussed in a wide range of titles – for instance, Oakland (1989) and Sallis (1993).

Quality assurance skills

The skills required for the two approaches overlap, but there are some important differences. QA systems are highly formalised (especially if they conform to the BS EN ISO 9000 standard) and involve some specific tools and processes, including:

- a written quality manual;
- written procedures;
- written work instructions;
- document control;
- auditing;
- corrective action; and
- management review.

Some of these terms will appear familiar since they have everyday connotations. In QA systems, however, these terms have quite precise meanings which need to be understood by staff at all levels.

TQM is harder to pin down at the skill level. True, it uses some specific techniques such as quality circles, but arguably the heart of TQM lies in its management philosophy. Jefferies *et al.* (1992: 165–7), describing the characteristics of 'TQM people', include such factors as 'understands the goals of the business' and 'expects to be involved in decision-making'. These are nebulous (but important) qualities, not easy to cultivate through training programmes.

Another valuable insight into the difficulty of defining the skills behind TQM comes from considering how the staff developer's role changes when TQM is introduced. Where once the developer had provided centrally determined courses, now the developer is 'concerned with facilitating learning and helping individuals and departments initiate, implement and come to terms with all this change' (Jefferies *et al.* 1992: 41). It does not devalue the process to say that TQM training is essentially a question of developing a participative management style. Hence, training for TQM is more likely to be indirect than direct.

Who needs QA system skills?

Because QA systems are formal, responsibilities are well defined, which in turn identifies who needs what training.

A QA system will involve the roles and training needs set out in Table 26.4. This matches the five distinct roles in a QA management system against the skills needed for each role. Often these are part-time roles, undertaken by people with other responsibilities in the organisation. Generally, then, QA system training is only needed by a few specialists who design and maintain the system. Everyone in the organisation will follow the written procedures and work instructions and, in a participative organisation, there will be widespread consultation in preparing these documents. A modest training requirement in the principles of the system is therefore needed.

Table 26.4 QA management system skills

Role	Skills needed
Management team review	Knowledge of the principles of QA management systems Strategic management skills
Quality manager	Knowledge of the principles of QA management systems Knowledge of the details of QA management systems
Quality officer	Administrative skills
Procedure writers	Procedure writing skills Work instruction writing skills
Auditors	Auditing skills
Other staff	Knowledge of the principles of QA management systems Ability to follow procedures and work instructions

Who needs TQM skills?

Inevitably, in view of what has been said above, the training requirement here is much vaguer, since the skills are less specific. Oakland (1989: 238–55) emphasises teamwork skills as the foundation of TQM, and discusses such skills as:

- communication;
- counselling and coaching;
- team selection;
- team leadership;

- setting objectives;
- running meetings; and
- participating in quality circles.

Methods of QA system training

Generic training for the skills in Table 26.4 is offered by commercial training organisations (often leading to the awards of the Institute of Quality Assurance) but these courses tend to focus on manufacturing or services and are unlikely to be designed for education. The same companies will provide in-house courses, tailored to the needs of the organisation. A skilled trainer with knowledge of quality assurance might provide such guidance for educational and training organisations (Freeman 1993).

QA system training typically needs to be spread over a lengthy period, supporting the organisation in developing its own QA system. Such a system may well take two years to set up, so half- or one-day workshops at intervals over the period may be appropriate. A minimal training programme would be:

Day 1: Introduction to quality systems;
Day 2: Procedure writing;
Day 3: Work instruction writing;
Day 4: Auditor training.

Methods of TQM training

Again, there are many generic open-access courses available, but it may be hard to find a course with an educational focus. Organisations may need to design their own courses and/or draw on outside specialists. Oakland (1989: 273–5) offers an outline programme at three levels:

1 for senior management (8–20 hours);
2 for middle management (20–30 hours);
3 for first-level supervisors (30–40 hours).

The suggested contents for these sessions could be adapted to match educational rather than manufacturing systems.

Jefferies et al. (1992) is another source of ideas for training and activities for trainers. Boore (1993), writing about quality assurance in university teaching, places less emphasis on staff development as a precursor to the use of TQM but describes the use of quality circles to develop standards for various teaching methods. Griffiths, by contrast, argues that in total quality management 'training and development [become] priority issues and powerful vehicles as a major part of the process, in creating the new culture of quality assurance thinking' (Griffiths 1993: 254).

Conclusion

Staff development for quality assurance systems is still in the early stages of development. Doubts about the applicability of quality assurance systems to ODL may partly account for this slow development. The continuing reliance on other, indirect approaches may also be an explanation.

References

Boore J. (1993) 'Teaching standards from quality circles', in R. Ellis (ed.), *Quality Assurance for University Teaching*, Bristol, PA, and Buckingham, UK, Society for Research into Higher Education/Open University Press.

British Standards Institute (1995) *BS EN ISO 9000*, Milton Keynes: British Standards Institute.

Davis, E.W. (1974) 'CPM use in top 400 construction firms', *Journal of the Construction Division*, American Society of Civil Engineers.

Freeman, R. (1993) *Quality Assurance in Training and Education: How to Apply BS5750(ISO9000) Standards*, London: Kogan Page.

Griffiths, S. (1993) 'Staff development and quality assurance circles', in R. Ellis, *Quality Assurance for University Teaching*, Bristol, PA, and Buckingham, UK, Society for Research into Higher Education/Open University Press.

Haynes, M.E. (1989) *Project Management: From Idea to Implementation*, London: Kogan Page.

Jefferies, D.R., Evans, B. and Reynolds, P. (1992) *Training for Total Quality Management*, London: Kogan Page.

Meredith, J.R. and Mantel, S.J. (1989) *Project Management: A Managerial Approach*, New York: John Wiley & Sons.

Munroe-Faure, L., Munroe-Faure, M. and Bones, E. (1993) *Achieving Quality Standards: A Step-By-Step Guide to BS5750/ISO9000*, London: Institute of Management/Pitman Publishing.

Oakland, J.S. (1989) *Total Quality Management*, Oxford: Heinemann Professional Publishing Ltd.

Sallis, E. (1993) *Total Quality Management in Education*, London: Kogan Page.

Project management software

MacProject. Available through computer software retailers. Further information can be found at http://www.claris.com/products/products.html

Microsoft Project. Available through computer software retailers. Further information can be found at http://www.windows.com/macoffice/ProductInfo/ Project Manager Workbench.

NAME INDEX

SUBJECT INDEX